Python for Teenagers

Learn to Program like a Superhero!

Second Edition

James R. Payne

apress®

Python for Teenagers: Learn to Program like a Superhero!, Second Edition

James R. Payne
Gainesville, GA, USA

ISBN-13 (pbk): 978-1-4842-9987-6
https://doi.org/10.1007/978-1-4842-9988-3

ISBN-13 (electronic): 978-1-4842-9988-3

Copyright © 2024 by James R. Payne

This work is subject to copyright. All rights are reserved by the Publisher, whether the whole or part of the material is concerned, specifically the rights of translation, reprinting, reuse of illustrations, recitation, broadcasting, reproduction on microfilms or in any other physical way, and transmission or information storage and retrieval, electronic adaptation, computer software, or by similar or dissimilar methodology now known or hereafter developed.

Trademarked names, logos, and images may appear in this book. Rather than use a trademark symbol with every occurrence of a trademarked name, logo, or image we use the names, logos, and images only in an editorial fashion and to the benefit of the trademark owner, with no intention of infringement of the trademark.

The use in this publication of trade names, trademarks, service marks, and similar terms, even if they are not identified as such, is not to be taken as an expression of opinion as to whether or not they are subject to proprietary rights.

While the advice and information in this book are believed to be true and accurate at the date of publication, neither the authors nor the editors nor the publisher can accept any legal responsibility for any errors or omissions that may be made. The publisher makes no warranty, express or implied, with respect to the material contained herein.

Managing Director, Apress Media LLC: Welmoed Spahr
Acquisitions Editor: Celestin Suresh John
Development Editor: James Markham
Editorial Assistant: Gryffin Winkler

Cover designed by eStudioCalamar

Distributed to the book trade worldwide by Springer Science+Business Media New York, 1 New York Plaza, Suite 4600, New York, NY 10004-1562, USA. Phone 1-800-SPRINGER, fax (201) 348-4505, e-mail orders-ny@ springer-sbm.com, or visit www.springeronline.com. Apress Media, LLC is a California LLC and the sole member (owner) is Springer Science + Business Media Finance Inc (SSBM Finance Inc). SSBM Finance Inc is a **Delaware** corporation.

For information on translations, please e-mail booktranslations@springernature.com; for reprint, paperback, or audio rights, please e-mail bookpermissions@springernature.com.

Apress titles may be purchased in bulk for academic, corporate, or promotional use. eBook versions and licenses are also available for most titles. For more information, reference our Print and eBook Bulk Sales web page at http://www.apress.com/bulk-sales.

Any source code or other supplementary material referenced by the author in this book is available to readers on GitHub (github.com/apress). For more detailed information, please visit https://www.apress.com/gp/services/source-code.

Paper in this product is recyclable

To my wife Whitney Payne, for always believing and pretending not to notice when I yell at the computer.

To my parents, Ronnie and Sharon Payne, and my brother, also Ronnie Payne, who all mysteriously have "ron" in their name and who always told me I could become whatever I wanted in life, even when I told them I wanted to be Batman.

To Dorjan Williams, who, years ago, helped me create a universe of ridiculous comic book characters. To Eric Miller, who helps me solve problems big and small, including slaying a dragon in my backyard, so that I can focus – sometimes – on getting work done. Nicholas Rini introduced me to both programming and comic books, and without him, this book would not exist. Nanci Packard and Wendy White provided inspiration with their use of words so big they couldn't possibly fit in a book. Thanks to members of the old Dev Shed crew: Jennifer Ruggieri – who got me the job that got me the book (more than once) – Charles Fagundes, and Keith Lee, for coding help and reminding me (frequently) that my cup overfloweth. Jose Escalante, I thank you here because you were the only one that could see John Cena. Enrique Stone… you know what you did.

Jacquelyn Jurian, for reminding me to write by making me remind you to write.

A special thanks to Sophie "the Bulldog" Payne for letting me use her likeness in this book and always being such a good helper in the kitchen. You will always be missed.

I would be remiss if I failed to thank the mad titan, Thanos, who helped me accomplish so much with just a snap of his fingers. Mister T pitied this fool, while Richard C. helped me "hit 'em with the Hein!" And lastly, thank you to a handful of the writers that inspire me: A. Lee Martinez, Neil Gaiman, Frank Miller, Alan Moore, Jim Starlin, and Stephen King – can't you guys write any faster?

Table of Contents

About the Author

James R. Payne was introduced to programming when he was just ten years old. He started off hacking text-based games like Lemonade Stand to gain an advantage while playing and soon started creating his own text-based role-playing games in the style of Dungeons & Dragons and inspired by his favorite comic books. The enjoyment of those early days stuck with him, and he continues to be drawn back into the programming world throughout his career.

Payne is the former Editor-in-Chief/Community Manager of Developer Shed, an online publication and community consisting of 14 websites and forums dedicated to programming, web development, and Internet marketing. He is presently the editor for the developer sites at TechnologyAdvice. He's written over a thousand articles on coding and marketing, covering virtually every language and platform available. His first book, *Beginning Python* (Wrox Press), was published in 2010. In addition, he has published over 3000 articles covering topics ranging from gaming to aerospace/aeronautics, and he also writes adult horror and young adult fantasy books.

Payne decided to write this book to pass on his love of development in the hopes that it would inspire future generations to code.

About the Technical Reviewer

 **Andrea Gavana** has been programming Python for more than 20 years, dabbling with other languages since the late 1990s. He graduated from university with a master's degree in chemical engineering, and he is now a Master Development Planning Architect working for TotalEnergies in Copenhagen, Denmark.

Andrea enjoys programming at work and for fun, and he has been involved in multiple open source projects, all Python based. One of his favorite hobbies is Python coding, but he is also fond of cycling, swimming, and cozy dinners with family and friends. This is his third book as a technical reviewer.

Acknowledgments

This book wouldn't have been possible without Todd Green, who reached out to me to write a book and listened to my ideas and, thankfully, chose the one I wanted to write the most.

Celestin Suresh reached back out to me and had me write this second version, for which I am eternally grateful.

James Markham and Andrea Gavana found all of my errors and proved to me that, even at this old age, I still have a lot to learn. Who knew – an old dog can learn new tricks.

Thank you to the entire editorial team at Apress, who were a pleasure to work with and helped me do what I love to do most: write. And make up stupid comic book characters.

Introduction

Who This Book Is For

This book is intended for teenagers looking to program in Python. While that technically means anyone aged 13 through 18, the truth of the matter is anyone of *any* age can (and should, if I do say so myself!) pick up this book if they want to learn either (a) how to program in Python, (b) how to program as a beginner, or (c) add Python to their current skill set.

Above all, if you are holding this book in your hand, intrepid adventurer, then this book is for *you*. The future is dependent on young heroes like yourself, eager to learn the art of coding and go out into the world and safeguard it from nefarious hackers, dubiously programmed applications, and the rise of artificially intelligent robots!

So, whether you are in sixth grade or in college, this book will grant you with superpowers galore. Sure, you won't be able to see through walls or lift cars over your head once you finish this book. However, you will be able to speak the language of computers and create some pretty cool programs.

And what could be better than that?

What You Will Learn in This Book

Chapter 1 provides an overview of programming and Python and then shows you how to install Python and a Python IDLE, which will allow you to create your own Python programs and test your code.

In Chapter 2, we will discuss mathematical functions (things like division, addition, and multiplication) and learn about the different *data types* used by Python. We will also begin to build the foundation of a fun superhero generator app – "Superhero Generator 3000"!

Chapter 3 delves into how to work with text – also known as *strings*. We take a look at the different types of *storage* Python offers as well. We wrap things up by looking at common string functions and build another section of our Superhero Generator 3000 application.

Sometimes a program will need to take a certain action depending upon feedback from a user or from other influences. This is known as decision-making and is the topic of Chapter 4.

Programming logic and loops – known as iterations, where code can "loop" or repeat itself based on certain conditions – are covered in Chapter 5.

Chapter 6 is a refresher course of what you have learned up until this point. We will use all the knowledge we've acquired to finish building the first complete version of Superhero Generator 3000. By the end, you will be able to randomly create heroes with unique superpowers, names, and battle statistics!

In Chapter 7, we begin to learn more advanced techniques. To be a real coder, you must learn efficiency and reduce mistakes in your code. That is where *modules* and *built-in functions* come into play. Learn what they are and why they will make your life a whole lot easier in this exciting chapter!

Chapter 8 looks at even more advanced topics: specifically, we will cover the basics of *object-oriented programming (OOP)* and cover *objects* and *classes* and define a thing called *polymorphism.*

To switch things up a little bit, Chapter 9 will look at some different types of data structures, including tuples and dictionaries.

Chapter 10 brings us up to speed on how to create – and work with – files inside of directories.

One of my personal favorite chapters is Chapter 11, which covers a topic that is near and dear to my heart: Python for Gaming. We will stroll through the world of video games and learn how to work with video game elements, including sound, animation, and more!

Learning how to create games that interact with a user's actions and making images move within a game are truly what make games enjoyable. Chapter 12 continues the topic of gaming and focuses specifically on game animation.

In Chapter 13 – don't worry, in this case 13 is lucky, for you at least! – we move into areas of Python we have not yet discussed that do not fit in their own chapter. This includes how to *debug* – or find broken code. We also look at advanced modules and other topics.

Finally, we sum everything up in Chapter 14 and cover a wide range of topics, including how to find work as a Python programmer, common interview questions, the future of Python, and career paths, and answer some of the *frequently asked questions (FAQs)* about our favorite programming language.

So now that we know what we will learn, let's put on our cape and superhero outfits and get ready to leap tall buildings – of knowledge.

Why I Started Programming

I started programming a long, long time ago – back before the Internet or cell phones existed and when wild dinosaurs roamed the earth. Back then, computers didn't have images on them like they do today. Everything was text-based – even most of our games – the horror! While we did have *some* computer games with animation and graphics, they were 8-bit and not cinematic like the ones of today.

I was fortunate enough to share a computer with my older brother. I'm pretty certain my parents didn't know what a computer was used for, but must have thought: "This future-device will surely make my children Men... of... the... Future... future... future... future..." (just pretend the word is echoing).

And to some degree, they were correct: if they hadn't purchased my brother and me a computer, who knows what I would be doing with my life right now? Certainly not writing this book and helping you to program like a hero!

But having a giant paperweight made of jumbled electronics – back then we called it an Apple IIe – wasn't enough to entice me to use it all that much. After all, I happened to own a Nintendo Entertainment System (NES) as well, and it had an amazing slew of games that I still – embarrassingly – play to this day.

What really got me into computers was this: I had a friend, Nicholas Rini, who knew all about programming computers. He showed me one day how to "hack" into the code of a few of our favorite text-based games to give ourselves an advantage. It was akin to creating your very own cheat code in a video game. In particular, we played a game called Lemonade Stand, which was exactly the same as standing outside your house and selling homemade Lemonade, only you never made real money and you didn't get a sunburn.

In the game, you started out with a couple of dollars – barely enough to make any real profit. However, once we looked at the code running the game, we figured out that we could start out with however much money we wanted if we just changed a few words around. Soon enough, I was the world's first millionaire Lemonade Stand mogul.

I was hooked.

From there, it was not a far stretch to conceive that we could actually create our own video games, and that is exactly what we did. From complex role-playing games (RPG) based off of our favorite comic books and Dungeons & Dragons to programs that would ask our friends a series of questions and then make fun of them based off of their answers – shenanigans!

While all of that seemed silly at the time, looking back on it I now know that it helped set the foundation for my love of programming and, to a degree, writing (though I began writing much earlier than that). Without that summer of programming fun, I would never have had the wonderful experiences, friends, jobs, and writing opportunities that have come my way ever since.

And, mostly, I would never have had the *fun* of programming either.

That is what I am hoping to pass on to *you*, dear reader: a lifetime love of programming and opportunities all based off of one thing – the fun and joy of writing computer programs and writing code.

Sure, programming applications can be a pain in the butt. You will find yourself banging your head against a keyboard on many nights and yelling at the computer screen for hours only to find that your program isn't working because you forgot a parenthesis () somewhere.

But – once you find that mistake that you or another programmer made – there isn't quite anything like that triumphant moment when you realize that you – YOU – are the greatest coder of all time!

Programming Dos and Don'ts

When reading this book, you may find yourself feeling the urge to skip ahead a little or might want to skip an exercise or two. As in all things in life, this piece of advice holds true in learning to program as well: if you cheat, you are only cheating yourself.

To help keep you on the straight and narrow, here are some dos and don'ts for reading this book and for learning how to program, in general:

Do read the book straight through. While you might be okay to skip a chapter or an exercise here or there, keep in mind that this book is all about building a foundation of not just coding language, but coding practices, theory, and an understanding of programming principles that you can take with you that apply to *other* languages as well.

Don't copy and paste code from this book or any other source (assuming you have a digital copy). Instead, take the time to type in the code so that you can begin to get a feel for writing code and, perhaps, commit some of the code to memory through repetition.

Do experiment with code. One of the best ways, I've found, to learn how to *truly* code is to experiment. If you come across an example in the book, feel free to change the parameters some and see what happens. The worst that can happen is that you can fail. The best? That you learn something new!

Don't be afraid to Google other tutorials and how-tos on Python. This book is supposed to build a beginner's foundation, but it does not teach you everything there is to know – that's what the sequel is for! If you do decide to look up comparative examples, be certain to look at the date of the article and the *version* of Python. If the version does not match the version we are using in this book (Python 3), odds are your code will not work, and you will find yourself very confused.

Do document your code. We have not covered this topic – yet – but for now, know that *documentation* means to leave little comments in *blocks*, or sections, of your code that lets you (or another coder in the future) know what you intended to do with a certain section of code. While Python is a very readable language, the way every programmer codes is different, and what might be apparent to you is not always apparent to others. Also, if you have to review your own code at a later date, it will make it easier for you to remember what, exactly, you were trying to do at 4 a.m. 10 years ago!

Do plan out your code. That is, write down how you want your overall program to work and then break that down into little sections. Then, take those little sections and map out what you need to code for each part. This way you will have a roadmap to follow and won't just be coding by the seat of your pants.

Finally, *do* test your code frequently and save your work often. When we programmers are in the thick of things, we like to carry on, plugging away, for hours at a time. However, if we don't stop to test our code and save our files, we risk losing hours of work and, worse, creating a program with problems that are difficult to trace.

CHAPTER 1

Introduction to Computer Programming and Python

Computer programming – commonly referred to as "coding" by the cool kids – is the art of creating applications or software. These programs allow us to do everything from solving simple math problems and watching our favorite TikTok videos (I can't get enough of skydiving bulldogs) to destroying hordes of rampant aliens in our favorite video games and even launching a real-life spaceship into outer space.

I call computer programming an "art" because it *is*. Anytime you create something, you are indulging in an art form. Sure, computer code, the words we type into a shell to create our programs (more on this later!), may not be pretty to look at for the common person on the street – your code will never see the inside of an art exhibit most likely – but when a part of your program does what you created it to, there is almost nothing more magical.

Well, maybe those skydiving bulldogs.

A computer program can come in many shapes and sizes. In addition to an application that runs on your desktop system or a game that plays on your go-to video game console, programs also take the form of mobile apps on a cell phone. You can even find pieces of software that operate things like refrigerators, your mom's minivan, and even something as simple as a toaster oven.

And robots. Armies of robots.

But more on that later.

For now, know that a computer program is a set of code, created in a *programming language*, that tells a device to carry out a set of instructions.

© James R. Payne 2024
J. R. Payne, *Python for Teenagers*, https://doi.org/10.1007/978-1-4842-9988-3_1

Programming Language Overview

As mentioned, a computer program is written using a programming language. Just like the real language you, I, and the rest of the world speak every day, computer languages come in all shapes and sizes. While most of them make sense to the trained eye, a newcomer to code would sound like a crazy person spouting gibberish if they tried to use it in everyday conversation. That dialogue might look something like this:

```
Normal person: Hello, how are you?
Programmer (you): Print I am fine! Input, how are you?
```

Fortunately for all involved, computers are fluent in programming languages (thanks, in part, to our friend *the compiler* – but more on this later!) and can easily understand the most complex of sentences you type in.

For the purpose of this book, we will stick to one of the most versatile, yet easy-to-learn, languages, *Python*. While the name sounds frightening, keep in mind, it could be worse: it could be called *Cobra*. In truth, the language was not named after a reptile at all, but, instead, an old television comedy from Britain called *Monty Python and the Flying Circus*.

Here's your first assignment: Go ask your parents about that show. See you in a few hours!

Oh, you are back. Great. Did what they said make any sense? Probably not. But that's okay; you don't need to understand the complexities of British comedy to learn how to program using this book. All you need is a desire to learn, a computer, and the pages in front of you.

Python Overview

Python is what is known as a high-level, dynamic, interpreted, object-oriented programming language. While all of that may sound a bit intimidating, never fear! By the end of this book, you will be able to impress your friends with sentences much more daunting than the one above! All that statement really means is that Python is not a basic machine-level language, and as such, it needs an "interpreter" to "compile" it to machine language so that the computer can understand what it is you are trying to tell it.

This interpreter takes your code and converts it – or *compiles* it – into a series of 1s and 0s that a computer can plainly understand. All of that happens in the background, so don't worry if you do not quite understand it just yet.

Python is a relatively new programming language that was created in the late 1980s – back when your dad had a big funny mustache and your mom listened to bands with names like *Wham!* and *Poison.*

The man that created the language was a computer genius named Guido Van Rossum, who was bestowed with the fancy, nonsensical title, Benevolent Dictator for Life. Like technology, programming languages evolve as well, and Python is no different. It has gone through several versions over the years and is currently known as Python 3. More specifically, the latest release is 3.11.4, with 3.12 in beta (or test mode).

The numbers following the decimal – the 11.4 – represent updates to the programming language. Prior to 3.11.4, there was version 3.11.3, and so on.

How Does Python Differ from Other Programming Languages?

Python differs from other programming languages in a number of different – yet important – ways. For starters, Python is typically easier to learn and use than languages in the same class, such as Java and C++. Programs created in Python also take less time to create, as it requires less code (in general). This is due, in part, to Python's *data types* – a term we will cover in great detail in an upcoming chapter.

Python is also extremely versatile. While it may not be the primary choice, Python *can* be used for applications in virtually every arena, including gaming, desktop software, mobile apps, and even virtual reality. It is also a must for network programming and an essential tool in a computer security toolbox.

The Benefits of Python

Python is currently the most-used programming language in the world today and is the fastest growing as well. And with good reason. Below are just a few ways in which Python can benefit a programmer:

- Increased productivity: By some reports, Python can increase a programmer's productivity – how much work they can accomplish in a given time – by as much as ten times! It literally is faster than a speeding bullet!

- Extensibility: One great advantage of Python is the fact that it has a very extensive library or, well, *libraries*. A library is a set of existing code you can *add-in* to your program. These libraries cover things that are common features of a program and save you from having to write the code over and over again yourself. For example, instead of having to write a section of code to perform a complicated mathematical equation, you can simply use a library and save yourself a huge headache.

- Python is easy to read: One tough part of being a programmer is the fact that, sometimes, your code does not work. When that happens, you might find yourself re-reading your code – or worse, someone else's – to try and figure out why your program is not behaving as it should. Fortunately, Python is easy to read, and most of the language makes sense at a glimpse. This makes finding issues a lot easier than more complicated languages.

- Portability: Python runs on many platforms and systems, meaning your programs can reach a wider audience.

- Internet of Things (IoT): The Internet of Things may sound like a magical world full of digital beasts, and in some ways, it is. The IoT consists of smart objects – light switches, doorknobs, toaster ovens, appliances – that you find in your everyday home. These household appliances are controllable by voice commands and mobile devices, making them more interactive than their primitive predecessors. I mean sure, your mom and dad yelled at the dishwasher all the time – but did it ever listen? Now, thanks to the IoT and languages like Python, it can! You still have to put your dishes inside of it, but still!

- Python frameworks: Frameworks are like skeletons for a program – they allow you to quickly set up the basics for certain types of applications without needing to code common elements that usually exist in the type of software you are developing. This saves programmers time and reduces the number of errors that can occur when you have to manually code. Python is supported by a large number of frameworks that can make launching a new program very rapid indeed!

- Python is fun: Python is a fun language to learn; as stated, not only is it easy to get started, but the Python community hosts many fun events and challenges. For example, many people write their Python code in poetry form, and there are numerous Python "challenges" released every year to help test a coder's skills.

- Python is flexible: Because Python has so many uses and is used by so many companies around the world, finding a job after learning Python is easier than with other languages. In addition, if you do not like a given field, you can always use your Python skills to try a different path. For example, if you find that coding applications is boring, you could switch to network administration or work at an IT security firm.

And those are just a few of the benefits and advantages that Python offers.

Examples of Python in the Wild

While it is impossible to say just how many companies around the world use Python, there are a number of interesting businesses that rely on the language. Below is just a smattering of them:

- Wayne Enterprises (Batman's Alter Ego's corporation): Well, we don't really know that, but wouldn't that be cool!

- Google: The search engine giant and one day ruler of the galaxy, Google, has been using Python since its inception, partially because developers can build programs so quickly with it and also because the code is easy to maintain.

- Facebook and Instagram: While Python is not the only language used at these two social media platforms, it is one of their most important ones. Facebook uses Python, in part, thanks to its extensive libraries. Instagram, meanwhile, is a firm supporter of one of Python's main web frameworks – Django. We cover web frameworks in great detail later in this book.

- Netflix: If you are a fan of streaming movies, then you are no stranger to Netflix. The company uses Python primarily for its data-analysis capabilities and for security purposes – among other areas.

- Video games: Battlefield 2 and Civilization 4 are just two video games that both rely on Python. Interestingly enough, Civilization uses Python for, among other things, its artificial intelligence (AI) scripts.

- Government agencies and institutions: Government agencies and institutions including NASA, The National Weather Service, and the CIA all use Python – though how it is used is Top Secret! Meet us in the garage with a briefcase full of money, and we'll tell you all about it!

Your First Python Program

By now, you are probably wondering what Python code looks like. Well, fear not! I am going to show you a sample snippet. Later, after we install Python and an IDLE (integrated development environment) on your computer, you can try and execute – or run – the code to see it in action. For now, though, I thought it would be a good idea to just give you a taste before delving any further into the language.

Traditionally, when a programmer writes their first *ever* line of code, they create a program called, "Hello, World," as a metaphorical way to introduce themselves to the world. However, as budding superheroes – or villains (no judgment here) – we need something a little flashier.

Behold, your first Python program!

```python
print("Look up in the sky! Is it a bird? Is it a plane?")
print("Dun dun dun dun dun dun dun dun dun dun dun dun dun dun dun")
print("No you dummy. That's just some guy flying around in his pajamas. Now get back to work!")
```

If you were to run this code, the result would be:

```
Look up in the sky! Is it a bird? Is it a plane?
Dun dun dun dun dun dun dun dun dun dun dun dun dun dun dun
No you dummy. That's some guy flying around in his pajamas. Now get back to work!
```

Let's examine the code a little more closely. The part that says *print()* is known as a *function*, whose job it is to tell the computer to – in this case – *print* something to the user's screen. The text in between the opening and closing parentheses () is the *parameter* that we are providing the function. The characters in between the quotation marks " " are known as a *string*.

Don't worry if this doesn't make all the sense in the world just yet – we go over this topic in great detail in the next chapter. For now, just know that this is what Python code looks like. Odds are, you were able to tell exactly what this program would do *before* I told you; that is just one of the things that make Python so great – its readability!

Installing Python

In this section, we are going to learn how to install Python on the various *operating systems*. An operating system is a piece of software that lets you interact with a computer. You are probably familiar with the more popular ones, such as *Microsoft Windows* (if you own a PC) and *macOS* if you own an Apple computer. The version of Python you install will vary depending upon which one of these your computer uses. In addition, we will learn how to install Python on *Linux* and *Ubuntu* systems as well.

Installing Python on Windows

To begin, open up a web browser, and navigate to the official Python website and its download page: www.python.org/downloads/ (Figure 1-1).

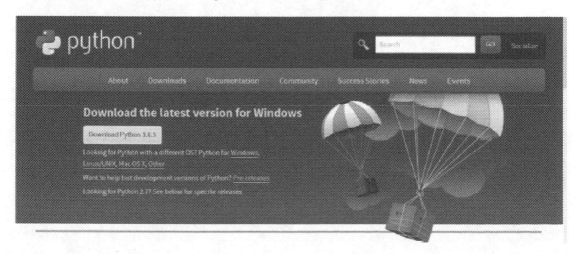

Figure 1-1. *Python.org website*

The current version of Python is 3.11.4; by the time you read this book, it may be higher than that. Whatever the case, click the "Download Python" button under the *Download the Latest Version for Windows* header. Optionally, you could scroll down and download previous versions (just make sure they are version 3.X or higher, as there are incompatibility issues between versions 2.X and 3.X); however, for the purposes of this book, it is always best to use version 3.11.4 or later.

Depending upon your system settings, an image may appear asking if you would like to save the file. If so, click "Save File," and save it to your Desktop or somewhere easily remembered.

Navigate to your Desktop or Downloads folder (or the location where you saved the file), and double-click it. It should appear similar to the image in Figure 1-2.

Figure 1-2. *Python .EXE install file icon*

The installer will launch and will ask you whether you wish to "Install Now" or "Customize Installation." For ease, we are going to allow the installer to "Install Now." Before you click that button, however, make sure that "Use admin privileges when installing py.exe" and "Add python.exe to PATH" are both checked. Then click the "Install Now" option (Figure 1-3).

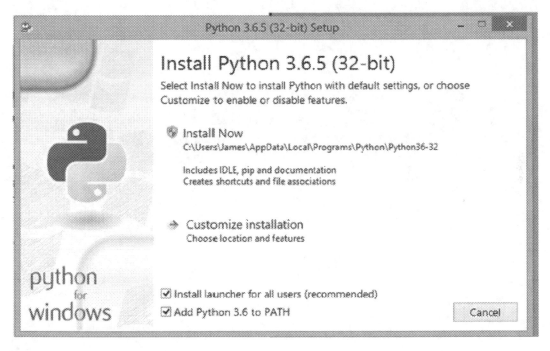

Figure 1-3. *Python install setup screen*

You may get a pop-up from Windows asking for permission to continue the installation. If so, allow the program to continue. A new pop-up will appear, showing you the Setup Progress (Figure 1-4).

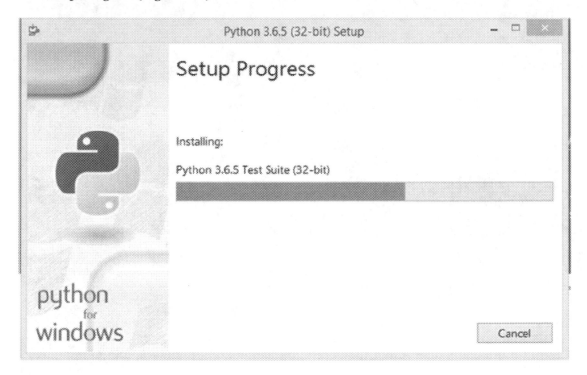

Figure 1-4. *Python installation progress screen*

Once Setup is complete, you will see a screen like the one below. Click the "Close" button to complete installation (Figure 1-5).

Figure 1-5. *Python install setup successful window*

You should now have Python installed on your computer. You can find it in your "Start" menu, labeled Python 3.11 (or whichever version you installed).

When you launch Python, the first thing you see is the *shell*, which is a piece of the development environment where you can write a line of code, test code, run code, and create Python files. Figure 1-6 shows an example of how the Python Shell will appear once launched.

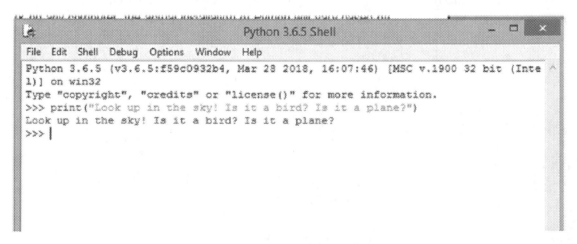

Figure 1-6. *The Python Shell*

At the top of this shell window, you can see the current version of Python and some other information. You will also see three greater-than symbols or arrows (>>>). These are known as the command *prompt*, and it is here that you will type in your instructions to Python.

Ready to dive in? Let's type in some simple code and see what happens! Enter the following into the prompt:

```python
print("Look up in the sky! Is it a bird? Is it a plane?")
```

When you finish, press *Enter* and you should see a result that looks like the following (Figure 1-7).

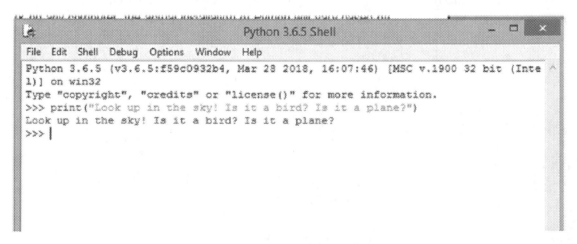

Figure 1-7. *Example code written in the Python Shell*

If not, re-check your code and make sure you spelled everything properly and remembered to insert your parentheses () and quotation marks " ".

Since we are working directly in the shell, our code gets *executed* – or run – in real time. In this instance, it ran a single line of code, which told the computer to print a line of text to the screen.

In the real world, we want to create actual Python files so that we can save our programs for later use and to help us save us from re-writing thousands of lines of code each time we want to run our program.

Fortunately, Python IDLE – Python's version of an IDE or integrated development environment – lets us create Python files, that is, files that end in the extension .py, quite easily.

To open IDLE, go back to your start menu and type in "IDLE." This will open the IDLE Shell.

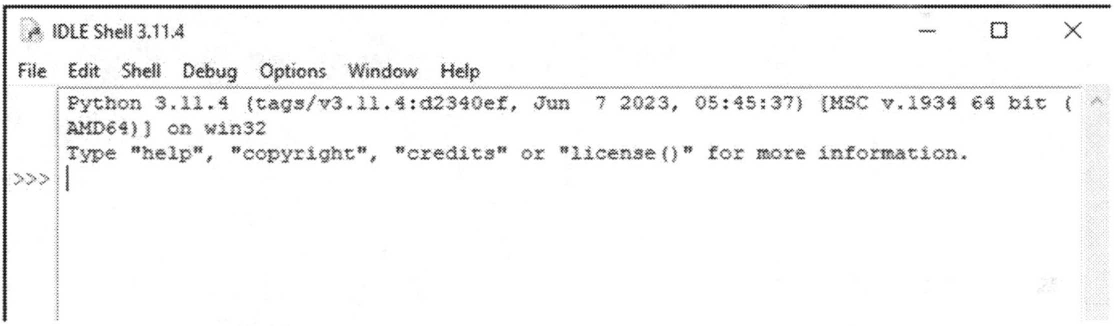

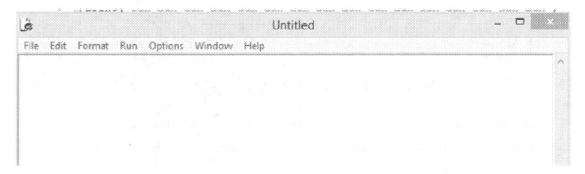

Figure 1-8. Example of Python IDLE

Now, to create a new Python file to add your code into, all you have to do is click *File*, then *New File* (see Figures 1-9, 1-10, and 1-11).

Figure 1-9. A newly created .py file

A new window will pop up. This is where you can write your code and save it for later. That being said, let's enter in the example code we just used. Then click *File*, then *Save*.

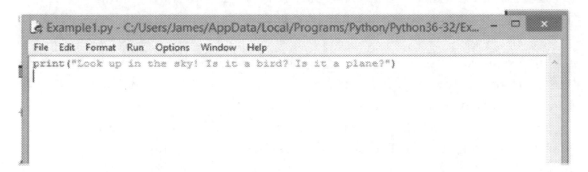

Figure 1-10. *Example code written in a .py file*

Next click *File*, then *Save*.

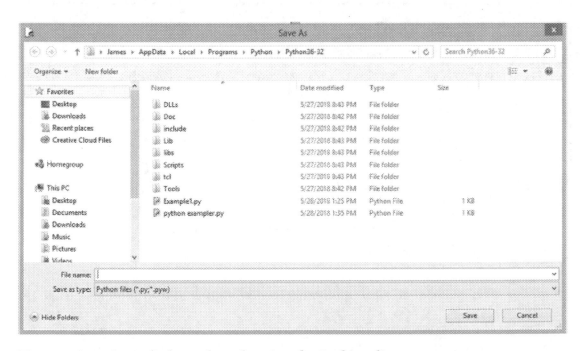

Figure 1-11. *Save dialogue box showing the Python directory*

Enter in the name of the file and click the *Save* button to finish creating the file. For the purposes of this book, let's keep things simple and name our file *Example1.py*.

There you have it – you created your very first real-world Python program. To run this program, click Run and then choose Run Module. Your program will now execute in the Python Shell (Figure 1-12)!

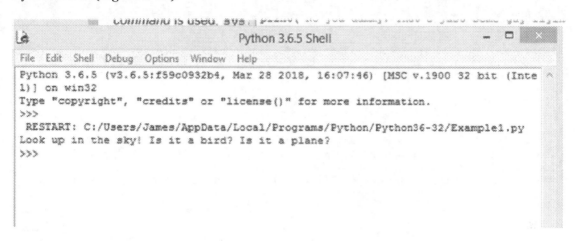

Figure 1-12. *Result of the .py file run in the Python Shell*

Now, let's wrap things up: remember the original first program we wrote at the beginning of this chapter? Let's enter that into our Example1.py file, and click *Save* once you are finished. Here is the code again:

```python
print("Look up in the sky! Is it a bird? Is it a plane?")
print("Dun dun dun dun dun dun dun dun dun dun dun dun dun dun dun dun")
print("No you dummy. That's just some guy flying around in his pajamas. Now
get back to work!")
```

Once you have saved the file, click *Run* and choose *Run Module* to see the full code in action (Figure 1-13)!

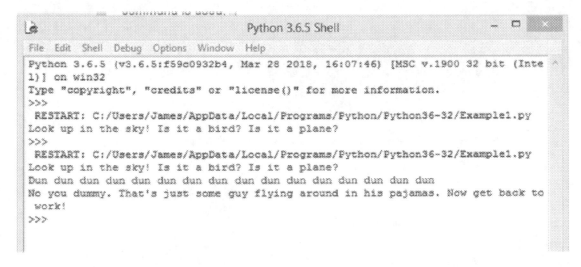

Figure 1-13. *Another example of a .py file running in the Python Shell*

Installing Python on Other Operating Systems

This book uses Python installed on a Windows-based computer; while the code inside will work on *any* computer, the actual installation of Python will vary based off of your operating system.

To install Python on macOS, open a web browser and navigate to `www.python.org/downloads/macos/`. Choose the "Latest Python 3 Release" link, and follow the instructions and prompts to complete the Setup and Installation process.

To install Python on Unix/Linux systems, open a browser and go to `www.python.org/downloads/source`. Click the link for the "Latest Python 3 Release," and follow the instructions to complete the Setup and Installation process.

In This Episode!

We certainly covered a lot in this chapter, but it is nothing compared to what we will unmask in the chapter to come! Here is a brief list – a summary if you will – of the things we covered thus far (hey, we are programming heroes now, we have to speak the lingo as well!):

- Python is a programming language that lets you program computers, mobile devices, video games, artificial intelligence systems, the Internet of Things (IoT) devices, web-based applications, and even virtual reality/augmented reality (VR/AR).

- A program or application is a group of code that lets you give a computer or device a set of instructions to carry out.

- Programmers that know Python can pursue careers in programming, network administration, IT security, video game development, mobile application creation, forensic computer science, and more.

- Python works across multiple platforms, including Windows PCs, Mac computers, mobile devices, Unix/Linux-driven computers, and more.

- Python can be used to prevent hacking via a set of skills and modules known as "ethical hacking" tools.

- IDLE stands for integrated development environment; it is where we create our Python code and files.

- Files created by Python end in the file extension ".py".

- The current – as of this writing – version of Python is 3.11.4. If you are reading this book, be sure to use this version or later.

- The `print()` function lets you print text to a user's screen. For example, `print("Hello Wall!")` would print the text: Hello Wall! to the computer screen.

- Many organizations and companies around the globe use Python, including Facebook, Google, Snapchat, NASA, the CIA, and more!

- Python is the most-used – and fastest-growing – computer programming language in the world.

CHAPTER 2

It All Adds Up

Now that we are all suited up in our metaphorical capes and superhero outfits (i.e., we have installed Python and learned how to use the IDLE); it is time to put our new superpowers to the test! Our first villain? Perhaps one of the most nefarious, vile, contemptuous beasts of all time; a criminal of the school system, running rampant and threatening to destroy – or bore – every student in its path. The villain's name?

Math.

I know, not the most exciting of topics. At least, not at first glance. However, the truth of the matter is math, and, more importantly, mathematical functions, are the bread and butter of the programming world. Without math, we wouldn't be able to do any of the nifty things that computers and mobile devices allow us to do. There would be no computer games, no spaceships in outer space, no robots of the future to help us clean our filthy rooms.

Without math, we would truly be a civilization lost.

The purpose of this chapter, therefore, will be how to deal with math and create simple or complex mathematical equations using some of Python's built-in *mathematical functions*.

Similar to the print( ) function we learned back in Chapter 1, the math functions we are about to discuss will let us perform pre-built actions on data without having to code common elements of an application. So, for example, instead of writing a lot code explaining to the computer what addition is and how to actually add numbers (remember, a computer can only do what we tell it; it can't think for itself – not yet anyway!), which would require thousands of lines of code were we to do it from scratch, all we have to do is type something simple, such as

1+1

Go ahead – type that into the Python Shell. When you do, it should dutifully return the answer: 2.

© James R. Payne 2024
J. R. Payne, *Python for Teenagers*, https://doi.org/10.1007/978-1-4842-9988-3_2

Like the math you learned in school, Python was built to inherently understand basic mathematical functions. If you see this: 8/2, your brain *knows* that this equation involves division. If you see a + symbol, it is obviously addition, and a - means subtraction. Python understands these symbols as well and will perform math based upon them. Try typing this into the Python shell:

```
2+2-1
```

Python will return 3 in this instance, showcasing that it can understand the common *mathematical operators*. An operator, in Python, includes the following: +, -, and / – to name but a few.

How about multiplication? Type this in:

```
2x2
```

What happened there? The program did not return 4 as we would have expected. Instead, it returned a *SyntaxError*: invalid syntax exception. SyntaxErrors mean that something is wrong in the Syntax – the written text – that you input into the shell or the Python file that prevents the program from running properly.

In other words, Python does not understand you.

Here, the solution is simple: in programming, the operator for multiplication is not an "x" – instead, it is an asterisk (*). To fix our SyntaxError, all we have to do is replace the wrong multiplication operator with the correct one, like so:

```
2*2
```

Now if you type that in, it will return the expected response – the number 4.

Operator Precedence

One of the evil villain Math's superpowers is to confuse us with concepts that seem too difficult to grasp. Never fear! With our superhero calculating powers, not even Math's most complex riddles can stump us.

Not that it won't try, mind you!

When performing calculations in Python, we always have to be aware of a thing called *operator precedence*. This is just fancy speak for the order in which Python performs mathematical problems. Certain operators have a higher precedence – meaning they go first in line – than other operators. As you can imagine, this can be confusing to a programmer, and even the most seasoned veterans can make mistakes when entering calculations.

To give you a clearer picture of how operator precedence works, here is a list of operators in Python, sorted by precedence or who gets to go first in an equation. Note: some of these operators may be unfamiliar to you – don't worry too much about that right now; we will cover them in great detail throughout this book.

- ** (Exponentiation)

- *, / (Multiplication and division)

- +, - (Addition and subtraction)

- in, not in, is, is not, <, <=, >, >=, !=, == (These are known as comparisons, which allow you to compare one value to another)

- not x

- and

- or

- if-else

To keep things simple, let's work with the basic operators: *, /, +, and - (multiplication, division, addition, and subtraction). Type the following into your shell:

```
10+10 * 20
```

In this equation, we are asking what the value of 10 *plus* 10 is when multiplied by 20. Normally, we would expect that the answer would be 400, because the first value – 10 plus 10 – should equal 20. Then, we would multiply that answer (20) by 20, resulting in 400. However, when we enter the code in the shell, we get a surprising result, as shown in Figure 2-1.

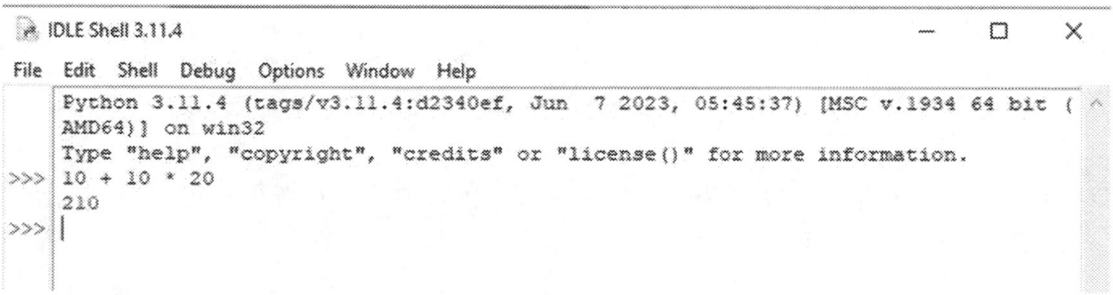

Figure 2-1. *Example of operator precedence*

Your first thought may be: is Python bad at math? How did it come up with the answer: 210? This occurs because of operator precedence. Remember from our list of operator precedence, multiplication goes first in line, ahead of addition. Therefore, Python *evaluates* the multiplication *first*, then does the math. In this instance, Python views our equation this way: 20 * 10 + 10.

I know what you are thinking: my head hurts.

This may seem confusing at first glance, but fortunately, there is a simple solution. We can force Python to use an *order of evaluation* – the order in which to perform calculations – by using parentheses. This has two effects: first, it ensures Python performs the calculation we want and doesn't confuse our precedence. Second, it lets other programmers know what you really intended with your equation, at a simple glance.

Let's try it out. Type the following into your shell:

```
(10+10)   * 20
```

As you can see in Figure 2-2, now we get the result we want. By placing (10+10) inside of parentheses, we are telling Python – and other coders – that we intended for that part of the equation to be performed first (see Figure 2-2).

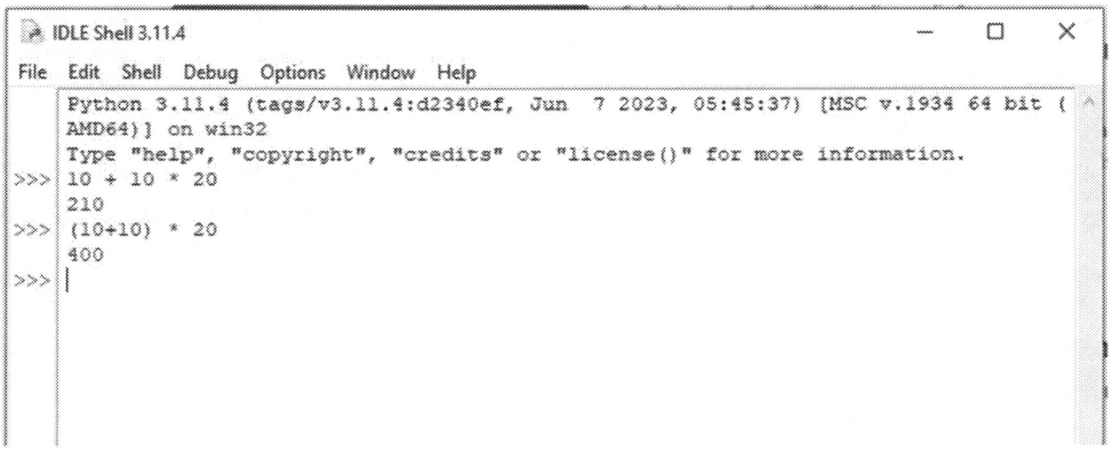

Figure 2-2. *Example of operator precedence using parentheses to force order*

To make matters a little more complicated, we can also do something known as *nesting*. This means that you place parentheses *inside* of other parentheses, to further dictate what order calculations should be performed. In a case such as this, the innermost parentheses are evaluated first, then the outer, then the rest of the equations. Consider this:

```
((10+5) * 10) / 2
```

If you were to type that equation into Python, it would perform the order of evaluation in the following manner:

- 10 + 5 equals 15

- 15 * 10 equals 150

- 150 / 2 equals 75

However, if we did not use parentheses, Python would read it this way:

10 + 5 * 10 / 2
Or

- 10 / 2 equals 5

- 5 * 5 equals 25

- 25 + 10 equals 35

This is, again, because Python performs multiplication and division *before* addition and subtraction when looking at operator precedence.

So, to avoid any confusion, always use parentheses when performing anything other than simple mathematics.

Data Types: Know Your Enemy

Super villains come in all shapes and sizes. You have your evil scientist, bent on destroying the world with death rays and genetically modified gorillas; there are the evil green ones, rippling with muscle and full of rage because, well, for no real good reason at all. Then there are the ones that laugh all the time even though no one has told a single joke.

There are thousands of types of villains, and as a fledgling superhero, you can bet it gets hard to keep them all in order. Is Mr. Mindblower a super smarty, or is he a misunderstood villain who just can't get his act together? What about the mysterious Stephen King Kong – half-gorilla, half-horror writer – what the heck is he? And how does he write so many books with those big gorilla knuckles?

It's enough to make you lose your mind.

Or is that Mr. Mindblower at work again?

Fortunately, there is a way to keep all of these villains organized. It's called archetypes.

In Python, we have a similar issue. There are all sorts of data floating around. We have numbers and text for starters. To make matters worse, we have different *types* of numbers. You have regular numbers, you have numbers with decimals, and you have numbers that represent things like time or money. There are even numbers that behave the same way that words behave.

Fortunately, in Python there is a thing known as *data types*. These are ways to define or classify what type of data you are entering into your programs. While it might seem that this should be common sense – and sometimes it is – the truth is, Python only knows what you tell it to know. The same goes for all computer languages. In fact, all computer languages have data types, just like Python, so the concept of data types is something you can bring with you as you learn other languages.

There are several forms of data types that we will be discussing in this book, but for this chapter, we are going to concentrate on one specific set: numbers.

In general, Python recognizes numbers as numbers, but, as you can imagine, not all numbers are created equal. To keep things simple, for now, know that any number you see that is a whole number or that does not have a decimal point in it is called an *integer*. Integers include numbers like 0, 2, 5, 10, 100, 1000, 1032, and so on.

Try out the following code:

```
print(122)
```

Your result should look like this (see Figure 2-3):

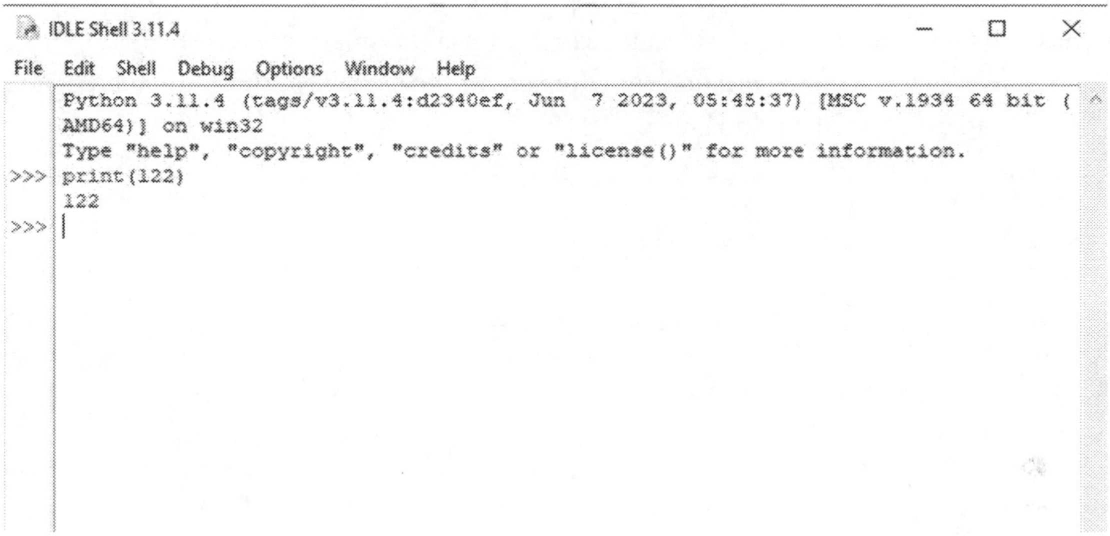

Figure 2-3. *Printing an integer*

As we saw earlier, integers are for more than just printing to the user's screen – we can do calculations, as you know. Let's try the following:

```
print(5/2)
```

Something interesting happens when this code runs, as shown in Figure 2-4:

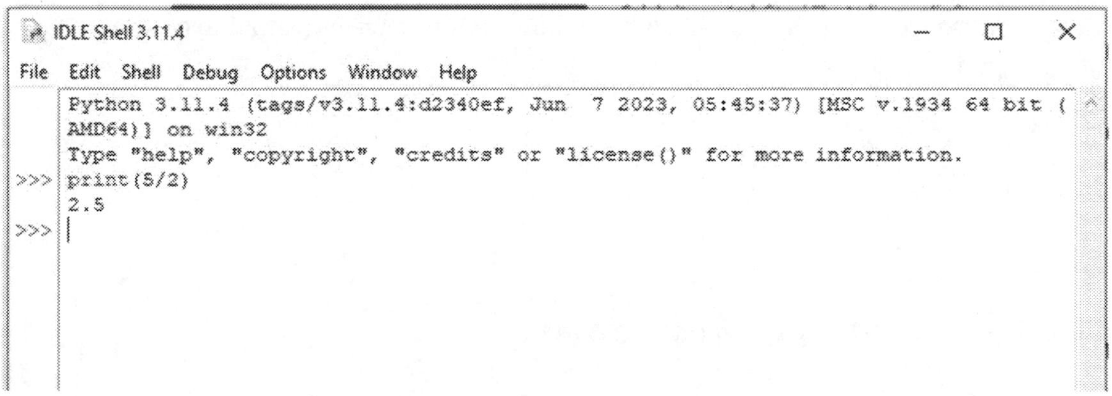

Figure 2-4. *Performing math inside of a print( ) function*

The number returned does not fit into the criteria of an integer, despite the fact that we performed math on *two* integers. Whenever a number has a decimal, it is no longer considered an integer data type; it is, instead, a *float* or *floating-point number*.

Just as we can perform equations on integers, so, too, can we perform them on floats. We show an example of this in Figure 2-5.

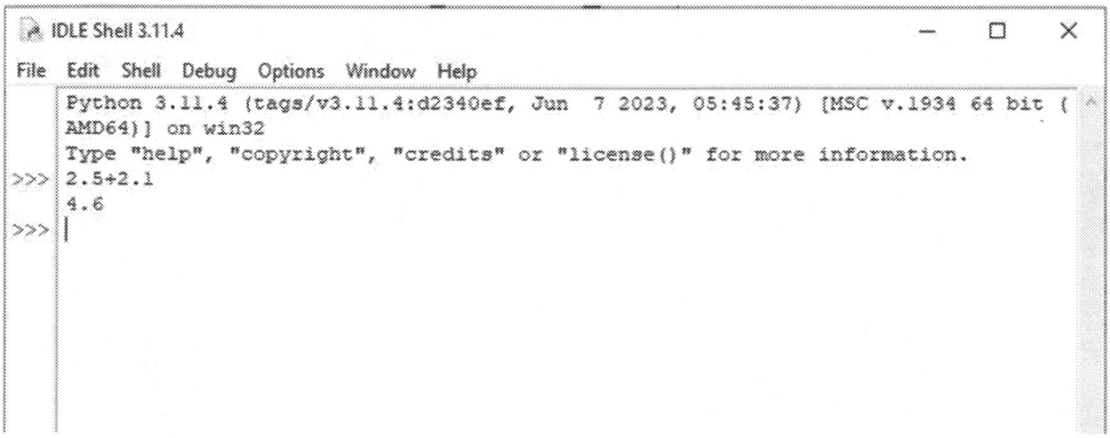

Figure 2-5. *A float data type*

When a float is added to another float, the result is another float. This holds true even if the number seems like it should be a whole number or integer. For example, if I asked for the result of 2.5 + 2.5, you would probably answer: 5. Let's see what Python has to say about that:

As you can see from Figure 2-6, Python did something we may not have expected: it returned 5.0 – a float.

```
>>> 2.5+2.5
5.0
>>> |
```

Figure 2-6. *Performing math on two floats*

While this is an appropriate result, we may find ourselves in a situation where we need to change the data type of our numbers. For example, we may have a program where we do not want to show decimal points or want to round up our numbers. In this case, one option would be to convert our numbers.

Before we learn about that, however, let's try one more thing. What happens when we perform math on an integer *and* a float? Try the following (see Figure 2-7):

```
print(5 - 2.5)
```

Your result should be the following.

```
>>> 5-2.5
2.5
>>>
```

Figure 2-7. *The result of a float subtracted from an integer*

Anytime you perform math on an integer and a float, the result will always be a float.

Converting Number Data Types

In this section, the first thing we are going to learn how to do is convert an integer into a float. In our previous example, we used a simple method to convert our integer into a float: division. Another way that we can achieve the same effect is to use one of Python's built-in functions known as `float()`.

Using `float()` is very simple – all you have to do is place the integer you want to convert inside of the parentheses ( ). Let's give it a go!

```
float(12)
```

If you type that into the Python Shell, you will get the following result.

```
>>> float(12)
12.0
>>>
```

Figure 2-8. *Converting an integer into a float*

As Figure 2-8 shows, your result should be *12.0* (instead of just regular 12 with no decimal point).

To do the reverse – convert a float into an integer – we use another of Python's super-duper handy built-in functions. Behold, `int()`!

The function `int()` works the same as `float()`. Just type in the number you wish to convert in between the parentheses, and Python does the rest. Try it out:

```
int(12.0)
```

This will return:

```
>>> int(12.0)
12
>>>
```

Figure 2-9. *Converting a float into an integer*

As shown in Figure 2-9, we took a floating-point number – 12.0 – and converted it to an integer, 12, by removing the decimal point.

What happens if we have a float that does not end in .0 though? Let's find out with a simple test. Type this into your Python Shell:

```
int(12.6)
```

When you press enter, you will get the result: 12. Why not 13? When you convert a float to an integer, Python removes everything after the decimal point and ignores it. If you wanted to round up (or round down), you would need to use a different function, which we will cover later in this book.

There are many data types that we can convert to other data types, and we will be covering the rest of them throughout this book. For now, however, give yourself a round of applause – you've added two new superpowers to your arsenal: the `int()` and `float()` functions!

What Are Variables?

So far, we have learned some basic math operators and functions that we can use to convert data types from one to the other. However, for us to have any *real* power, we need to learn about a secret weapon known as the *variable*.

There are several easy ways to think of variables that will make them easier to understand. One way is to think of them as a box that you store something in. In our case, the thing that we store in them is data. That data can be numbers, it can be text, it can be a monetary value, the name of your dog, a paragraph of text, or the security code to your secret lair.

Variables serve many functions in Python, as well as other programming languages. One of the greatest uses of variables is to store information so that we do not have to continuously type it over and over again. For example, you might have a long list of numbers that you use frequently. Instead of typing that long list out every time you need it, you could just store it in a variable and call upon the variable instead.

To use a variable, all you do is give it a name and then define its value. For example:

```
a = 8675309
```

This code creates the variable name – "a" – and then assigns it a value, which, in this case, is 8675309.

Of course, storing data is one thing; using that data is another. Let's go ahead and create a simple program that will give two variables some data and then print it out to the user's screen. Remember how to create a new Python file from our first program example? In the Python Shell, click *File*, then *New File*. A new window will pop up. Enter the following code into the new window:

```
a = 500
b = 250
print(a)
print(b)
```

Next, click *File*, then *Save*. Give the file the name *VariableTest.py*. To see the code in action, click *Run*, then *Run Module*.

The code will run in the Python Shell, as shown in Figure 2-10:

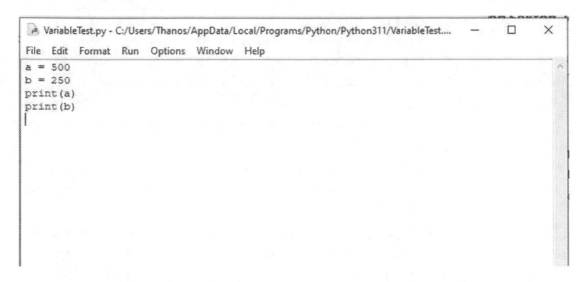

Figure 2-10. *Printing the values of two variables*

So, as you can see, we assigned the variable "a" the value of 500 and then assigned variable "b" the value of 250. Then, using the print function, we printed out the values of both variables. Now for some real fun!

Printing out the value of variables is pretty boring, let's be fair. However, printing is not the only thing that we can do with our variables. Let's modify the code of VariableTest.py. Add the following code to the file, so that it looks like this:

```
a = 500
b = 250
print(a)
print(b)
print(a+b)
```

Save the file and then run it again to see the result, which should match Figure 2-11.

```
500
250
750
>>> |
```

Figure 2-11. *Showing the results of adding – and printing – two variables*

Here, we created our two variables and gave them a value, just as before. We also printed them out. However, this time we also performed some math on them and printed out the result. The code in the line: print(a +b) tells Python to print whatever is inside of the print( ) function's parentheses( ) – in this case, we are saying to print the equation (a) + (b), which is 750.

Note that this *does not* change the value of the data in variable "a" or "b" – it simply performs math using them. To change the data inside of a variable, we have a few different options. Let's create a new file and name it VariableChange.py. Enter this code into it:

```
a=500
b=250
a=a+b
print(a)
```

Run the code to see the result (shown in Figure 2-12):

```
750
>>>
```

Figure 2-12. *Assigning the result of two variables to a variable*

So what happened here? First, we named and defined the values of variables "a" and "b." Then we added the values of the two variables together and reassigned the value of variable "a" to match the result of that equation. Then, we printed out variable "a" to show the new value, which was 750.

When we type in a=, we told Python to change the value of "a" to whatever came after the equal (=) sign. Next Python added "a" and "b" together and assigned that value back to "a." The equal sign (=) is known as the *assignment operator*.

We can also create a whole new variable if we did not want to change the value of variable "a." Let's modify the code in VariableChange.py so that it matches the following:

```
a=500
b=250
c=a+b
print(c)
```

This time, instead of changing the value of "a," we simply created a new variable "c" and gave it the value of "a" + "b," then printed out the contents of "c."

Superhero Generator 3000

Now that we have some code experience under our belt, let's use it to build the basis of a program that we are going to create by the end of this book. The program is going to be a superhero generator that lets users create heroes (or villains) complete with statistics, random names, and randomly generated powers and statistics.

Some of the following code will add text to our program, which we will be covering in greater detail in Chapter 3. For now, we will be using this text as labels only, so you should have no trouble understanding the code.

Every hero has certain physical and mental attributes. If you have played role-playing games – or RPGs – before, then you are familiar with this concept. If not, no worries! Just look around at the people near you and observe them. Your Phys Ed coach, for example, may have muscles and be in really good shape. This would mean he has more *strength* and *endurance* than, say, your science teacher.

On the flip side, your science teacher is probably smarter and wiser than your P.E. coach, meaning that he has more *intelligence* and *wisdom*. Let's start with these attributes as our first four stats – or statistics. We can always add more later.

To determine the value of each, we need to assign a range of low to high. We can use a range of 0–20 for now, with 0 being low and 20 being high. So, if we were discussing strength, then 0 would be extremely weak and 20 would be Hercules. An average, therefore, would be 10.

Likewise, for intelligence, we could say 0 would be a doorknob (hence the phrase "dumb as a doorknob"), and 20 would be Albert Einstein. Anyone falling in the 10 range would be considered of average intelligence.

Now, we could allow players to set their own attribute scores, but then, we know that everyone would just set them to 20 and be the strongest, smartest person alive. And while that does define you and I perfectly, other mere mortals just don't measure up to those high standards.

Instead, what we would want to do is assign the values to their attributes *randomly*. Python is capable of creating random numbers fairly easily using a function called – you guessed it – random().

Using `random()` is a bit different than other functions. To use it, we first have to `import` it into Python. We do this with a simple line of code:

```
import random
```

The `random()` function works like other functions, in that you can assign parameters to its parentheses. Create a new Python file called RandomGenerator.py, and type in the following code:

```
import random
strength = random.randint(1,20)
print(strength)
```

In this code, we first import the random() module, then create a variable named "strength." One important thing to note about variables. There is a thing called *naming conventions* in the programming world. What that means is that there are certain "rules" you should follow when naming things. With a variable, you always want to name them something that will let you or a future programmer know what type of data is being held in the variable. Naming a variable "a," for instance, does not give us much information. Naming it "strength" tells us exactly what the data inside is for.

If your variable name has more than one word in it, always keep them as one word and simply capitalize the first letter of the second word. For example, if our variable were "Hero Strength," we would name it heroStrength. If it were "Hero Strength Stats," we would use heroStrengthStats.

A second rule of thumb is to always keep it as short and simple as possible. Remember, variables are used to save time typing code, so long names defeat the purpose.

Back to the code….

After creating our variable "strength," we want to assign a value to it. The next part of the code calls upon the random() module and uses an attribute called `randint`. Randint is a part of random() and tells Python not just to create a random number but to create a random integer. The value that we place in parentheses is the range of the random number. Remember, we want our stats to range between 1 and 20, so therefore, the value that we input was (1,20).

Try running the code from RandomGenerator.py several times. You should get a random number each time:

Now that we have our random number generator working and understand how to use it, let's add some more stats:

```
import random
strength = random.randint(1,20)
intelligence = random.randint(1,20)
endurance = random.randint(1,20)
wisdom = random.randint(1,20)
```

Next, we need to print these values to the screen to test them. For that, we are going to use some text as labels, then print the value of each variable after its respective label. Add this code after your variables:

```
print("Your character's statistics are:")
print("Strength:", strength)
print("Intelligence", intelligence)
print("Endurance", endurance)
print("Wisdom", wisdom)
```

Here we encounter a different use of the print( ) function. Before, we were using print( ) to print numbers and variables. However, now we are using a new data type, known as the *string*. A string is simply text. It can contain any letter, special character (!, @, #, $, %, ^, &, *, -, +, =, etc.), and any number. However, for it to be considered text, it *must* be placed between quotation marks " ". If not, Python will interpret it as something else. Don't worry too much about this right now – we go over it in great detail in Chapter 3. For now, let's examine one line of code:

```
print("Your character's statistics are:")
```

This code literally tells the computer to print "Your character's statistics are:" to the screen.

The next instruction is a little different:

```
print("Strength:", strength)
```

This print( ) function does two things. First, it says print the text between the parentheses: "Strength:". Then, we add a comma (,), which tells Python there are further instructions for the print( ) function. Next, we include the name of the variable whose contents we want to print – in this case, the variable *strength*. Note that the variable is not in quotation marks. If it were, it would only print the word "strength" vs. the contents of the variable named strength.

So now, your RandomGenerator.py file should look like this:

```python
import random
strength = random.randint(1,20)
intelligence = random.randint(1,20)
endurance = random.randint(1,20)
wisdom = random.randint(1,20)
print("Your character's statistics are:")
print("Strength:", strength)
print("Intelligence", intelligence)
print("Endurance", endurance)
print("Wisdom", wisdom)
```

Let's run the code a few times. Keep in mind that our program creates randomly generated numbers, so the results will vary each time we execute the code. Figure 2-13 shows a sample of what it should look like:

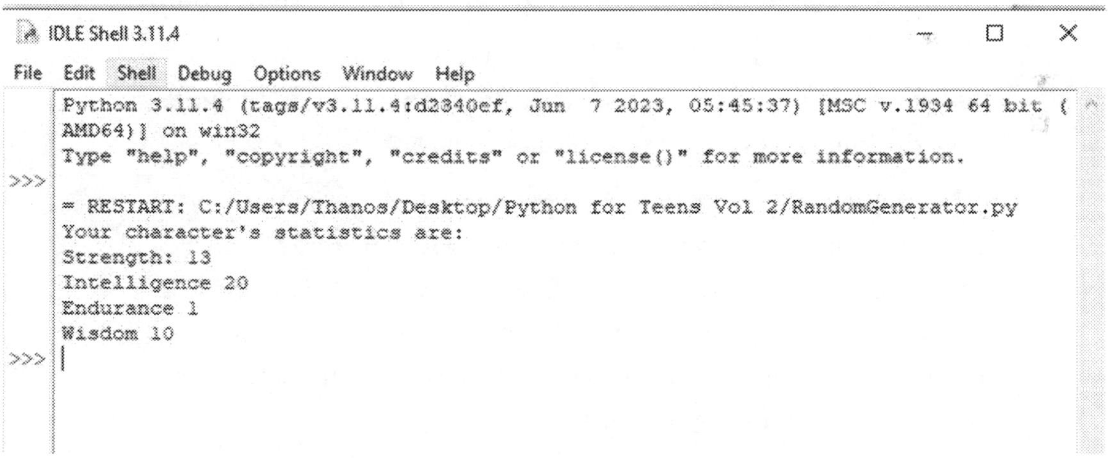

Figure 2-13. *Generating random statistics*

Congratulations, you just created the beginning part of the Superhero Generator 3000 application!

In This Episode!

We covered a lot of ground in this exciting episode. You started out as a young sidekick, but your powers are steadily growing! Soon you'll transform from Wonder Boy to... Wonder Man? I don't know – we'll work on the name. All that really matters is that you have made your first steps onto the path of coding like a superhero.

What perils lie ahead? Next chapter, we will look at working with text and continue to build upon our Superhero Generator 3000 application. We will also begin to document and comment on our work, a programming practice that is mandatory if you ever hope to be one of the greats!

Before we can move forward though, let's look at what we learned in this installment:

- Data types: Data types exist in all programming languages and help define the sort of data a program is handling. Integer – or int – is a data type for whole numbers, while float is the data type for floating, point numbers, or numbers with decimals.

- Operator precedence: Certain operators take precedence over – or go before – other operators when equations are performed.

- Operators: Common operators include + (addition), - (subtraction), * (multiplication), and / (division).

- Assignment operator: The equal sign (=) is known as an assignment operator, allowing you to assign a value to a variable.

- Order of operation: The order that mathematical operations are performed is known as order of operation. We can control which math is performed in an equation first by encapsulating sections in parentheses. For example, (1+1) * 10 ensures that 1+1 is performed prior to the multiplication, despite the fact that multiplication has operator precedence over addition.

- Converting data types: int( ) and float( ) allow us to convert a floating-point number to an integer and an integer to a floating-point number, respectively.

- Variables: Variables are storage units for data. You can also think of them as labels that point to the location of data, but it may be easier to think of them as a box that can contain a piece of information. We create variables by naming them and assigning value to them with the assignment operator. For example, a = 12.

- Naming conventions: Naming conventions are loose rules that help make coding easier – for you and any future programmers reading your code. Think of them as a "best practice." When naming a variable, for instance, always use lowercase letters for the first word and capital for any words following. Be sure to group multiple words into one word. For example, socialSecurity is good. Social Security is bad and will result in a SyntaxError. Also, try to name variables with short names that describe what the data in them is used for.

- random( ) and randint( ): random( ) is a module that lets you generate random numbers. You must import it into your program using the code: import random. To randomly generate an integer with a given range of numbers, type random.randint(1,20) or random. randint(5,100) if you wanted to generate numbers randomly from 1 to 20 or 5 to 100, respectively. If you wanted to generate numbers from 0 to 20, you must specify that in code, such as random.randint(0,20).

CHAPTER 3

Stringing Things Along

Welcome back intrepid hero! One thing you should know about superheroes and villains (especially villains) – they tend to blather on. Thankfully, this chapter is all about increasing your abilities and granting you the new superpower to handle all things text and text-related!

We will learn the basics of handling and manipulating text, including common text functions and details about the text data type. We will also cover formatting text and converting text to different data types. Finally, we will cover the importance of good documentation and how to comment on your code to save you – and future programmers – a lot of headaches.

So, slip into you bright green tights and pop on that Day-Glo orange mask. Clean the ketchup stain off your Wonder Boy (or Girl) logo, and get your fingers nice and limber.

Prepare to code!

Leave Your Comments at the Door

Before we delve any further into the language of programming, it is important to cover a topic that we have alluded to, yet avoided, thus far. Just like proper naming conventions, the art of *commenting* – or documenting – your code is one of those best practices that a good coder always, well, practices. It's sort of like ironing your cape before you leave the house. Sure, you can skip it, but then you risk your arch-nemesis making fun of you.

There are several reasons to comment on your code. First of all, programmers often have to look back through their code at a date later than when they first programmed it. This can be days, weeks, months, and even years. Looking back through thousands of lines of code can be taxing, especially if you have to identify what each section does. If you have your sections labeled and sporting a brief description, it becomes easier to navigate and find problem areas or sections that you may need to update later on down the line.

© James R. Payne 2024
J. R. Payne, *Python for Teenagers*, https://doi.org/10.1007/978-1-4842-9988-3_3

Another reason you should practice documenting your code is that other programmers will likely need to review it at some point in time. These programmers could be your boss, your co-workers, or a coder in the future who needs to make changes to something you wrote before they were even hired.

Finally, there are times where you will reuse code from one program in another one – we call this efficiency (so long as your company allows you to do this of course!). In these instances, finding the code snippet you are looking for will be much faster if you have commented/documented your work.

There are many different ways that programmers leave comments – every person has their own style. Some companies may require that you document your code in a very specific, formatted style, while others leave it up to you.

One other thing: while a comment is written in your code, the interpreter or compiler implicitly ignores them. This means that they do not affect your code at all – unless you enter them using the wrong syntax.

To comment, you use the hashtag or # symbol. Anything appearing after the # on the rest of that line is considered a comment. Here is an example of a comment:

```
# This block of code randomly calculates a hero's stats.
```

If you run that code, nothing will happen, again, because Python ignores comments. They are not there for computer consumption, only for humans and sub-humans (a.k.a. programmers).

Let's look at how commenting looks next to code. Remember our RandomGenerator. py file from the last chapter? Open it up and add the following text to it:

```
import random
# This block of code randomly calculates a hero's status.
strength = random.randint(1,20)
intelligence = random.randint(1,20)
endurance = random.randint(1,20)
wisdom = random.randint(1,20)
print("Your character's statistics are:")
print("Strength:", strength)
print("Intelligence", intelligence)
print("Endurance", endurance)
print("Wisdom", wisdom)
```

As you can see, this makes it easier to see what, exactly, that section of code is for. We could add another comment at the end of the code snippet to make it even clearer:

```
import random
# This block of code randomly calculates a hero's status.
strength = random.randint(1,20)
intelligence = random.randint(1,20)
endurance = random.randint(1,20)
wisdom = random.randint(1,20)
# End random calculation code
print("Your character's statistics are:")
print("Strength:", strength)
print("Intelligence", intelligence)
print("Endurance", endurance)
print("Wisdom", wisdom)
```

The idea here is to notate the end and start point of each section of code that does something different. As you can imagine, it can get easy to get carried away with this sort of documentation, but it does have its benefits. How much or how often you comment is up to you, but as a rule, it is better to document than not.

Block Commenting

In addition to regular commenting, there is also a form of commenting known as *block commenting*. This type of comment is used when you need more than a single line to explain a section of code. It can also be used if you need to document things like the date you wrote the code, who wrote it, and so forth. Look at the following code demonstrating block commenting:

```
# Importing the random function
import random
# This code was written by James Payne
# To be published in Python for Teenagers by Apress Books
# This block of code randomly calculates a hero's status.
strength = random.randint(1,20)
intelligence = random.randint(1,20)
endurance = random.randint(1,20)
```

```
wisdom = random.randint(1,20)
# End of random number generator code
#Prints out player statistics
print("Your character's statistics are:")
print("Strength:", strength)
print("Intelligence", intelligence)
print("Endurance", endurance)
print("Wisdom", wisdom)
```

As you can see, to block comment, all you need to do is add a hash symbol (#) to the beginning of each line that you are going to leave a comment on.

Inline Commenting

Another way to comment is known as *inline commenting*. This means that you leave a comment on the same line as your code. They are not as common as other forms of commenting, but they can be useful if you need to document what a specific line of code does. For instance, in our RandomGenerator.py file, we start off by importing random. While that line of code should be obvious to a programmer looking at your code, we *could* leave an inline comment to explain it.

Here is how that would look:

```
import random      # Importing the random module
```

As a rule, try to avoid using inline commenting except in situations where you feel you need to explain what a single line of code does.

Other Uses for Commenting

One final use for leaving comments in your code: to find errors. While this may sound unconventional, it is actually pretty practical. Sometimes your code may be giving you errors, and you might need to narrow down which portion of the code is the culprit. Instead of wholesale deleting sections of Python, you can always just comment out sections. Remember, when Python sees the # symbol, it ignores any characters following it on that line.

If we were to comment out the following code, it would run differently than before:

```
import random
strength = random.randint(1,20)
intelligence = random.randint(1,20)
endurance = random.randint(1,20)
wisdom = random.randint(1,20)
print("Your character's statistics are:")
# print("Strength:", strength)
# print("Intelligence", intelligence)
print("Endurance", endurance)
print("Wisdom", wisdom)
```

With this code, we would not see the character's strength or intelligence print to the screen since we commented out that part of the code. Instead, only the endurance and wisdom would show.

To return the program back to its normal state, we would simply remove the # symbols. Feel free to add comments to your code and comment out sections of your code to see what effect it has on your program.

Texting – Without Your Phone

Now that we understand the importance of – and how to make – comments to document our code, we can move on to working with our next data type, *strings*.

The string data type consists of any character you can type, so long as it is contained within quotation marks " ". In essence, it is any letter, number, or special symbol. It can be a single letter, a sentence, or a mixture of letters, numbers, and special symbols.

Let's create a new file called LearningText.py. Add the following text to it:

```
# This is how you print text
print("Holy smokes, it's the Grill Master!")
```

You could also choose to write the code using single quotes if you prefer:

```
# This is how you print text
print('Holy smokes, it's the Grill Master!')
```

If you run the second version of the code, however, you will get an *Invalid SyntaxError*. Can you figure out why this occurs? Let's examine the code a little more closely. We know that the print( ) function will print anything contained between quotation marks. While our sentence ends and begins with a single quote, if you look closely, you will see a third quotation mark – in the word "it's."

When we use single quotes in a print function, we have to be careful, because Python cannot differentiate between a quote and an apostrophe being used in a contraction. When it sees the first quotation before the word Holy, it begins the parameter. Then, when it encounters the apostrophe in the word it's, the interpreter gets confused and sees it as the closing quotation. Finally, it encounters a third single quotation and throws an error.

There are several ways to avoid this type of issue. The first is to, as a rule, always use double quotation marks. Second, in cases where you need or want to use single quotes, an *escape* can solve your problem.

An escape key is essentially a backslash (\) character that tells Python to treat a single quote as a regular character. To use it, you simply add it before the character you want Python to treat as plain text. Here is how you would code it:

```
# This is how you print text
print('Holy smokes, it\'s the Grill Master!') # Notice the use of the
escape key
```

Now if you run the code, you will get the result shown in Figure 3-1:

```
Holy smokes, it's the Grill Master!
>>> |
```

Figure 3-1. *Using escape keys to format print statements*

For simplicity's sake, let's revert back to using double quotation marks in the code for now. Go ahead and make that change – I'll be here waiting.

Finished? Great. Let's add a few more lines of text:

```
# This is how you print text
print("Holy smokes, it's the Grill Master!")
print("His sizzling meats are too good to resist!")
print("Quick Wonder Boy! Get some Wonder Bread and make me a sandwich!")
print("To quote a genius: 'Man Cannot Live On Bread and Water Alone!'")
```

The purpose of this code is twofold. First, it shows you how to print several lines of text. Second, it showcases an instance of when you might interchangeably use double quotes and single quotes. When using proper grammar, you must use single quotes when using a quote from a person.

In this instance, the single quote does not need to be escaped. This is because we *started* our print( ) function with a double quote. It is only when we start it with a single quote that we need to worry about escaping another single quote that is not intended to end the function.

Working with Strings and Variables

Just as we do with numbers, strings can be stored in variables. The method is similar to storing a number, only slightly different:

```
name = "Grillmaster"
print(name)
```

We first create the variable, which we called, "name," and then added some text to it. Note that, unlike we did with a number, we surrounded our value with quotation marks. This signifies that we are adding a string to our variable. Next, we print our variable to the user's screen using the print( ) function.

Here is where things get interesting. Create a new file and try out the following code:

```
age = "42"
graduation = 27
print(age + graduation)
```

If you were to try and run this code, you would get an error message. Why? The reason is simple: when we declared our variable named "age," we assigned the value "42" to it. However, since we enclosed the value in quotations, Python interpreted that data as a string data type. The "graduation" variable, meanwhile, was assigned a number data type. When we tried to perform math on the two variables, it would not work, because you cannot perform math on a string.

Interestingly enough, you *can* use certain math operators on strings. In Python – and other languages – there is a thing known as *concatenation*. Concatenation occurs when you add one string to another, or join them together. We do this using the addition (+) operator – or *joining operator* when using on strings. Here it is in code:

```
print("Wonder" + "Boy")
```

When you test that bit of code, your result will be:

WonderBoy

The same thing happens if you use the + operator on two variables that contain strings:

```
firstName = "Wonder"
lastName = "Boy"
print(firstName + lastName)
```

The result?

WonderBoy

An important note: if you want to add two strings together, you may want to consider using a space in between. This can be achieved by simply adding a space at the end of the first string you are joining:

```
print("Wonder " + "Boy")
```

or by adding a space before the second string you are joining:

```
print("Wonder" + " Boy")
```

Of course, there is nothing to stop you from inserting a third string that contains a blank space:

```
print("Wonder" + " " + "Boy")
```

This works because even a blank space is considered a string or character in Python's eyes.

Another math operator that you can use on strings is the multiplication (*) operator – or, as it is referred to when working with text, *the string replication operator*. Try typing this code into the Python Shell:

```
print("WonderBoy" * 20)
```

This results in what is shown in Figure 3-2:

```
>>> print("WonderBoy" *20)
WonderBoyWonderBoyWonderBoyWonderBoyWonderBoyWonderBoyWonderBoyWonderBoyWonderBo
yWonderBoyWonderBoyWonderBoyWonderBoyWonderBoyWonderBoyWonderBoyWonderBoyWonderB
oyWonderBoyWonderBoy
>>>
```

Figure 3-2. *Example results of string replication*

You would get a similar result if you created a file with this code, performing string repetition on a variable containing a string, as seen in Figure 3-3:

```
sidekick="WonderBoy"
print("You ruined the Grill Master's barbeque!")
print("The crowd is chanting your name!")
print(sidekick *20)
```

```
You ruined the Grill Master's barbeque!
The crowd is chanting your name!
WonderBoyWonderBoyWonderBoyWonderBoyWonderBoyWonderBoyWonderBoyWonderBoyWonderBo
yWonderBoyWonderBoyWonderBoyWonderBoyWonderBoyWonderBoyWonderBoyWonderBoyWonderB
oyWonderBoyWonderBoy
>>> |
```

Figure 3-3. *Performing string replication on a variable*

Longer Strings

Strings would not be very powerful if they were limited to single characters or a single word. As mentioned previously, strings can consist of entire sentences, and we declare them in a variable the same way we would a single word:

```
joke = "Why did Spiderman get in trouble with Aunt May?"
punchline = "He was spending too much time on the web."
print(joke)
print(punchline)
```

Strings on Multiple Lines

Sometimes you may find that you wish to print text in a particular way or structure it as you would a poem or song lyrics. In that case, you could create a multi-line string. To do this, all you need to do is use three double quotes (" " ") or three single quotes (' ' '). Here is a sample of how that would look in code. Feel free to create a new file and test it for yourself. You should see the same result that is showcased in Figure 3-4:

```
print("""My name is Grill Master
and I have an appetite
For destruction
That is well done!""")
```

```
My name is Grill Master
and I have an appetite
For destruction
That is well done!
>>>
```

Figure 3-4. *Creating multi-line string print statements*

The same result could be achieved using three single quotes as well:

```
print('''My name is Grill Master
and I have an appetite
For destruction
That is well done!''')
```

Formatting Strings

While using multiple line strings can help you format your text and strings, there are other – arguably better – methods you can use as well. Perhaps you want to impress a girl or boy by inviting them to the Sidekick Appreciation Ball with a fancy invitation or are hard at work on the lyrics to your new theme song. Either way, without the proper *string formatters*, your text will be bland and uninspiring.

And uninspiring is the last thing a hero should be.

Earlier we discussed the *escape character* (\). We learned how to use it to have Python treat an apostrophe as just that, vs. the end of a print( ) function. In truth, there are several different escape characters, each capable of formatting text in a particular way. They are as follows:

- \ Allows you to create a new line in multi-line strings

- \\ Used to format a backslash

- \n Creates a line break

- \t Creates a tab or indentation

- \' or \" Used for single or double quotes

To better understand the use of the escape characters listed in our table, let us take a peek at "\n" or the line-break escape. This escape character allows us to create a new line whenever we insert it into some text.

Create a new Python file and name it WonderBoyTheme.py. Enter this code into the file:

```
print("My name is\nWonder Boy\nAnd it is a wonder\nThat I can fit in these tights!")
```

At first glance this code looks very jumbled and confused. When we run the program, however, we can see exactly how \n works (Figure 3-5).

```
My name is
Wonder Boy
And it is a wonder
That I can fit in these tights!
>>>
```

Figure 3-5. *Formatting strings in a single print( ) function*

Normally when we view this line of code, we would expect everything inside of the print( ) function to print out on a single line. However, the \n escape forces a line break each time Python encounters it and instead formats our text so that it appears on separate lines.

The \t escape works in a similar method, except that it does not create a new line; instead, it makes an indent or tab in the text. Let's add some more text to our WonderBoyTheme.py file:

```
print("My name is\nWonder Boy\nAnd it is a wonder\nThat I can fit in these
tights!")
print("There trunks are \ttight")
print("tight \ttight \ttight \tso very tight!")
```

If you run this code, it would return the results shown in Figure 3-6.

```
My name is
Wonder Boy
And it is a wonder
That I can fit in these tights!
There trunks are         tight
tight    tight    tight    so very tight!
>>> |
```

Figure 3-6. *More example of using the escape character*

Spiderman only *wished* he had a theme song like that!

Notice in the example figure how the words "tight tight tight so very tight" are all indented with a tabbed space? That is all thanks to \t.

Finally, let's revisit the \" and \' escape characters. As noted prior, sometimes you may want to use quotations as part of the actual text that you print to the screen, which causes an issue because Python can't differentiate what you *intend* the quotations to be used for *unless you tell it*.

To let Python know you want to use your quotation marks in the grammatical sense vs. the programmatic sense, you simply escape them. Let's add some more text to our WonderBoyTheme.py file. Make sure yours matches mine:

```
print("My name is\nWonder Boy\nAnd it is a wonder\nThat I can fit in these
tights!")
print("There trunks are \ttight")
print("tight \ttight \ttight \tso very tight!")
print("\n")
print("And when the people see me they all shout and agree:")
print("\"Boy, those tights are too tight for he!\"")
```

Run this program and take a look at the result, as seen in Figure 3-7.

```
My name is
Wonder Boy
And it is a wonder
That I can fit in these tights!
There trunks are          tight
tight    tight    tight    so very tight!


And when the people see me they all shout and agree:
"Boy, those tights are too tight for he!"
>>> |
                                                    Ln: 107  Col: 4
```

Figure 3-7. *Using the escape \t to create tab indents*

Pay particular attention to this portion of the code:

```
print("\"Boy, those tights are too tight for he!\"")
```

The first double quote (") tells Python that anything following it is to be printed to the screen. Then, Python encounters the backslash (\) and knows to treat the character following it as regular text. Then, Python encounters another backslash (\) and once more treats the character following it as simple text. Finally, it comes across the final double quotation and, since there is no escape character or backslash preceding it, knows that you are intending for it to signify the end of the text you wish to print.

Note that this code would work the same exact way if we were to replace all of the double quotes with single quotes (').

Introducing a New Weapon to Your Arsenal: Lists

Let's face it – fighting crime is tough business. A superhero (or sidekick... let's slow down there rookie!) sometimes needs to rely on something more than bravery, theme songs, and their inherent superpowers. Every hero worth their tights has some sort of super weapon or gadget they can fall back on when all else fails. To that end, we need to start equipping you with some more tools for your futility belt (it's similar to Batman's utility belt, only, well, you bought yours at the flea market).

One of our first gadgets will be *lists*. Just as a variable is a data structure, so, too, are lists. However, unlike variables, lists can contain more than one piece of data. Whereas a variable can be thought of as a label or a box, lists are more like a closet filled with a bunch of boxes.

We can fill lists with the same data types that we can store in variables, including strings, numbers, integers, floating-point numbers, and so forth. To assign values to a list, we place our values between two `square brackets` [ ] and separate them with commas (,).

Let's create a list:

```
superPowers = ['flight', 'cool cape', '20/20 vision', 'Coding Skillz']
```

In this code, we created a list named superPowers and assigned it four separate pieces of information – in this case, the string values: flight, cool cape, 20/20 vision, and Coding Skillz.

If we wanted to print this list, all we have to do is use our handy-dandy print( ) function:

```
print(superPowers)
```

When we print this list, something interesting happens – instead of printing just the contents of the list as we would expect, it prints the entire structure (see Figure 3-8):

```
['flight', 'cool cape', '20/20 vision', 'Coding Skillz']
>>>
```

Figure 3-8. *Printing a list*

Remember, a list is a group of items, stored individually. Each item in our list corresponds to what is known as an *index number*. All lists start at index number 0 and continue in sequence after that. So, therefore, in our list, "flight" would be located at 0, "cool cape" at 1, "20/20 vision" at 2, and so forth.

If we wanted to just print the item located at index number 3, for instance, we could do so like this:

```
superPowers = ['flight', 'cool cape', '20/20 vision', 'Coding Skillz']
print(superPowers[3])
```

This would result in *Coding Skillz* printing to the screen, because it is located in the third position of our list (remember, lists start at position 0). To get a better understanding, let's print out each item in our list individually:

```
superPowers = ['flight', 'cool cape', '20/20 vision', 'Coding Skillz']
print(superPowers[0])
print(superPowers[1])
```

```
print(superPowers[2])
print(superPowers[3])
```

Figure 3-9 shows us the results.

Figure 3-9. *Printing the values in a list*

Alternatively, you could also code the print( ) function on one line like so:

```
superPowers = ['flight', 'cool cape', '20/20 vision', 'Coding Skillz']
print(superPowers[0], superPowers[1], superPowers[2],superPowers[3])
```

And achieve the same result.

Let's create a file and name it ListExample.py. Add the following code to it and then run the program (results shown in Figure 3-10):

```
superPowers = ['flight', 'cool cape', '20/20 vision', 'Coding Skillz']
print(superPowers[0], "is located at Index 0")
print(superPowers[1], "is located at Index 1")
print(superPowers[2], "is located at Index 2")
print(superPowers[3], "is located at Index 3")
```

Figure 3-10. *Another method to print the values in a list*

In this example, we append or add some text to the end of our print( ) function. Notice that we separate the first print parameter with a comma and then define the second part of our print( ) function. We could also use this method if we wanted to print some text prior to the value(s) in our list:

```
print("The item located at index 0 is", superPowers[0])
```

This would give us: *The item located at index 0 is flight.*

Finally, there is an easy, more efficient way to print out all of the items in our lists. Let's create another file and call it PowersWeaknesses.py. Add the following code to it:

```
superPowers = ['flight', 'cool cape', '20/20 vision', 'Coding Skillz']
superWeaknesses = ['bologna', 'lactose intolerance', 'social settings',
'tight trunks']
print("Behold our fledgling hero/sidekick, \"Wonder Boy!")
print("His super powers include:", *superPowers)
print("And his weaknesses are:", *superWeaknesses)
```

Using the list name with a * symbol in front tells Python to use the entire list. For instance, if you type: print(*superPowers), the program would print out every item in the superPowers list. The result of our previous code is shown in Figure 3-11.

```
Behold our fledgling hero/sidekick, "Wonder Boy!
His super powers include: flight cool cape 20/20 vision Coding Skillz
And his weaknesses are: bologna lactose intolerance social settings tight trunks
>>>
```

Figure 3-11. *Printing the entire contents of a list*

Changing Lists

Lists, like variables, can change. We can add things to them, remove them, rearrange them, and so forth. For instance, in our PowersandWeaknesses.py file, we have a list of super weaknesses, one of which is the dreaded "lactose intolerance" (the inability to drink dairy products or eat ice cream – oh no!). Fortunately for you, there is a way to eliminate that particular weakness: they have medication that can help you digest the enzymes in milk. So now you can stuff your face with ice cream bars again – hooray!

Having that knowledge in hand, we might want to delete that particular weakness from our superWeaknesses list. To achieve this, we would use the del statement.

```
superWeaknesses = ['bologna', 'lactose intolerance', 'social settings',
'tight trunks']
del superWeaknesses[1]
print(*superWeaknesses)
```

This would remove the item located at index 1 – in our case, "lactose intolerance." When we print the contents of superWeaknesses out, we would now see bologna, social settings, and tight trunks.

We could also use the remove method to delete a value from our list. Instead of telling Python the position of the item, we simply supply it with the value:

```
superWeaknesses = ['bologna', 'lactose intolerance', 'social settings',
'tight trunks']
superWeaknesses.remove('lactose intolerance')
```

This would give us the same result as using the del statement.

In addition to deleting items from a list, we can also add them. There are a few methods to do so. The first is to use the append statement. This method appends – or adds – the item to the end of the list:

```
superWeaknesses = ['bologna', 'lactose intolerance', 'social settings',
'tight trunks']
del superWeaknesses[1]
superWeaknesses.append('Taco Meat')
print(*superWeaknesses)
```

In this example, we first create our superWeaknesses list and then use the del statement to remove the item at position 1, as we did before (keeping in mind that lists start at position or index 0). Then we discover that we have a new enemy – the stomach cramping "Taco Meat" – and so we use the append statement to add it to our list. When we print the results, we get:

bologna social settings tight trunks Taco Meat

Additionally, we can insert an item into our list. The insert method works a little differently than append. It allows us to add our item at any position within the list, where append just places it at the very end. Here is how it looks in use:

```
superWeaknesses = ['bologna', 'lactose intolerance', 'social settings',
'tight trunks']
del superWeaknesses[1]
superWeaknesses.insert(1,'Taco Meat')
print(*superWeaknesses)
```

The insert method uses two arguments or parameters. The first tells Python where to place the item you are adding in the list – that is, what index position you would like it to be in. The second argument tells Python what value you want to add to the list. Running the preceding code prints out:

```
bologna Taco Meat social settings tight trunks
```

Other List Methods

In total, there are eleven – count them, 11 – list methods. Each one allows you to perform some bit of wizardry on the data stored in a list. While we have reviewed a good number of them, space does not permit us to cover all of them in this chapter. Below, however, you can find a table of the different list methods and what they are used for. Feel free to try them out on your own as an exercise.

- list.pop( ): The pop method lets you return – or print – a value from a list and remove it afterward. This lets you confirm that you are removing the correct item. Example:

```
print(superWeaknesses.pop(1))
print(*superWeaknesses)
```

- list.reverse( ): It is possible to sort the items in a list. One way to do so is by using the reverse method. This will change the order of your items, moving the first item to the end and the last item to the front, and so forth, essentially reversing their order. Example:

```
superWeaknesses.reverse()
print(*superWeaknesses)
```

- list.sort: Another way to change the order of items is by using the sort method. This method simply sorts the items in your list in alphabetical order. Example:

```
superWeaknesses.sort()
print(*superWeaknesses)
```

- list.count( ): This method is used to count the number of times a given value appears in a list. For instance, you may wish to know how many sidekicks have a weakness for "Taco Meat." We could figure this out using count. Example:

```
print(superWeaknesses.count('Taco Meat')
```

- This will return the number of times "Taco Meat" appears in our list. In this case, just once.

- list.extend( ): The use of this method is pretty straightforward. It is used to combine one list into another. For example, if you have a table called moreSuperWeaknesses that listed even more things that can defeat our heroes, you could combine it with our old list, superWeaknesses. That way you would only have one list to contend with. Example:

```
superWeaknesses.extend(moreSuperWeaknesses)
```

- list.copy( ): There are times you may want to copy a list and have a duplicate on hand. Maybe this is for testing purposes, or if you have similarly named data, it would be faster to edit the text than to re-write it. Whatever the case, you can copy a list by using the copy method. Example:

```
superWeaknesses2 = superWeaknesses.copy()
```

Note: list.copy is only available in versions of Python 3.3 and greater. Using an earlier version of Python will result in an AttributeError.

- list.index( ): Oftentimes we need to know where a specific item is within our lists so that we can call upon it as needed. Instead of looking back through your code, you can use the index method to find a value's location in a list. Example:

```
print(superWeaknesses.index('Taco Meat'))
```

- Would return the number 3, because "Taco Meat" is in position 3 in our list. (Note: if you have been experimenting with these methods – particularly with the sorting methods – "Taco Meat" may be in a different position for you).

- list.clear( ): The last method we will cover is the `clear` method. We have saved this one for last because if you practice using it, it will do exactly what it sounds like it would do: clear your list of any data. Sometimes it might be necessary to erase all of the data in a list – that is what this method is used for. Example:

```
superWeaknesses.clear()
```

In This Episode!

We covered a ton of ground in this exciting episode. By now, your powers are growing by – dare I say it – leaps and bounds! Soon enough you will be up and running in your own superhero car – the Wonder Boat maybe, or, better yet, the Wonder Car!

That is, if you have your Learner's Permit. If not, it's back to the Wonder Cycle or Wonder Skates for you.

Let's recap what we learned in this chapter, shall we?

- Comments allow us to document our code for future reference – by us or another programmer.

- We create comments by using a hash or # and a blank space. Any text after this is ignored by Python.

- We can leave an inline comment after a specific line of code if we feel it needs further clarification. Use this sparingly.

- Commenting out code helps us to locate errors without deleting existing code. We simply uncomment the code once we are certain it is not the problem.

- Escape characters let you print special characters that would normally not be treated as text. They also allow you to format your strings.

- Escape characters include \t, \n, \', \", and \\.

- Strings are a data type that can consist of letters, numbers, or symbols.

- You can add one or more strings together – called concatenation – using the + symbol.

- You can replicate strings – create multiple copies of them – using the
  * symbol.

- Lists are storage units that act like a closet full of boxes; you can store
  many items in them vs. just one (in the case of a variable). You define
  them in this manner: superPowers = ['flight', '20/20 vision'] and
  so forth.

- Lists contain items – pieces of data – that are indexed. The items
  begin at index 0 and carry on sequentially.

- You can print lists several ways, including print(superPowers[1]) –
  for a single value – or print(*superPowers), if you wish to print the
  entire list.

- The del statement lets you delete an item from a list.

- There are 11 list methods, including insert(), append(), pop(),
  reverse(), sort(), count(), extend(), copy(), index(),
  clear(), and remove().

## CHAPTER 4

Making Decisions

When it comes to fighting crime and dealing with villainous villainy (trademark pending!), we superheroes often find ourselves facing forks in the road: should we save the helpless damsel being thrown off the side of the building, or do we let her plunge to the ground so that we can nab the bad guy? Do we wash our cape today, or can we go one more day without it smelling too funky?

At the end of the day, the majority of fighting crime – and programming for that matter – comes down to one thing: making decisions.

You have probably heard the statement, "Every action has a reaction." Well, that is especially true in programming. Think about it: every time you engage a computer, you are forcing it to make a decision. When you move your mouse, when you press a key, when you bang your head against the screen for an hour straight because your code won't work (okay, maybe not this last one) – all of these require the computer to interpret what you want and, hopefully, perform an action.

Here is an easy example: if you press the letter "a" or the letter "k," the computer must know what to do for either scenario. If you are using a word processing application, this particular scenario is simple – print one of those two letters to the screen.

More often than not, however, when we discuss decision-making in relation to computer programming, we mean it more in the context of a multiple-answer pop quiz. The program will present the user several options – Choose A, B, or C, for example, and then react according to which option is chosen.

To truly understand one of the most powerful functions in all of programming, let's put on our superhero masks, summon our super brains, and dig into our next developing superpower: decision-making.

© James R. Payne 2024
J. R. Payne, *Python for Teenagers*, https://doi.org/10.1007/978-1-4842-9988-3_4

Making Decisions

Imagine your life as a computer program. It's lunch time and a fledgling sidekick/soon-to-be hero needs lunch to ensure their muscles grow. Before you is a set of items: two slices of bread, two jars of peanut butter, and three jars of jelly. Let's put that into a list so we can see it better!

- Bread (two slices)
- Crunchy peanut butter
- Creamy peanut butter
- Apple jelly
- Grape jelly
- Strawberry jam

As you can see, decisions must be made before you can eat your lunch. We have the bread figured out, but what type of peanut butter will we use? How about the jelly?

This sort of scenario is known as decision-making or, better yet, a *conditional statement*. That is, how will we/the program react if certain conditions are met? To look at this in a programmatic way, let's turn to something called *pseudocode*.

No, pseudocode is not some old Phil Collins song your parents used to jam out to back in the 1980s. It is a method of planning out code using language that sounds like code but that *is not*. If we were to apply our sandwich scenario to pseudocode, it would look something like this:

```
if making sandwich, get bread
Then choose peanut butter type;
if peanutButterType = "Creamy"
print "That's gross. Don't be gross."
else print "Crunchy is the correct choice! You win deliciousness!"
Next choose jelly type;
If jellyType = "Grape"
print "You really aren't good at this are you?"
else if jellyType = "Strawberry Jam"
print "Sure, if you want to ruin your peanut butter, go ahead."
```

```
else print "Apple Jelly is the only Jelly! The golden nectar of the Gods!
You are so wise!"
Next put peanut butter and jelly on bread, smash together, leave the crusts
on, and eat.
```

If you put that code into Python, you will get a ton of errors, because remember, it isn't working code. It's pseudo, which means fake or mock. We use pseudocode to lay out our programs sometimes prior to real coding so that we can map out important sections. This helps us with our programming logic and allows us to avoid errors in our coding. It can be like a set of directions your friend wrote down detailing how to get to the comic book store. It may not be pretty (though some pseudocode is beautiful, full of charts and graphs), but it gives you the idea of where you need to go.

Conditional Statements

In the most basic of terms, conditional statements are snippets of code that determine whether a piece of code will run or not – depending upon whether the condition is met or not. From a programming standpoint, conditional statements could be used in simple examples, such as these:

- If user chooses to be a superhero, enter him/her into the "hero" category; otherwise, enter them into the villain slot.

- If a superhero gained their superpowers by touching toxic waste, classify them as "mutated." If not, classify them as "inherited superpowers."

- If a superhero has a tragic background, make their personality type "Dark and Brooding." Otherwise, make their personality "Quick-Witted and Funny."

These are the most basic uses of conditional statements. In the real world, there could be multiple conditions that must be met for a certain portion of a program to execute (or not). We will get into the more advanced types soon enough, but for now, let's look at the most basic conditional statement of them all: the If statement.

Behold – The If Statement!

The previous examples are all part of what is known as an `if` statement. `If` statements basically state that *if* something occurs, do *this*. The implication, also, is that if that *something* does not occur, the program will do something else – which could mean the program does nothing at all.

To make matters more clear, let's try out a little code. Create a new Python file called `ConditionalStataments.py` and enter in this code:

```
superHeroType="Dark and Brooding"
print("Let's see what sort of hero we have here...")
if superHeroType=="Dark and Brooding":
    print("Ah, it says here you are 'Dark and Brooding'.")
    print("I bet you had a tragic event in your past!")
    print("Your voice sounds pretty rough by the way...")
    print("Here, have a cough drop. Or two.")
```

There are several things to note in this code. For starters, we created a string variable called `superHeroType` and filled it with some text. The text in this variable is what we will be testing our `If` statement against.

After printing some text, we begin our if statement with the line:

```
if superHeroType=="Dark and Brooding":
```

When the interpreter sees this line of code, it enters the conditional statement and checks to see if it is TRUE or FALSE. If the condition is met – meaning the result is true – the program runs the remainder of the code that is *indented* (and therefore part of) – the `if` statement.

In this case, the condition is met: the text in `superHeroType` is *equal to* "Dark and Brooding," so the program prints out the `print()` functions that are part of the `if` statement. Since that is the case, the program results in the following (see Figure 4-1).

```
Let's see what sort of hero we have here...
Ah, it says here you are 'Dark and Brooding'.
I bet you had a tragic event in your past!
Your voice sounds pretty rough by the way...
Here, have a cough drop. Or two.
```

Figure 4-1. *Working with conditional statements*

One other thing to note: the == sign is known as a *comparison operator*. In this instance, it means that the value being compared must equal *exactly* what is in the preceding quotation marks (" "). We use the == symbol when evaluating text and numbers.

But what happens if our conditional is not met? What if the value of superHeroType does not equal "Dark and Brooding"? To find out, all we have to do is edit our code to change its value and run the program again:

```
superHeroType="Quick-Witted and Funny"
print("Let's see what sort of hero we have here...")
if superHeroType=="Dark and Brooding":
    print("Ah, it says here you are 'Dark and Brooding'.")
    print("I bet you had a tragic event in your past!")
    print("Your voice sounds pretty rough by the way...")
    print("Here, have a cough drop. Or two.")
```

```
Let's see what sort of hero we have here...
>>>
```

Figure 4-2. *Results of an if statement that is not triggered*

Now when we run our code, all that gets returned is the opening print() function (see Figure 4-2).

Why does this happen? Because we changed the value in our superHeroType variable, when Python encounters our if statement, it checks the conditional and finds that it is not met and returns false. Since the condition is not met, Python skips the remainder of the if statement block and moves on to the next part of the program.

Since there is no next part of the program, Python exits and the program ends.

We could, of course, create multiple if statements in our program. If we did, Python would evaluate each of those statements and execute the block of code, so long as the condition is met. Let's open up our ConditionalStatements.py file and modify the code so it matches the following:

```
superHeroType="Quick-Witted and Funny"
print("Let's see what sort of hero we have here...")
if superHeroType=="Dark and Brooding":
```

```
    print("Ah, it says here you are 'Dark and Brooding'.")
    print("I bet you had a tragic event in your past!")
    print("Your voice sounds pretty rough by the way...")
    print("Here, have a cough drop. Or two.")
if superHeroType=="Too Polite":
    print("It says here that you are 'Too Polite'")
    print("How are you ever going to catch that criminal if you keep
holding the door?")
    print("Don't say sorry to him - he's the villain!")
if superHeroType=="Quick-Witted and Funny":
    print("Oh boy. I can tell by all the puns that you are the Quick-Witted
and Funny Type.")
    print("I have a joke for you:")
    print("What has 8 fingers, two thumbs, and isn't funny?")
    print("You!")
```

With this modified code, we are adding not one but three total conditional if statements to our program. The program begins by printing out some text, and then it encounters the first if statement, which checks to see if the value of superHeroType is equal to "Dark and Brooding." Since it isn't, our program ignores the rest of the indented code for that block.

Whenever we have a block of code with indented text, Python knows that the indented code belongs to that specific group of code. Once it runs out of indented code, it knows that the particular block is over and it moves on to the next set.

Don't get hung up too much on code indentation yet – we will cover it in greater detail soon. For now, just know that blocks of code have a hierarchy – that is, a structured order – that relies on indentation (typically four spaces or a tab press) to denote which part of the code belongs to which section.

Next, Python runs into our second if statement and again checks the criteria: does superHeroType equal "Too Polite"? Again, it doesn't, so the interpreter moves on to the next block of code, which happens to be our third if statement.

In this third if statement, we check to see if the value of superHeroType is equal to "Quick-Witted and Funny." This time, the result is true, and so the interpreter executes the indented print() functions that are part of that block of code. The result can be seen in Figure 4-3.

```
Let's see what sort of hero we have here...
Oh boy. I can tell by all the puns that you are the Quick-Witted and Funny Type.
I have a joke for you:
What has 8 fingers, two thumbs, and isn't funny?
You!
>>>
```

Figure 4-3. *Example of an if statement that evaluates as True*

Boolean Logic and Comparison Operators

Before we delve further into conditional statements, there are some funny words that we need to define. Not only are these funny words fun to say over and over to your friends and family, but they are also yet another handy tool in your futility belt.

The first word is `Boolean`. Go ahead, say it out loud and get the giggles out of your system. Then, run around the house a few times, and see how many times you can work the word – Boolean – into your conversations. I'll wait here.

Booleans are another data type, and as you may have surmised from our earlier explanation of the `ConditionalStatements.py` code, this particular data type can have one of two different values: `true` and `false`.

When we work with conditional statements like `if`, we are ultimately asking if a certain condition is `true` or `false`. No matter how we may word those conditions or criteria, at the end of the day, the answer can only be one of those two choices.

Of course, we can't just play a game of Truth or Dare with the computer, so Python (and other programming languages) uses something known as *comparison operators* to help us compare data and figure out if the end result is `true` or `false`.

We already discussed one of the comparison operators – the equal to operator ==. In addition to this, there are five other comparison operators available to us. They are as follows:

- == Used to see if a value is equal to another value

- != Used to see if a value is NOT EQUAL to another value

- < Used to determine if a value is less than another value

- > Used to determine if a value is greater than another value

- <= Used for less than OR equal to another value

- >= Used for greater than OR equal to another value

So far we have worked with strings for our conditional statement examples. To better understand our new tools, the comparison operators, let's switch to working with numbers instead. To begin, create a new file named MathIsHard.py. Enter the following code into it:

```
wonderBoyAllowance = 10
newCape = 20
print("That new cape sure is shiny. I wonder if you can afford it...")
if wonderBoyAllowance > newCape:
    print("Congrats! You have enough to buy that new cape!")
if wonderBoyAllowance < newCape:
    print("Looks like you'll have to keep wearing that towel as a cape...")
    print("Maybe if you ask nicely Wonder Dad will give you a raise...")
```

Let's examine this code a little more closely, shall we? We begin by creating two variables: wonderBoyAllowance and newCape. We then print some text that says, "That new cape sure is shiny. I wonder if you can afford it...."

To find out if Wonder Boy can, indeed, afford that new cape, we have to compare the value in wonderBoyAllowance (which represents your allowance) to the value of newCape (which represents the cost of that shiny new cape).

Our first if statement looks to see if wonderBoyAllowance is > (or *greater than*) newCape. If so, it would print out the text, "Congrats! You have enough to buy that new cape!" However, since the allowance is *not* greater than the cost of the new cape, the program skips to the next if statement to see if its value is true.

When the second if statement is evaluated, the program notes that the value of your allowance is less than the cost of the new cape. Since that condition is met and returns a value of true, it proceeds to execute the rest of the if statement, resulting in the following (see Figure 4-4).

```
That new cape sure is shiny. I wonder if you can afford it...
Looks like you'll have to keep wearing that towerl as a cape...
Maybe if you ask nicely Wonder Dad will give you a raise...
>>>
```

Figure 4-4. *Evaluating multiple if statements*

To see how Boolean logic really works, create a new Python file and name it BooleanExamples.py. Enter this code:

```
# Creating two variables with different values
a=10
b=20
# Compare values using the different Comparison Operators
print("Is the value of a EQUAL to b?  ", a == b)
print("Is the value of a NOT EQUAL to b?  ", a != b)
print("Is the value of a GREATER than b?  ", a > b)
print("Is the value of a LESS than b?  ", a < b)
print("Is the value of a GREATER THAN or EQUAL to b?  ", a >= b)
print("Is the value of a LESS THAN or EQUAL to b?  ", a <= b)
```

Running this program will show you which comparisons are true and which are false. A value of true means the comparison is correct, while false means that it is not.

Else Statements

Now that we understand the if statement and comparison operators, we can move on to another type of conditional statement: else. So far, we have used conditional statements that execute a set of code *only* if a given condition is met. What happens, however, if we want to have one outcome if the result is true and another if it is false? While we could, technically, achieve this result using multiple if statements, there is a better, more efficient way to write your program. Let's edit the code of our MathIsHard.py file and change it so that it matches the following:

```
WonderBoyAllowance = 10
NewCape = 20
print("That new cape sure is shiny. I wonder if you can afford it...")
if WonderBoyAllowance > NewCape:
    print("Congrats! You have enough to buy that new cape!")
else:
    print("Looks like you'll have to keep wearing that towel as a cape...")
    print("Maybe if you ask nicely Wonder Dad will give you a raise...")
```

In this version, we have replaced our second if statement with an else statement. The else statement only gets triggered if the if statement's condition is not met. Basically, what you are saying to the program is, "If this happens, do this, otherwise, do that."

The result of this program is the same as it was earlier; however, now there is less code involved, and since there is no second if statement, Python doesn't need to perform another comparison. This saves on computing power and processing. While that might not seem like a big deal here, you can imagine how much it could save in a program with tens of thousands of lines of code and hundreds of if statements.

One more thing to note: when using an else statement, Python will always execute either your if block or your else block; your program will never end without going down one of those two paths.

But what would happen if you needed to have more than an if and else option? What if there were three choices? Or four? Or four bazillion? For that, you would need something a little stronger than a measly if and else statement.

Are you ready to upgrade those powers once more? *If* so (get it – a pun!), prepare to learn – the else-if!

Else-If Statements

I know what you are thinking – else-if is not a real phrase. In fact, it is probably the name of a farmer that spends his days milking cows and wiping the sweat from his tired forehead – call him Uncle Elseif!

Well, I hate to break the news to you, but else-if is a real phrase and it is a real member of the conditional statement family. It is highly versatile, efficient, and will be one of your best friends as a coder. With it, you can create any number of conditional scenarios vs. the regular one or two you get with a boring mix of regular if/else statements.

As usual, the best way to learn this new power is to suit up and try it out. So, with that in mind, create a brand new file called UncleElseIf.py and pop in this code:

```
# Create our variables representing our allowance and the cost of a
new cape
wonderBoyAllowance = 20
newCape = 20
print("That new cape sure is shiny. I wonder if you can afford it...")
```

```
if wonderBoyAllowance > newCape:
    print("Congrats! You have enough to buy that new cape!")
    print("And it looks like you have some money left over.")
    print("How about getting a hair cut? You hair is covering your mask!")
elif wonderBoyAllowance == newCape:
    print("You have exactly enough money to purchase the cape!")
    print("No change for you!")
    print("Eh...and no tip for me I see...")
else:
    print("Looks like you'll have to keep wearing that towel as a cape...")
    print("Maybe if you ask nicely Wonder Dad will give you a raise...")
```

This code may look familiar, because it is – it is a modified version of our MathIsHard.py file. For starters, we changed the value of wonderBoyAllowance to 20 (congrats on the raise!); you will understand why in a few moments. Next, we do our introductory print() statement, followed by our first if block. This first if checks to see *if* our allowance is *greater* than the cost of the new cape. Since that comparison returns a false, the program skips the print() functions and moves on to the next block.

Now hold on a second! This next block is not an if or an else at all. In fact, it doesn't even say else-if – what gives? Well, the guru who created Python decided to make the else-if statement using a hybrid of else and if in the language, hence, elif.

When the interpreter sees elif, it once more evaluates the comparison – in this case, it checks to see if our allowance is *exactly* the same as the cost of the new cape. Since it is – both variables hold the value 20 – the rest of the else-if executes and the indented print() functions do their magic.

Since the else-if evaluated as true, the program knows there is no need to look any further and exits out of this particular block of code. And since there is no code after our if/else/else-if block, the program ends.

Here is where things get interesting. Even though we refer to the if, else, and else-if as their own blocks, in reality, they are all part of the *same* block. Think about it: you can't have an else-if without the else and the if, right? Well, you could, but then your program might not function in the way you intended!

As stated, else-if statements allow us to create any number of options. Let's add a few more elif to our code and examine the results. Modify the text of UncleElseIf.py so that it matches the following:

```
# Create our variables representing our allowance and the cost of a
new cape
wonderBoyAllowance = 20
newCape = 20
print("That new cape sure is shiny. I wonder if you can afford it...")
# Check to see if allowance is greater than the cost of the new cape
if wonderBoyAllowance > newCape:
    print("Congrats! You have enough to buy that new cape!")
    print("And it looks like you have some money left over.")
    print("How about getting a hair cut? You hair is covering your mask!")
# Check to see if allowance is the same exact price as the new cape
elif wonderBoyAllowance == newCape:
    print("You have exactly enough money to purchase the cape!")
    print("No change for you!")
    print("Eh...and no tip for me I see...")
# Check to see if allowance is zero dollars
elif wonderBoyAllowance == 0:
    print("Oh boy, you are broke!")
    print("Maybe it's time to hang up the cape and grab an apron!")
    print("Time to become...Bag Boy!")
# If all other conditions fail, this else will trigger
else:
    print("Looks like you'll have to keep wearing that towel as a cape...")
    print("Maybe if you ask nicely Wonder Dad will give you a raise...")
```

In this version of the code, we've added comments (#) to each section to make our snippets of code clearer. We also added a second elif to our conditional block; it checks to see if the value of wonderBoyAllowance is 0 and, if so, prints out some text suggesting you get a new job.

In theory, we could add as many elif as we wanted to this conditional block, so long as we meet the condition that needed to be met. For instance, we could check the value of wonderBoyAllowance in increments of 1 until we reached 20. Here is an example of how that would look:

```
# Create our variables representing our allowance and the cost of a
new cape
wonderBoyAllowance = 20
```

```
newCape = 20
print("That new cape sure is shiny. I wonder if you can afford it...")
if wonderBoyAllowance == 0:
        print("Nope. You need 20 more dollars.")
elif wonderBoyAllowance == 1:
    print("Nope. You need 19 more dollars.")
elif wonderBoyAllowance == 2:
    print("Nope. You need 18 more dollars.")
elif wonderBoyAllowance == 3:
    print("Nope. You need 17 more dollars.")
elif wonderBoyAllowance == 4:
    print("Nope. You need 16 more dollars.")
elif wonderBoyAllowance == 5:
    print("Nope. You need 15 more dollars.")
# Keep adding elif until you reach 19
# Then use an else for if the value equals 20 or higher
else:
        print("Looks like you have just enough!")
```

In this code sample we added 5 elseif to cover the first 5 dollars of your allowance. I could have added 19 total elseif, but that would take up several pages in this book. Instead, feel free to fill in the blanks yourself and test out the program. Alternate the value of wonderBoyAllowance or newCape a few times so that you can see how the results change based on the value in the variables that we are testing our conditions against.

Logical Operators

As powerful as the elif statement is, there is one more ability you need to learn to truly become the *Master of Conditional Statements...atements...atements...*(is there an echo in here?). And that ability is known as *logical operators*.

So far we have covered a number of different operator types – including comparison operators earlier in this chapter. There are only three logical operators, but they will give a whole new level of power to your programs.

Like comparison operators, logical operators have one purpose: to help you compare values to one another. Also like comparison operators, logical operators seek a Boolean answer: true or false. They are primarily used to determine if two or more comparisons are true or false. Unlike our other operators, logical operators are not made up of special characters or symbols, but, instead, actual words that are self-explanatory: and, not, or.

The first of these – and – is probably the easiest to grasp. It simply looks at the statement and tries to determine if "this AND that" are both true. If both are, it evaluates as true; if one or more conditions are not met, it evaluates as false.

Let's examine it a little closer in code. Create a new file called LogicalOperatorsExample.py and enter in the following code snippet:

```python
# Create a few variables to evaluate
wonderBoyAllowance = 20
newCape = 20
oldCape = 'smelly'
# Check to see if allowance is equal to the cost of a new cape AND
# that the old cape is "smelly"
if wonderBoyAllowance >= newCape and oldCape == 'smelly':
    print("Wow...you can afford to buy a new cape!")
    print("And your old cape IS really stinky!")
    print("Why not treat yourself to a new cape?")
# If the if fails, this else statement will trigger
else:
    print("Sorry kid, it just isn't time for a new cape yet.")
```

Before Wonder Boy can purchase a new cape, two conditions must be met. First, he has to have the 20 bucks to cover the cost. Second, his old cape has to be smelly – it's the only way he can justify spending his life savings on a new cape!

After setting up our variables that are to be evaluated, we pop in an if statement to check if wonderBoyAllowance is greater than or equal (>=) to the value of newCape. In this instance, it *is* equal, so the interpreter moves on and sees the and operator and knows that the next part of the evaluation must *also* be true in order for the entire if statement to evaluate as true. It checks that the value of oldCape is equal to "smelly" – which it is! – and since both conditionals are true, it proceeds to print out the rest of the if statement.

Had either of the conditions not been true, the else statement would have been triggered instead.

Here is the result (Figure 4-5).

```
Wow...you can afford to buy a new cape!
And your old cape IS really stinky!
Why not treat yourself to a new cape?
>>>
```

Figure 4-5. *Using else statements and the "and" logical operator*

Next up in our logical operators list is **or**. When used for conditional statements, an **or** operator requires that at least one condition evaluates as true – the other condition(s) can be false, but so long as one is true, the whole statement evaluates as true.

Here is an example of an or operator at work:

```
# Variables to check
wonderBoyAllowance = 20
newCape = 20
newShoes = 50
# Checks if you can afford a new cape OR if you can afford new shoes
if wonderBoyAllowance >= newCape or wonderBoyAllowance >= newShoes:
    print("Looks like you can either afford a new cape or new shoes.")
    print("That's good, because one of them are really stinky!")
# If both of the conditionals fail, the else below triggers
# If even one of the conditionals are true, the else does not trigger
else:
    print("That's a shame, because one of them is really stanky!")
```

This example program is designed to check whether or not one or both conditions are true. If both are true, great – our print() functions still trigger. If only one condition is true – still great; our print() functions will trigger. Remember: an or operator only requires one conditional to be true.

Only if *neither* condition is met would the program trigger the else statement.

Keen observers may notice a small problem with those programs – while we know that Wonder Boy can afford a pair of shoes or a new cape, we don't know which one he will choose. Further, we don't know if he can afford both together; we only checked to see if he could afford either one.

There are several ways that we could remedy this problem and expand our program. We could add a few more if statements to figure things out. However, now would probably be a good time to discuss something called *nesting*. And no – it has nothing to do with birds!

Nesting – Not Just for the Birds

Sometimes checking if one conditional (or two) is true in a given block is not enough. For example, we may wish to check if a second or third (or fourth, etc.) condition is met *if* the first evaluates as true. Consider our code that determines if Wonder Boy can purchase a new cape and shoes or not. We know that Wonder Boy can purchase either one of those items, but we do not know if he has enough money to purchase both. We also don't know which one he needs more – the cape or the shoes.

We can programmatically answer some of these questions – meaning, we can use our program to unlock the answers. When we check multiple statements within one if, we call this nesting.

By now you have noticed how code gets indented automatically when we use our if statements; after we insert a colon (:) and press the enter key, the development environment skips a line and then indents four spaces. This tells us, as programmers, visually, that the indented code is part of the if statement above it. It also tells the interpreter the same thing. This is known as code hierarchy, which states (1) execute this code before that code and (2) this indented code belongs to the code above it.

To better understand how nesting works, let's re-work our previous example:

```
# Variables to check
wonderBoyAllowance = 20
newCape = 20
newShoes = 50
# Checks if you can afford a new cape
if wonderBoyAllowance >= newCape:
    print("You can afford a new cape.")
    print("But how about new shoes?")
# When the if check to see if you can afford the new cape passes it
does this
    if wonderBoyAllowance >= newShoes:
        print("Looks like you can afford new shoes as well.")
        print("That's good, because the old ones are really stinky!")
        print("But can you afford both together?")
#If you cannot afford the shoes, but can afford the cape, it does this
    else:
        print("You can only afford the new cape, sorry.")
```

```
# If both of the conditionals fail, the else below triggers
# If even one of the conditionals are true, this else does not trigger
else:
     print("That's a shame, because one of them is really stanky!")
```

The first thing to note in the updated example is the indentation of our if statements. The first if checks to see whether Wonder Boy can afford the new cape. Since he can (meaning wonderBoyAllowance is greater than or equal to newCape), the program moves on to the indented – or nested – if statement. Once more, the program checks to see whether the condition of the nested if statement is true (whether wonderBoyAllowance is equal to or greater than newShoes). If so, it would execute the indented print() functions.

Notice how even the print( ) functions under our nested if statement get indented as well.

In this case, our nested if statement does not evaluate to true, so the nested else statement – the one that is indented – triggers.

Only when the original if statement returns a false would the else statement at the bottom trigger. The result of this program?

```
     You can afford a new cape.
But how about new shoes?
You can only afford the new cape, sorry.
```

What would happen if you had more than two if statements? When that occurs, you must use elif for each additional if statement. Let's use a simple math example to truly illustrate the power of nested if statements. Create a new file named SuperHeroQuiz.py and type in this code:

```
# Variable representing Wonder Boy's Test Score
wonderBoyScore = 100
# Introduction text
print("Congratulations on finishing your Superhero Quiz Intelligence/
Reasoning Test.")
print("Or, S.Q.U.I.R.T. for short.")
print("Let's see if you passed or failed your exam!")
```

```
print("A passing grade means you are licensed to be a Sidekick!")
# Comparison block to see if Wonder Boy passed his S.Q.U.I.R.T. Exam
if wonderBoyScore > 60:
    print("Here are your results: ")
    if wonderBoyScore > 60 and wonderBoyScore < 70:
        print("Well, you passed by the skin of your teeth!")
    elif wonderBoyScore >= 70 and wonderBoyScore < 80:
        print("You passed...average isn't so bad. I'm sure you'll make up
for it with heart.")
    elif wonderBoyScore >= 80 and wonderBoyScore < 90:
        print("Wow, not bad at all! You are a regular B+ Plus player!")
    elif wonderBoyScore >= 90:
        print("Look at you! Top of your class. Yer a regular little
S.Q.U.I.R.T. if I ever saw one!")
else:
print("Nice try fella, but I'm sorry you didn't pass.")

    print("I hear the Burger Blitz needs a security guard - you are a
shoo-in!")
```

In this scenario, Wonder Boy is not yet a full-fledged sidekick. In order to become one, he/you must pass the S.Q.U.I.R.T. Exam. Only a score of greater than 60 indicates a passing grade.

In addition to figuring out if Wonder Boy has passed the exam, we want to give him a little feedback on his test score. For every 10-point range, we created an if/elif statement that will print out some text based on where the score falls.

In the event that Wonder Boy does not pass the exam (he scores 60 or below), all of the nested if/elif statements will be skipped, and the else statement will be triggered instead.

An important note: in the event that the first if statement conditional is not met, none of the other conditionals will be evaluated; instead, the program will skip to the else statement automatically. When the program runs into the first if statement, it checks the value of wonderBoyScore and asks whether it is greater than 60. If it were *not*, the program would end and execute the else statement.

However, since wonderBoyScore *is* greater than 60, the program goes to the next if/elif statement to evaluate it. It continues this process until it finds a condition that evaluates to true.

The program results in:

```
Congratulations on finishing your Superhero Quiz Intelligence/
Reasoning Test.
Or, S.Q.U.I.R.T. for short.
Let's see if you passed or failed your exam!
A passing grade means you are licensed to be a Sidekick!
Here are your results:
Look at you! Top of your class. Yer a regular little S.Q.U.I.R.T. if I
ever saw one!
```

Feel free to change the value of wonderBoyScore a few times and re-run the program to see how the results change.

In This Episode!

This exciting episode was jam-packed with action. Of all of the chapters so far, I would venture to say that this one elevated your powers the most! There was a lot to cram into one episode (sort of like how you cram all that jelly into your PB&J and hope it doesn't spill on your shirt), but with your super brain, keen insight, and ability to read corny superhero jokes, I am certain that you will have absorbed all of the information contained within this tomb thus far.

Will you use it for good, or evil? Only time will tell!

Here is a recap that you can share with your parents when they ask what it is that is so fascinating about that wonderful book – written by that amazing author James Payne – and why you can't stop reading it!

- Decision-making is the process by which a program must decide to take one path or another, based on certain defined criteria.

- Pseudocode is a made-up language used to describe sections of a program; it is a shorthand for laying out programs to better understand the layout and different parts your program will need.

- Conditional statements allow your program to proceed down one branch of your program or another if certain conditions are met/not met. They include the if, else, and elif statements.

- If statements allow you to create decisions in your program. For instance, you can have a program execute a snippet of code *if* "x" happens.

  Example:

  ```
  if 10 < 20:
      print("Yes, 10 is less than 20")
  ```

- Else statements enhance if statements by adding an else clause. For instance, you can have a program execute a snippet of code *if* "x" happens, or else you can have it execute a different code block if "x" *doesn't* happen.

  Example:

  ```
  if 10 < 20:
      print("Yes, 10 is less than 20")
  else:
      print("Maths are hard! Numbers bad for brain!")
  ```

- Else-if/elif statements are used for adding additional if conditionals to your code.

  Example:

  ```
  if 10 < 20:
     print("Yes, 10 is less than 20")
  elif 10 == 20:
     print("10 shouldn't be equal to 20, but if you say!")
  else:
      print("In our backwards world, 10 is greater than 20!")
  ```

- Comparison operators allow you to compare values. They are as follows: equal to (==), not equal to (!=), less than (<), greater than (>), less than or equal to (<=), and greater than or equal to (>=).

- Logical operators allow you to check for multiple conditions. They are and, not, or.

CHAPTER 5

Loops and Logic

Sometimes fighting crime can make you feel like you are running around in circles. Day in and day out you seem to have to tackle the same struggles: a bank robber here, a cat stuck in a tree over there, an evil genius trying to take over the universe. It is almost as if you are stuck in some sort of...loop.

While being stuck in a proverbial Groundhog Day – a day that repeats itself over and over and an excellent flick starring Bill Murray (ask your parents) – is a bad thing, using loops in your computer programs can be a *great* thing. One of the prime purposes of computer programs is to repeat repetitive tasks day in and day out. One of the methods we use to enslave our programs and have them perform these tedious tasks is known as a *loop*.

Loops, as you may have guessed by now, cause a snippet of code to repeat over and over again while a certain condition is true. Just like conditional statements (covered in Chapter 4), loops require a condition to be met – or not met – in order to execute or not execute, depending upon the programmer's needs.

There are several types of loops, and we will be covering each type in this very adventurous chapter. So, ready yourself young hero – as we prepare to get loopy!

What Are Loops?

As programmers, one of our overall goals is to write code efficiently. Everything we do should center around providing a good user experience, decreasing processor resources, and creating programs with the least amount of code possible. One way we can achieve this is through the use of loops, of which there are two types in Python. As stated in the introduction to this chapter, loops are magical creatures that allow us to repeat a section of code any number of times, so long as a condition that we define is met.

© James R. Payne 2024
J. R. Payne, *Python for Teenagers*, https://doi.org/10.1007/978-1-4842-9988-3_5

One example of how a loop would work in programming is if you created an application where someone had to guess the number you were thinking. The code would keep asking the user to guess a number until they guessed right, at which point the loop would exit and the rest of the program would execute.

As always, let's head into the *Ominous Room of Danger!* and test out some new code. To begin, create a file named SinisterLoop.py, and add the following code:

```
# Create an empty variable. We will store data in it later.
numberGuess = ''
# create a while loop that continues until the user enters the number 42
while numberGuess != '42':
    print("Sinister Loop stands before you!")
    print("I'll only let you capture me if you can guess the number in my
    brain!")
    print("Enter a number between 0 and 4 gajillion:")
    numberGuess = input() # Stores the number the user types into
    numberGuess
print("Sinister Loop screams in agony!")
print("How did you guess the number in his head was " + numberGuess + "?")
```

In the scenario of this code snippet, the evil Sinister Loop confronts our hero, Wonder Boy, and forces him to guess the malevolent number residing in the villain's mind. If Wonder Boy succeeds, Sinister Loop will allow you to capture him. If not? Well, if not, then he will keep asking you to enter a number over and over again. Fun, right?

We learned several new things in this code example. We start off by doing something we have not done thus far – we created a blank (or empty) variable named numberGuess. We leave this variable blank because we are going to have the user fill it with data later on.

Next, we create a block of code known as a while loop. The line

```
while numberGuess != '42':
```

tells the program to run *while* the value of variable numberGuess is *not equal* – or != – to "42." We then print a few lines of text and finally request that the user enters in a number. The actual line that stores the number is in the code:

```
numberGuess = input()
```

The input( ) function is similar to the print( ) function, except that it accepts input or data from the user. This input is collected through keystrokes on the user's keyboard. These keystrokes get stored in the variable to the left of the assignment operator (=) – in this case, `numberGuess`.

Go ahead and run the code and type in different numbers several times before finally typing in the number 42, to see the program in action.

All finished fooling around? Good. A quick note: in this example, we used the not equal to (!=) operator for our `while` criteria. You may be asking yourself why we did not use an equal to or == operator instead. The reason is because we want the program to loop – or iterate – while something is not true. If we used an == instead and asked the program to loop while the value equaled 42, we would have created a serious looping logic error.

This is where loops can become dangerous. If we told the program to loop while the variable value equaled 42, the program never would have executed our loop at all. Why? Because we were telling it to loop while numberGuess was equal to 42. However, remember: we never set the value of numberGuess. Therefore, when Python goes to check if the value is 42, it determines it is not and exits out of the loop, because it will only loop if the value is 42!

If you think that is tricky, consider this: what would have happened if we set the value of numberGuess to 42 and kept the while loop condition at ==42?

In that scenario, the program would loop forever. Why? Because we are telling it "while the value of numberGuess is 42, loop through this code." This is what is known as the dreaded infinite loop, and it is the bane of every programmer's existence. For fun, let's create a new file called InfiniteLoop.py and enter in the following code:

Note   When you run this program, an infinite loop will occur. To exit out of it, you will have to close your IDLE window and restart the IDLE.

```python
# Create a variable with the value of 42.
numberGuess = 42
print("Sinister Loop stands before you!")
print("Behold my infinite loop!")
# create a while loop that continues while the value of numberGuess is 42.
while numberGuess == 42:
    print("Loop!")
```

Run the code to see what happens. Congrats – you created your first infinite loop! Now, never do that again!

Let's try something a little different. Instead of using a number for our value, let's use text instead. Create another new file named WonderBoyPassword.py and type in this code:

```
# create a variable to hold Wonder Boy's password
password = ''
print("Welcome to Optimal Dad's Vault of Gadgets!")
while password != "wonderboyiscool2023":
    print("Please enter your password to access some fun tech!")
    password = input()
print("You entered the correct password!")
print("Please take whatever gadgets you need!")
print("Don't touch the Doom Canon though - that belongs to Optimal Dad!")
```

This code operates much as you would expect it to. Just like our example using the number '42', this program creates an empty variable and prints out some introductory text. Then we create a while loop that is set to run until the value of password is *not equal* to "wonderboyiscool2018." Once the user inputs that specific value, the program exits the loop and moves on to the other print statements.

However, there is a slight difference here. Since we are working with text and not number data types, the value that is input must equal exactly the same as the condition. That is to say, password must contain the exact text "wonderboyiscool2018." Capitalized letters must be capital and lowercase letters must be lowercased.

Why is that? Without getting into too much boring detail, know that every character in your program has a specific value assigned to it. Remember, the computer does not see text, but, instead, a series of 1s and 0s that are translated into machine language. Because of this, computers see "H" and "h" as two separate things.

Run the program and try typing "WonderBoyIsCool2018" or "WONDERBOYISCOOL2018" when prompted and observe what happens.

As you can see, the program continues the while loop and keeps asking for a password. Only when you enter "wonderboyiscool2018" will the program exit the loop.

Coding loops with this type of "loop logic" is perfectly normal. In fact, when it comes to passwords or secure information, this is exactly the way the program should behave. But what if you did not care about capitalization? What if you wanted the input to work no matter how it was capitalized?

There are a few ways you can achieve this. One of them involves converting the text to lowercase letters. To do this, you would use a new string function called str.lower( ). Change the code of WonderBoyPassword.py so it matches the following:

```
# create a variable to hold Wonder Boy's password
password = ''
print("Welcome to Optimal Dad's Vault of Gadgets!")
while password != "wonderboyiscool2018":
    print("Please enter your password to access some fun tech!")
    password = input()
    password = password.lower()
print("You entered the correct password: ", password)
print("Please take whatever gadgets you need!")
print("Don't touch the Doom Canon though - that belongs to Optimal Dad!")
```

In this code, we added a new line to our previous snippet:

```
password = password.lower()
```

This line of code takes the data inside of the variable password and converts it to lowercase. This way, when the loop checks to see if the password is correct, it does not need to worry if the user typed any of the letters in capital or not.

Note   To make all of a string lowercase, you use `str.lower()`.

For example: `password.lower()`

To make a string uppercase, you use `str.upper()`.

For example: `password.upper()`

Limiting Loops

While we can allow our loops to execute indefinitely, oftentimes we want to limit the number of times they run. For example, in our `WonderBoyPassword.py` code, we allow the user to guess the password as many times as they like; the program only exits once the correct password is given. However, that may not be the best way to write such a program.

When dealing with passwords – or when you need to limit the number of times a loop executes – you can create a conditional that causes the loop to break if a given criterion is met.

To see break in use, edit the code in WonderBoyPassword.py so that it matches the following:

```
# create a variable to hold Wonder Boy's password
password = ''
passwordAttempt = 0
print("Welcome to Optimal Dad's Vault of Gadgets!")
while password != "wonderboyiscool2018":
    print("Please enter your password to access some fun tech!")
    password = input()
    password = (password.lower())
    passwordAttempt = passwordAttempt + 1
    if password == "wonderboyiscool2018":
        print("You entered the correct password: ", password)
        print("Please take whatever gadgets you need!")
        print("Don't touch the Doom Canon though - that belongs to
        Optimal Dad!")
    elif passwordAttempt == 3:
        print("Sorry, you are out of attempts!")
        break
```

In this version of WonderBoyPassword.py, we added several new lines of code. For starters, we defined a new variable named passwordAttempt and gave it the value of 0. This variable will be used to track the number of attempts made at guessing the password. Each time a user guesses incorrectly, the loop repeats itself, and thanks to this code:

```
passwordAttempt = passwordAttempt + 1
```

adds 1 to the value of passwordAttempt. We then added two if statements. The first prints out some text if the user guesses the correct password. The elif statement triggers once the value of passwordAttempt is equal to 3 (after three attempts). Once triggered, it prints out some apologetic text and then uses the break statement to exit out of the while loop.

Try out the code a few times, being sure to improperly guess the password at least three times and guess it accurately at least once.

For Loops

Another way to make sure a loop only iterates a certain number of times is by using the for loop. This type of loop is typically used when you know how many times you want to repeat a snippet of code. A popular method to introduce the for loop is to create a program that counts through a list of numbers – such as 1–10. However, we are no ordinary programmers – we are superheroes who *happen* to code. Therefore, we need a special type of program. Behold vile villains! The Count10.py example!

```
print("Sinister Loop, I know you are in there!")
print("If you don't come out of the cafeteria freezer by the time I count
to 10...")
print("You won't get any of that delicious stop-sign shaped pizza!")
for x in range(1,11):
    print(x)
print("I warned you! Now all the pizza belongs to Wonder Boy!")
```

The important part of this code occurs here:

```
for x in range(1,11):
    print(x)
```

The for begins the loop. The 'x' is a variable (you can name this variable any way you like; traditionally programmers name it 'i' or 'x') that will hold the value of the number of iterations. In fact, when used this way, it is known as an *iterating variable*. Next, we use the range function to tell the loop the *sequence* to use. A sequence can be made up of a number range or using text (more on this below).

The numbers in parentheses following range are the start and stop parameters of the function. For our example, we want to count to 10, so we put the start at 1 and the stop at 11. We choose to use 11 here, even though we want the range to stop at 10, because range stops at the number *before* our end point. We could have the start at 0 and the stop at 10, or the start at 12 and the stop at 1,000,000 if we wanted to give Sinister Loop a long time to come out of that freezer (but then, he would probably freeze to death!).

Finally, we `print(x)` to print out the number of times the iteration occurs. Once "10" is reached, the program breaks from the for loop and skips to the next part of the code, which happens to be a final print statement.

If you run the program, you get the result:

```
Sinister Loop, I know you are in there!
If you don't come out of the cafeteria freezer by the time I count to 10...
You won't get any of that delicious stop-sign shaped pizza!
1
2
3
4
5
6
7
8
9
10
I warned you! Now all the pizza belongs to Wonder Boy!
```

If we wanted to jazz the code up a little, we could add some text to the `print` statement that is part of the `for` loop, like so:

```
print("Sinister Loop, I know you are in there!")
print("If you don't come out of the cafeteria freezer by the time I count
to 10...")
print("You won't get any of that delicious stop-sign shaped pizza!")
for x in range(1,11):
    print(x, "Mississippii")
print("I warned you! Now all the pizza belongs to Wonder Boy!")
```

All we did here was change:

```
print(x)
```

to

```
print(x, "Mississippii")
```

This gives us a new result of:

```
Sinister Loop, I know you are in there!
If you don't come out of the cafeteria freezer by the time I count to 10...
You won't get any of that delicious stop-sign shaped pizza!
1 Mississippii
2 Mississippii
3 Mississippii
4 Mississippii
5 Mississippii
6 Mississippii
7 Mississippii
8 Mississippii
9 Mississippii
10 Mississippii
I warned you! Now all the pizza belongs to Wonder Boy!
```

All we did here was add the word "Mississippii" to our print out of the iteration loop.

In addition to counting up, range has the ability to count down as well. To achieve this, we need to use something called step. Step is an optional parameter of range() and is used to "step" numbers up or down. For example, if we wanted to count down from 10 to 1, we would write a for loop that looked like this:

```
for x in range(10,0, -1):
print(x)
```

The -1 part of the loop is the step and basically tells the program to subtract one each time. If you ran this code, it would result in:

```
10
9
8
7
```

```
6
5
4
3
2
1
```

If we made the step -2, the countdown would "step" down by subtracting 2 each time.

```
for x in range (10,1, -2):
print(x)
```

Then the result would be:

```
10
8
6
4
2
```

If we wanted to count up in increments of 2, we don't need to add the + symbol – we just add the step as 2, like so:

```
for x in range(1,10,2):
    print(x)
```

This would produce:

```
1
3
5
7
9
```

More Fun with For Loops

Of course, printing out numbers is not the only thing we use for loops to achieve. As stated, any time we know the number of times we want to loop through code, a for loop is our best bet.

For example, maybe we want to be annoying and print the same text to the screen a whole bunch of times. Our friend the for loop can help with that!

```
for x in range(1,10):
    print("Wonder")
print("Boy!")
```

This little code snippet will print out the text "Wonder" nine times before exiting the loop and ending with "Boy!" If you were to put some cool theme music behind that, you would be all set for your own television series!

Another way we can use for loops is to iterate through lists. Let's say we had a list of nefarious villains, and we want to print out their names. We could use code similar to this to do so:

```
nefariousVillains = ['Sinister Loop', 'The Pun-isher', 'Jack Hammer',
'Frost Bite', 'The Sequin Dream']
print("Here is a list of today's villains, brought to you by:")
print("Heroic Construction Company. You destroy the city, we make it
almost, sort of new.")
print("Villains Most Vile:")
for villains in nefariousVillains:
    print(villains)
```

Here, we create a list (we originally discussed lists back in Chapter 3 as you will recall). We then populated the list with various villains. Next, we printed out some text and then made our for loop:

```
for villains in nefariousVillains:
    print(villains)
```

This time, the for begins by creating a variable name villains, whose job it will be to hold the values (temporarily) of each value in our list. Since we have not set a range, the loop will execute one time for each value in the nefariousVillains list. Each time through it will assign a different value to the villains variable. For example, the first

91

time through the loop, 'Sinister Loop' gets passed to villains then printed. Then the loop continues a second time and passes 'The Pun-isher' to villains, which once again prints. This continues until the loop runs through all of the values in the list. The final value in villains will be 'The Sequin Dream'. Its value will remain that until you change the data.

If we were to run this code, the result would be:

```
Here is a list of today's villains, brought to you by:
Heroic Construction Company. You destroy the city, we make it almost,
sort of new.
Villains Most Vile:
Sinister Loop
The Pun-isher
Jack Hammer
Frost Bite
The Sequin Dream
```

Break, Continue, and Pass Statements

Although loops are used to iterate through portions of code, sometimes we may find that we need a way to end the loop early, skip a section of a loop, or handle some data that is not specifically part of our loop(s). There are three statements, in particular, that can help us in these endeavors: break, continue, and pass.

We learn about break earlier; with this statement, we can exit out of our loops early, provided certain conditions occur. For instance, in our WonderBoyPassword.py program, we used break to exit the program after three attempts at entering the password were made. Since we covered this statement earlier, let's move onto the continue statement.

The continue statement lets you skip part of a loop without actually breaking completely out of it, like the break statement. Consider this: what if you had a program that counted down from ten, but at the halfway mark you wanted to print some text; you could achieve this with continue.

Let's create a new file called DoomsdayClock.py. In this program, Sinister Loop has begun a countdown timer that will signal your...well, doom. However, villains are always so long-winded, so don't be surprised if he has something to say at some point during the countdown!

Enter this code into your file:

```
print("The nefarious Sinister Loop stands before you, greedily rubbing his
hands together!")
print("He has his hand on a lever and has a large grin on his face.")
print("Sinister Loop opens his mouth and says:")
print("'You are doomed now Wonder Boy!'")
print("'You have ten seconds to live! Listen as I count down the time!'")
for x in range(10,0,-1):
    print(x, "Mississippii!")
# When x is equal to 5, print some text, then continue with the count down.
    if x==5:
        print("'Any last words, Wonder Boy?!?'")
        continue
print("You wait for your inevitable doom as the count reaches 0...")
print("But nothing happens!")
print("Sinister Loop screams, 'Foiled Again!'")
```

Run the example and observe the result – it should look like this:

```
The nefarious Sinister Loop stands before you, greedily rubbing his hands
together!
He has his hand on a lever and has a large grin on his face.
Sinister Loop opens his mouth and says:
'You are doomed now Wonder Boy!'
'You have ten seconds to live! Listen as I count down the time!'
10 Mississippii!
9 Mississippii!
8 Mississippii!
7 Mississippii!
6 Mississippii!
5 Mississippii!
'Any last words, Wonder Boy?!?'
4 Mississippii!
3 Mississippii!
2 Mississippii!
1 Mississippii!
```

```
You wait for your inevitable doom as the count reaches 0...
But nothing happens!
Sinister Loop screams, 'Foiled Again!'
```

This code works like our other for loops, with a small exception. Once the program hits our if statement, it checks to see if 'x' is equal to 5. Since we set the range to count down from 10 to 1 by increments of -1, we know that 'x' will equal 5 around the sixth time the code repeats. When it does, our condition is met and we print out the text, "Any last words Wonder Boy?!?" effectively pausing the loop for a moment (in reality, we are skipping an iteration so that we can print some text), before re-entering the loop once more.

After the continue statement, the program finishes its normal loop cycle and then exits out of the program normally.

So far, we have looked at how to exit out of a loop if a certain condition applies or how to skip an iteration through a loop (using break and continue, respectively). The next statement we learn won't seem nearly as useful, but, in truth, it does serve a purpose in the grand scheme of things.

The pass statement is particularly useful when working with things called classes – a subject we will broach in Chapter 8. In terms of loops, however, the pass statement is primarily used as a placeholder. It is a great tool when you are planning out a section of code but are not entirely certain what your criteria will be.

For example, in our DoomsdayClock.py program, we placed an if statement within our loop to execute some text once our variable held the number 5. However, what if we were not sure what we wanted that text to or where in the countdown we wanted to have the text print? Maybe we were waiting for feedback from a colleague and would have to come back to that section of code.

The pass statement would let us place our conditional without defining what, exactly would happen if it was met, without having to worry about getting errors because we did not complete the code. That way, later, when we figured out what we wanted to happen in that section of the loop, we could fill in the rest of the code later.

Here is how the pass statement would look if we inserted it into our DoomsdayClock.py program:

```
print("The nefarious Sinister Loop stands before you, greedily rubbing his
hands together!")
print("He has his hand on a lever and has a large grin on his face.")
print("Sinister Loop opens his mouth and says:")
```

```python
print("'You are doomed now Wonder Boy!'")
print("'You have ten seconds to live! Listen as I count down the time!'")
for x in range(10,0,-1):
    print(x, "Mississippii!")
# When x is equal to 5, print some text, then continue with the count down.
    if x==5:
        pass
print("You wait for your inevitable doom as the count reaches 0...")
print("But nothing happens!")
print("Sinister Loop screams, 'Foiled Again!'")
```

If you run this code, you will see that nothing occurs when the if statement is reached – the program just runs normally. However, if you were to remove pass from the statement, you would receive an error, because Python is expecting more code to finish the if statement. Try it out and see for yourself!

In This Episode!

We covered quite a bit in this chapter, and I would not blame you one bit if you were feeling a little...loopy (insert cricket sounds here). While this chapter may have been the most difficult to grasp thus far, the good news is, once you have mastered using loops, you really do have just about every tool you need to create some decent real-world programs.

Sure, you may not be able to walk into an office and get a high-paying gig as the World's Greatest Programmer – WGP for short – but hey, you are still a teenager; you are already far ahead of the curve of future competition. Plus, let's not forget, there are a whole nine other chapters left!

At this point in the book, you should feel comfortable dabbling on your own and creating your own code snippets and mini-programs. Like anything in life, practice makes perfect, so be sure to put your new superpowers to the test often. The more you code, the better you will understand programming.

Speaking of, in the next chapter, we will be putting everything we have learned so far to good use, as we create our first full-fledged program! It is going to be called Superhero Generator 3000, and it will incorporate loops, variables, if-else statements, string and math functions, and so much more; invite your friends and you will be the life of the party!

As for this current chapter, let's recap what we learned in this *quick In This Episode* reference sheet!

- Loops allow you to repeat – also known as iterate – through portions of code if given conditions are met/not met.

- For loops can be used to iterate while a condition is not met or by using the range function. For example:

```
for x in range(1,10):
    print("Wonder Boy is here!")
```

- Range() is a function that allows you to iterate through a loop a certain number of times. It has three parameters and is defined in the following manner:

```
range(1, 10, 1)
```

The first number is the starting point. The second number is the end point. The third number – which is optional – is known as the step and controls the increment in which range() counts. For example, using 2 for the step would increase the numbers by 2 each iteration through the loop.

- While loops repeat so long as a condition or criteria is met or evaluates as Boolean true. For example:

```
    salary = 0
while salary < 10:
    print("I owe, I owe, so off to work I go.")
    salary = salary +1
```

Infinite loops are naughty and to be avoided most of the time. They occur when you have a flaw in your loop programming logic or make a mistake typically. They are loops that never end and go on forever – like a bad algebra lesson. Here is an example (don't try this at home kids!):

```
x = 0
while x == 0:
print:("You down with L-O-O-P?")
print("Yeah, you know me!")
```

Since the variable x is equal to 0, and the criteria say to loop while x is equal to 0, this loop will go on forever.

- Str.lower( ) is a function that converts a string to lowercase. For example:

```
name = "Wonder Boy"
print(name.lower())
```

Would print "wonder boy" in all lowercase letters.

- Str.upper( ) works the same as str.lower( ), except it changes all letters in a string to uppercase. Example:

```
name = "wonder boy"
print(name.upper())
```

- The break statement forces a loop to exit – or break – out of its iteration if a certain condition is met, and you want it to end the loop early.

- The continue statement lets you skip an iteration in a loop without exiting the loop entirely.

- The pass statement is a sort of placeholder that lets you create loops without defining certain conditions within them until later. This way you can create the loop structure and decide what your criteria will be later on without receiving errors when you test your code.

CHAPTER 6

Using What We've Learned

You've come a long way thus far. You started off being bitten by a radioactive programmer when you made the unfortunate mistake of trying to grab his microwaveable pizza bites. From there, your powers began to blossom, and you proved yourself a worthy sidekick. But now it is time to truly test your knowledge and your l33t cod3r skillz. Are you up for the challenge?

In this chapter, we are going to recap everything you have learned so far and put it to use creating your very own full-length program. In addition, you will learn a few more new tricks, and, by the end of this chapter, you will have graduated from faithful sidekick to full-blown hero status.

You'll still be Wonder Boy, but at least you won't have to shine Amazing Dad's shoes any longer!

Creating Your First Real Program

Before we begin to create our first fully functional application – which we will be naming the Superhero Generator 3000 – we have to first understand what, exactly, we want the program to do. The basic concept is simple enough: we want an app that will randomly generate a superhero character for us – no big deal, right?

That is a start, but clearly, we need more details than that. For instance, what constitutes a hero? Do they have any attributes? Any superpowers? How about a name? The answer to all of that is yes.

As good, heroic programmers, we always want to plan out any programs that we create. We need to know the purpose of the program, how it will function, and any details that will help keep us on track as we code and build it.

© James R. Payne 2024
J. R. Payne, *Python for Teenagers*, https://doi.org/10.1007/978-1-4842-9988-3_6

For example, we know that in this program, we are going to need the following:

- Superhero first name (randomly generated)

- Superhero last name (randomly generated)

- Code to join the Superhero first name/last name into a single string

- Code to randomly generate a set of statistics or STATS within a given range.

- A random power generator

In addition, we will need variables to hold all of our STATS data; our first, last, and combined names; and our superpowers. We also need a data structure – in this case lists – to hold the values for our names and superpowers, from which we will randomly select names/powers to give to our hero.

Sound complicated? Don't worry – it is not. We will be walking through each section of the program, step-by-step with refreshers for everything we have already covered. That said, let's put on our capes and masks and start the first part of the Superhero Generator 3000!

Importing Modules

To begin with, our program will rely on two *modules* – pieces of pre-existing code designed to perform a common task that we can use to save time and reduce human error. The first of these is random, which we have worked with already. To refresh your memory, random can be used to randomly generate numbers. It can also allow you to randomly choose a value (or values) from a list – among other things. We use it for both purposes in our program.

The second module we import is known as time and is something we have not covered thus far. One of its primary functions is that it allows us to create a "pause" in our program's execution. There can be many reasons why you wish to delay a portion of code from executing. For our purposes, we are using time to build suspense and make it appear that our program is calculating something complicated.

Let's create a new file called SuperheroGenerator3000.py and add the following code to it:

```
# Importing the random module to use for randomizing numbers and
strings later
import random
# Importing the time module to create a delay
import time
```

Creating Our Variables

As noted previously, this program will rely on quite a few variables and lists to store data. To hold our STATS (or statistical) data, we are going to use variables for our storage needs. By now, you should be familiar with their use and how to define them. That being said, let's add this code to our SuperheroGenerator3000.py file, just below where we imported the time and random modules:

```
brains = 0
braun = 0
stamina = 0
wisdom = 0
power = 0
constitution = 0
dexterity = 0
speed = 0
answer = ' '
```

The first set of variables will be used to hold stats such as how intelligent your character is, how strong they are, and so forth. Notice that the initial values are all set to 0. Later in the application, we will be using random to change these values. For now, however, we have to assign them a value, so 0 it is!

You may notice that we have a variable sitting outside of the group of stats, called answer. Once the program runs, it will ask the user a question to continue – we will be using the answer string variable to hold the user's response. For now, we assign it with no value; the user's input will fill it in later.

Defining Our Lists

Lists are used to hold more than one piece of data. The SuperheroGenerator3000.py app relies on three lists: one will hold a list of possible superpowers – named superPowers – while the other two will hold lists of possible first and last names.

Later in the program, we will be using random to choose values from these lists to give our hero a name and superpower. For now, we need to create the lists and assign them with some values.

For now, use the values that I provide. However, after you have tested the program several times, feel free to add your own wacky name combinations and superhero powers to these lists – be creative and have fun!

Here is the code for the lists – add it to your file beneath the list of variables:

```
# Creating a list of possible super powers
superPowers = ['Flying', 'Super Strength', 'Telepathy', 'Super Speed', 'Can
Eat a Lot of Hot Dogs', 'Good At Skipping Rope']
# Creating lists of possible first and last names
superFirstName = ['Wonder','Whatta','Rabid','Incredible', 'Astonishing',
'Decent', 'Stupendous', 'Above-average', 'That Guy', 'Improbably']
superLastName = ['Boy', 'Man', 'Dingo', 'Beefcake', 'Girl', 'Woman', 'Guy',
'Hero', 'Max', 'Dream', 'Macho Man','Stallion']
```

Now that we have our data structures in place, it is time to move on to the next portion of our code.

Introductory Text and Accepting Input from the User

The next section of our code is designed to greet the user and accept some input from them. As we learned in Chapter 5, we can accept input from the user by using the `input()` function. Add the following code to your file, right underneath your newly created lists:

```
# Introductory text
print("Are you ready to create a super hero with the Super Hero
Generator 3000?")
# Ask the user a question and prompt them for an answer
```

```
# input() 'listens' to what they type on their keyboard
# We then use upper() to change the users answer to all uppercase letters
print("Enter Y/N:")
answer = input()
answer = answer.upper())
```

To make life easier, after we accept input from the user, we convert their `answer` to all uppercase letters. Why do we do this? To keep us from having to check for both lowercase and uppercase combinations when they answer. If we did not convert the text to all uppercase, we would have to check for "yes," "Yes," "yEs," "yeS," and so on. It is much easier – and more efficient – to convert the string and check for a simple "YES" (or in this instance, a "Y").

We check the user's answer by using a `while` loop that repeats while the value of `answer` is *not equal* to "YES." Once the condition is met and the loop exits, the program continues, and the fun really begins!

Add the `while` loop to your code, right beneath the introductory text and `input()` section:

```
# While loop to check for the answer "Y"
# This loop will continue while the value of answer IS NOT "Y"
# Only when the user types "Y" will the loop exit and the program continue
while answer != "Y":
    print("I'm sorry, but you have to choose Y to continue!")
    print("Choose Y/N:")
    answer = input()
    answer = answer.upper())
print("Great, let's get started!")
```

Creating Suspense!

Just as in real writing, sometimes in our computer programming, we want to add suspense or pause dramatically to make the user think that something really cool is happening. Or we may wish to pause a program intermittently to give the user time to read the text on the screen instead of having it scroll by too quickly.

Whatever the case, we can achieve this dramatic effect by using a new module that you have not learned yet: time( ).

While we will be using time( ) in our code, we will not be covering the function in its entirety just yet – for now we only want to use one aspect of this handy new tool and that is by taking advantage of its sleep function.

Like any other method, the time.time( ) function accepts parameters – six common ones and a few others that are not so commonly used. Sleep creates a pause in your program, measured in seconds, and looks like this in us:

```
time.sleep(3)
```

The number in parentheses is the number of seconds you want to pause. We could type that and be done with it, but – as stated – we want some dramatic flair! So instead of using time.sleep( ) on its own, we want to print some ellipses (...) to the user's screen to simulate some wait time as well. It just looks cooler!

To do this, we are going to place our time( ) function in a for loop that repeats three times. Each time through the loop, our program will print to the user's screen.

Add this code to your .py file:

```
print("Randomizing name...")
# Creating suspense using the time() function
for i in range(3):
    print("...........")
    time.sleep(3)
print("(I bet you can't stand the suspense!)")
print("")
```

Theoretically, if we were to run our program at this point, we would see the following output on the screen:

```
Are you ready to create a super hero with the Super Hero Generator 3000?
Enter Y/N:
y
Great, let's get started!
Randomizing name...
...........
...........
...........
(I bet you can't stand the suspense!)
```

When the `time()` function kicks in, each of the "........." lines takes exactly three seconds to print, creating our "dramatic pause."

Now that we have our introductory text, understand how to pause or create a hesitation in our programs, and have our initial variables/lists in place – as well as our modules imported – it is time to get to the meat of the application!

In this next section, we will create the portion of our code that randomizes all of the different parts of our generated superheroes. For that, we rely on the good old `random()` module.

Randomizing Superhero Names

There are five things that every superhero needs:

- Cool outfit

- Superpowers

- Innocuous source of income that allows them to never be seen working a day job

- Tissues to wipe away the tears from all those lonely microwave dinners (superheroes don't have time to date!)

- And, of course, an awesome name

The next step in the SuperheroGenerator3000 code is to program the name generation section. Earlier, you may recall, we created two lists full of superhero first and last names. As a reminder, here are those lists:

```
superFirstName = ['Wonder','Whatta','Rabid','Incredible', 'Astonishing',
'Decent', 'Stupendous', 'Above-average', 'That Guy', 'Improbably']
superLastName = ['Boy', 'Man', 'Dingo', 'Beefcake', 'Girl', 'Woman', 'Guy',
'Hero', 'Max', 'Dream', 'Macho Man','Stallion']
```

The idea behind our name generation portion of code is that we want to pull one name from each of these two lists and combine them into one, creating our hero's name. There are many ways we could achieve this, but for our purposes, we want to randomly select the two values – that way every time the program is run, it creates a unique combination of names.

Let's look at the code we use to achieve this effect before we delve any deeper. Add the following code to your SuperheroGenerator3000.py file, right below the time() code:

```
# Randomizing Super Hero Name
# We do this by choosing one name from each of our two name lists
# And adding it to the variable superName
superName = random.choice(superFirstName)+ " " +random.
choice(superLastName)
print("Your Super Hero Name is:")
print(superName)
```

This section of code is pretty simple to understand. We start it off by creating a variable named superName, whose job will be to hold the combined first and last names of our hero (which we get from the lists superFirstName and superLastName).

Next, we use random() – and specifically random.choice – to randomly choose a value from our list superFirstName and a value from superLastName.

The part of the code line that reads

```
+ " " +
```

may seem confusing; its purpose is simple, however. In this instance, the + symbol is used to *concatenate* – or add – our two strings together. Since we want a space in between the first and last names, we also have to add – or concatenate – a space by adding " " in between. Otherwise, we could have just written random.choice(superFirstName) + random.choice(superLastName).

Finally, we finish this part of our program by printing out the value of the newly created superName by using: print(superName).

Now if we were to run our program, it would result in something like:

```
Are you ready to create a super hero with the Super Hero Generator 3000?
Enter Y/N:
y
Great, let's get started!
Randomizing name...
...........
...........
```

```
...........
(I bet you can't stand the suspense!)
Your Super Hero Name is:
Improbably Max
```

Or

```
Are you ready to create a super hero with the Super Hero Generator 3000?
Enter Y/N:
y
Great, let's get started!
Randomizing name...
...........
...........
...........
(I bet you can't stand the suspense!)
Your Super Hero Name is:
Stupendous Hero
```

Note   Since the values are randomly generated, your superhero name will likely appear different than the example I've provided.

A Quick Check-In

Before we go any further, let's check to see that your code matches mine at this point in the game. If you have been following along and placing your code in the right order, your program should look like the following. If not, no worries – just modify your code to match mine and re-read the sections to figure out what went wrong!

Here is how your code should presently look:

```python
# Importing the random module to use for randomizing numbers and
strings later
import random
# Importing the time module to create a delay
```

```
import time
# Creating - or initializing - our variables that will hold character stats
brains = 0
braun = 0
stamina = 0
wisdom = 0
power = 0
constitution = 0
dexterity = 0
speed = 0
answer = ''
# Creating a list of possible super powers
superPowers = ['Flying', 'Super Strength', 'Telepathy', 'Super Speed',
'Can Eat a Lot of Hot Dogs', 'Good At Skipping Rope']
# Creating lists of possible first and last names
superFirstName = ['Wonder','Whatta','Rabid','Incredible', 'Astonishing',
'Decent', 'Stupendous', 'Above-average', 'That Guy', 'Improbably']
superLastName = ['Boy', 'Man', 'Dingo', 'Beefcake', 'Girl', 'Woman', 'Guy',
'Hero', 'Max', 'Dream', 'Macho Man','Stallion']
# Introductory text
print("Are you ready to create a super hero with the Super Hero
Generator 3000?")
# Ask the user a question and prompt them for an answer
# input() 'listens' to what they type on their keyboard
# We then use upper() to change the users answer to all uppercase letters
print("Enter Y/N:")
answer = input()
answer = (answer.upper())
# While loop to check for the answer "Y"
# This loop will continue while the value of answer IS NOT "Y"
# Only when the user types "Y" will the loop exit and the program continue
while answer != "Y":
    print("I'm sorry, but you have to choose Y to continue!")
    print("Choose Y/N:")
    answer = input()
```

```
    answer = answer.upper()
print("Great, let's get started!")
print("Randomizing name...")
# Creating suspense using the time() function
for i in range(3):
    print("...........")
    time.sleep(3)
print("(I bet you can't stand the suspense!)")
print("")
# Randomizing Super Hero Name
# We do this by choosing one name from each of our two name lists
# And adding it to the variable superName
superName = random.choice(superFirstName)+ " " +random.choice(superLastName)
print("Your Super Hero Name is:")
print(superName)
```

Randomizing the Superpowers

Now comes the fun part – randomly generating our hero's superpowers! After all, he wouldn't be all that super if he couldn't shoot laser beams out of his nose or grow a full beard in less than a day, now, would he?

As with our superFirstName and superLastName lists, you will recall that we already created a list to hold superpowers, aptly named superPowers. It is from this list that we will be choosing what power our superhero has in his arsenal.

Note   After we complete the program in its entirety and you have tested it several times, feel free to add your own mix of superpowers to the superPowers list – have fun and be as creative as possible!

Add the following code to your SuperheroGenerator3000.py file, placing it directly beneath the portion of code that randomly generated your hero's name:

```
print("")
print("Now it's time to see what super power you have!)")
print("(generating super hero power...)")
```

```
# Creating dramatic effect again
for i in range(2):
    print("...........")
    time.sleep(3)
print("(nah...you wouldn't like THAT one...)")
for i in range(2):
    print("...........")
    time.sleep(3)
print("(almost there....)")
# Randomly choosing a super power from the superPowers list
# and assigning it to the variable power
power = random.choice(superPowers)
# Printing out the variable power and some text
print("Your new power is:")
print(power)
print("")
```

As you can see, this code starts out by printing some text to the user's screen, informing them that the hero's superpower is about to be generated. After this, we use `time.sleep()` not once, but twice, to create more dramatic effect and slow the program down. This time, we only print two lines of "......." each time through our `for` loop – each of which lasts for three seconds.

The next portion of the code

```
power = random.choice(superPowers)
```

creates a new variable named `power` and then assigns it a random value from the `superPowers` list. Finally, the section of code finishes up by printing out the value of `power` so the user can see what superpower was chosen.

If we were to run the program at this point, in theory, we would receive results that are similar to:

```
Are you ready to create a super hero with the Super Hero Generator 3000?
Enter Y/N:
y
Great, let's get started!
Randomizing name...
```

```
. . . . . . . . . . .
. . . . . . . . . . .
. . . . . . . . . . .
(I bet you can't stand the suspense!)
Your Super Hero Name is:
Astonishing Dingo
Now it's time to see what super power you have!)
(generating super hero power...)
. . . . . . . . . . .
. . . . . . . . . . .
(nah...you wouldn't like THAT one...)
. . . . . . . . . . .
. . . . . . . . . . .
(almost there....)
Your new power is:
Flying
```

Or

```
Are you ready to create a super hero with the Super Hero Generator 3000?
Enter Y/N:
y
Great, let's get started!
Randomizing name...
. . . . . . . . . . .
. . . . . . . . . . .
. . . . . . . . . . .
(I bet you can't stand the suspense!)
Your Super Hero Name is:
Astonishing Stallion
Now it's time to see what super power you have!)
(generating super hero power...)
. . . . . . . . . . .
. . . . . . . . . . .
(nah...you wouldn't like THAT one...)
```

```
...........
...........
(almost there....)
Your new power is:
Can Eat a Lot of Hot Dogs
```

Remember, your results may differ, as the superpowers and superhero names are generated randomly.

Finishing Our Program

We are almost finished creating your first, full-fledged program! In the words of the incomparable Stan Lee – Excelsior!

The final part of our application will randomly generate our hero's statistics. You may recall that at the beginning of our code, we created seven variables (brains, braun, stamina, wisdom, constitution, dexterity, and speed) and assigned them each a value of 0.

In the following code, we will now assign each of these seven variables that represent the hero's stats with a random integer value, ranging from 1 to 20. We do this using the random.randint() function, which we discussed in Chapter 2.

Add the following to your SuperheroGenerator3000.py file:

```python
print("Last but not least, let's generate your stats!")
print("Will you be super smart? Super strong? Super Good Looking?")
print("Time to find out!")
# Creating dramatic effect and slowing the program down again
for i in range(3):
    print("...........")
    time.sleep(3)
# Randomly filling each of the below variables with a new value
# The new values will range from 1-20
brains = random.randint(1,20)
braun = random.randint(1,20)
stamina = random.randint(1,20)
wisdom = random.randint(1,20)
constitution = random.randint(1,20)
```

```
dexterity = random.randint(1,20)
speed = random.randint(1,20)
# Printing out the statistics
print("Your new stats are:")
print("")
print("Brains: ", brains)
print("Braun: ", braun)
print("Stamina: ", stamina)
print("Wisdom: ", wisdom)
print("Constitution: ", constitution)
print("Dexterity: ", dexterity)
print("Speed: ", speed)
print("")
# Printing out a full summary of the generated super hero
# This includes the hero's name, super power, and stats
print("Here is a summary of your new Super Hero!")
print("Thanks for using the Super Hero Generator 3000!")
print("Tell all your friends!")
print("")
print("Character Summary:")
print("")
print("")
print("Super Hero Name: ", superName)
print("Super Power: ", power)
print("")
print("Brains: ", brains)
print("Braun: ", braun)
print("Stamina: ", stamina)
print("Wisdom: ", wisdom)
print("Constitution: ", constitution)
print("Dexterity: ", dexterity)
print("Speed: ", speed)
```

If we examine this part of the new code

```
brains = random.randint(1,20)
braun = random.randint(1,20)
stamina = random.randint(1,20)
wisdom = random.randint(1,20)
constitution = random.randint(1,20)
dexterity = random.randint(1,20)
speed = random.randint(1,20)
```

we can see how easy it is to randomly assign a random integer value to our variables. The numbers in parentheses represent the lowest value of the allowable range and the highest number allowed; the number will always be between 1 and 20.

The SuperheroGenerator3000 Code – Completed!

Now it is time to bask in the glory of our first completed program! Pat yourself on the back, and run and tell all of your friends what a great teacher I am and how this book is the best thing since sliced cheese! Who am I kidding – cheese is just as awesome in giant chunk form!

The last thing we need to do is make sure that your code matches exactly what is in this book. Once we do that, you are free to run the program over and over, change the values of the lists, and invite all of your friends and teachers over to generate their own superheroes!

Here is the code of SuperheroGenerator3000.py in its entirety – compare your code and make sure it matches:

```
# Importing the random module to use for randomizing numbers and
strings later
import random
# Importing the time module to create a delay
import time
# Creating - or initializing - our variables that will hold character stats
brains = 0
braun = 0
stamina = 0
wisdom = 0
```

```
power = 0
constitution = 0
dexterity = 0
speed = 0
answer = ''
# Creating a list of possible super powers
superPowers = ['Flying', 'Super Strength', 'Telepathy', 'Super Speed', 'Can
Eat a Lot of Hot Dogs', 'Good At Skipping Rope']
# Creating lists of possible first and last names
superFirstName = ['Wonder','Whatta','Rabid','Incredible', 'Astonishing',
'Decent', 'Stupendous', 'Above-average', 'That Guy', 'Improbably']
superLastName = ['Boy', 'Man', 'Dingo', 'Beefcake', 'Girl', 'Woman', 'Guy',
'Hero', 'Max', 'Dream', 'Macho Man','Stallion']
# Introductory text
print("Are you ready to create a super hero with the Super Hero
Generator 3000?")
# Ask the user a question and prompt them for an answer
# input() 'listens' to what they type on their keyboard
# We then use upper() to change the users answer to all uppercase letters
print("Enter Y/N:")
answer = input()
answer = answer.upper()
# While loop to check for the answer "Y"
# This loop will continue while the value of answer IS NOT "Y"
# Only when the user types "Y" will the loop exit and the program continue
while answer != "Y":
    print("I'm sorry, but you have to choose Y to continue!")
    print("Choose Y/N:")
    answer = input()
    answer = answer.upper()
print("Great, let's get started!")
print("Randomizing name...")
# Creating suspense using the time() function
for i in range(3):
    print("...........")
```

```
    time.sleep(3)
print("(I bet you can't stand the suspense!)")
print("")
# Randomizing Super Hero Name
# We do this by choosing one name from each of our two name lists
# And adding it to the variable superName
superName = random.choice(superFirstName)+ " " +random.
choice(superLastName)
print("Your Super Hero Name is:")
print(superName)
print("")
print("Now it's time to see what super power you have!)")
print("(generating super hero power...)")
# Creating dramatic effect again
for i in range(2):
    print("..........")
    time.sleep(3)
print("(nah...you wouldn't like THAT one...)")
for i in range(2):
    print("..........")
    time.sleep(3)
print("(almost there....)")
# Randomly choosing a super power from the superPowers list
# and assigning it to the variable power
power = random.choice(superPowers)
# Printing out the variable power and some text
print("Your new power is:")
print(power)
print("")
print("Last but not least, let's generate your stats!")
print("Will you be super smart? Super strong? Super Good Looking?")
print("Time to find out!")
# Creating dramatic effect and slowing the program down again
for i in range(3):
    print("..........")
```

```
    time.sleep(3)
# Randomly filling each of the below variables with a new value
# The new values will range from 1-20
brains = random.randint(1,20)
braun = random.randint(1,20)
stamina = random.randint(1,20)
wisdom = random.randint(1,20)
constitution = random.randint(1,20)
dexterity = random.randint(1,20)
speed = random.randint(1,20)
# Printing out the statistics
print("Your new stats are:")
print("")
print("Brains: ", brains)
print("Braun: ", braun)
print("Stamina: ", stamina)
print("Wisdom: ", wisdom)
print("Constitution: ", constitution)
print("Dexterity: ", dexterity)
print("Speed: ", speed)
print("")
# Printing out a full summary of the generated super hero
# This includes the hero's name, super power, and stats
print("Here is a summary of your new Super Hero!")
print("Thanks for using the Super Hero Generator 3000!")
print("Tell all your friends!")
print("")
print("Character Summary:")
print("")
print("")
print("Super Hero Name: ", superName)
print("Super Power: ", power)
print("")
print("Brains: ", brains)
print("Braun: ", braun)
```

```
print("Stamina: ", stamina)
print("Wisdom: ", wisdom)
print("Constitution: ", constitution)
print("Dexterity: ", dexterity)
print("Speed: ", speed)
```

When you run this program, you should see a result similar to the following, keeping in mind that the superhero's name, superpowers, and stats will be different, as they are all randomly generated – I know, I sound like a broken record!

Possible outcome:

```
Are you ready to create a super hero with the Super Hero Generator 3000?
Enter Y/N:
y
Great, let's get started!
Randomizing name...
...........
...........
...........
(I bet you can't stand the suspense!)
Your Super Hero Name is:
Wonder Man
Now it's time to see what super power you have!)
(generating super hero power...)
...........
...........
(nah...you wouldn't like THAT one...)
...........
...........
(almost there....)
Your new power is:
Good At Skipping Rope
Last but not least, let's generate your stats!
Will you be super smart? Super strong? Super Good Looking?
Time to find out!
...........
```

```
..........
..........
Your new stats are:
Brains:  8
Braun:  13
Stamina:  5
Wisdom:  15
Constitution:  20
Dexterity:  11
Speed:  9
Here is a summary of your new Super Hero!
Thanks for using the Super Hero Generator 3000!
Tell all your friends!
Character Summary:
Super Hero Name:  Wonder Man
Super Power:  Good At Skipping Rope
Brains:  8
Braun:  13
Stamina:  5
Wisdom:  15
Constitution:  20
Dexterity:  11
Speed:  9
```

## CHAPTER 7

Saving Time with Functions, Modules, and Built-Ins

Now that we have officially created our first ever, full-blown Python application (back in Chapter 6 if you are skipping around!), it is time to begin learning how to truly harness our programming powers and become the best programm we can be.

Throughout this book so far, we have touched upon the importance of being as efficient with our code as possible. Not only does coding efficiently increase the amount of work we can accomplish throughout the day, it also has several other benefits. First, it helps ensure that our programs use as little memory and processing power as possible, and second, it helps reduce the amount of errors in our code. The latter is achieved because, naturally, the less we type, the fewer chances there are of typing something wrong or making a programming logic or syntax error.

Part of working efficiently involves reusing tested and proven snippets of code over and over again as we create new programs. These pieces of code are often written to perform common tasks and can range from a few simple lines of code to thousands of lines. The key point, however, is that we know that they work, and instead of typing all of that code over and over again, we can simply save them in their own little file and import them into our programs as needed, saving us tons of time and mistakes.

When used this way, these snippets of code are referred to as modules. Simply put, a module is a file containing code. That's it.

We have used several modules throughout this book thus far, including time and random. In this chapter, we will not only learn how to create our own modules but will also look at some of the more popular and most commonly used modules that Python has to offer. After all, the wide array of tried-and-true Python modules that are built-in

© James R. Payne 2024
J. R. Payne, *Python for Teenagers*, https://doi.org/10.1007/978-1-4842-9988-3_7

to Python – and the ones created by the large Python community – are one of the things that make Python such a powerful and important programming language to begin with!

So put down those delicious corn-flavored potato chips and wipe that cheese dust from your fingers (be certain not to get any on that new fancy cape!), and prepare to extend your programming powers even further, as we delve into the ultimate weapon of any superhero coder – modules!

Defining Modules

Now that we know what a module is, you may find yourself wondering what, exactly, a module can contain. Working off of our previous definition, a module can contain any code at all. It might have a set of functions, be a script to write a bunch of text to the user's screen, contain a list of variables, or even be a few lines of code that import other modules into your program.

So long as it is a Python file (.py) and contains code, it is a module.

There are technically three types of modules in Python. They are

- Built-ins

- Packages

- Self-defined/custom-created

Built-Ins

Built-ins refer to modules and functions that are already a standard part of the Python library. These modules come pre-installed when you perform an install of Python. They include helpful functions such as `datetime` (which lets you work with date and time data types), `random` (used to randomly generate numbers), and socketserver (for creating network server frameworks).

You will be familiar with a few of the built-ins already, as we have used them in examples throughout this book. There are quite a few built-in modules that come standard with Python. To view a complete list, you can visit `https://docs.python.org/3.11/py-modindex.html`. Note, however, that this list changes with each version, so be sure to check the version of Python you are working with when visiting the Python.org website.

Of course, an easier way to see a list of built-in Python modules is to simply use the following bit of code:

```
# Print a list of Python Built-in Modules
print(help("modules"))
```

When you run this code, Python prints out a list of all of the built-in modules you currently have installed, similar to this:

Please wait a moment while I gather a list of all available modules...

BooleanExamples	_testmultiphase	gettext	reprlib
BooleanLogic	_thread	glob	rlcompleter
ConditionalStatements	_threading_local	grep	rpc
Count10	_tkinter	gzip	rstrip
DoomsdayClock	_tracemalloc	hashlib	run
Example1	_warnings	heapq	runpy
InfiniteLoop	_weakref	help	runscript
LearningText	_weakrefset	help_about	sched
ListExample	_winapi	history	scrolledlist
LogicalOperatorsExample	abc	hmac	search
MathIsHard	aifc	html	searchbase
MultipleElifs	antigravity	http	searchengine
OrExample	argparse	hyperparser	secrets
PowersWeaknesses	array	idle	select
RandomGenerator	ast	idle_test	selectors
...			

Of course, seeing a list of built-ins is great, but it would be better still to know what they actually do, without having to log onto the Internet and Google them. Fortunately, Python has two built-ins that help with that as well!

The first is .__doc__ – also known as a *docstring* or documentation string. Every module you encounter should have a docstring as part of its definition that basically serves that "document" what the function or module is used for. To read a module's documentation, we can call this docstring in the following manner:

```
# First we must import the module
import time
```

```
# Then we can print out its documentation
print (time.__doc__)
```

The name of the module whose documentation you wish to view goes before the .__doc__ command.

If you were to put that code in a file and run it, your result would look like the following:

```
This module provides various functions to manipulate time values.
There are two standard representations of time.  One is the number
of seconds since the Epoch, in UTC (a.k.a. GMT).  It may be an integer
or a floating point number (to represent fractions of seconds).
The Epoch is system-defined; on Unix, it is generally January 1st, 1970.
The actual value can be retrieved by calling gmtime(0).
The other representation is a tuple of 9 integers giving local time.
The tuple items are:
  year (including century, e.g. 1998)
  month (1-12)
  day (1-31)
  hours (0-23)
  minutes (0-59)
  seconds (0-59)
  weekday (0-6, Monday is 0)
  Julian day (day in the year, 1-366)
  DST (Daylight Savings Time) flag (-1, 0 or 1)
If the DST flag is 0, the time is given in the regular time zone;
if it is 1, the time is given in the DST time zone;
if it is -1, mktime() should guess based on the date and time.
```

Another option exists to see documentation – and in fact, you may wish to use both options, as the documentation for the two commands can be different. For example, if you enter this code

```
# First we must import the module
import time
# Then we can print out its documentation using our second method
```

```
help(time)
```

and run it, you will get a different, more wordy response than you did when you used
.__doc__:

```
Help on built-in module time:
NAME
    time - This module provides various functions to manipulate
    time values.
DESCRIPTION
    There are two standard representations of time.  One is the number
    of seconds since the Epoch, in UTC (a.k.a. GMT).  It may be an integer
    or a floating point number (to represent fractions of seconds).
    The Epoch is system-defined; on Unix, it is generally January
    1st, 1970.
    The actual value can be retrieved by calling gmtime(0).
    The other representation is a tuple of 9 integers giving local time.
    The tuple items are:
      year (including century, e.g. 1998)
      month (1-12)
      day (1-31)
      hours (0-23)
      minutes (0-59)
      seconds (0-59)
      weekday (0-6, Monday is 0)
      Julian day (day in the year, 1-366)
      DST (Daylight Savings Time) flag (-1, 0 or 1)
    If the DST flag is 0, the time is given in the regular time zone;
    if it is 1, the time is given in the DST time zone;
    if it is -1, mktime() should guess based on the date and time.
```

This result is actually just a tiny fraction of the entire document that will print.

To see the difference, try using both at the same time. Enter this code into a new Python file named printDocumentation.py and run it, examining the results to see the differences:

```
# First we must import the module whose documentation we wish to view
import time
# Printing documentation using .__doc__ or docstring
print (time.__doc__)
# Creating a dividing line so that we can see where the next set of
# Documentation begins.
 print("Here is what using HELP looks like...")
 print("####################################")
# Printing documentation using help()
help(time)
```

The result of this code is too large to include in this book, but feel free to run the program for yourself to see all of the documentation. Make sure to note which documentation belongs to which method we used to read the docstring.

Packages

Before you can import a module, you have to first install it – that is, if it did not come pre-packed in your Python installation. One method we can use to install a package that does not come standard (or that is developed by the community) is to use a built-in function known as pip. pip comes installed automatically in most current versions of Python, so unless you are using a legacy version of the language, then you should be all set.

pip is an installer program that comes bundled with Python versions 3.4 and up. To use the program, you must launch your command line window (you can do so by accessing Start, then run, then typing CMD). From there, you can see a list of possible pip commands by simply typing "pip" in the command prompt.

For now, you only need to understand one simple pip command: install. Before we use it however, we always want to check to see if we have the package we want to install already installed.

To do that, we head back over to IDLE and type in:

```
import <nameofmodule>
```

For example, if we wanted to see if we had the time module installed, we would type:

```
import time
```

If we receive an error, we know that that particular module is not installed already.

To fix this, we head back over to our command line – or CMD – and install the module. For our example, let's use the Pygame package, which is a popular package that helps in video game development (a topic we cover in a later chapter).

At the command prompt, simply enter:

```
python -m pip install Pygame
```

After a few seconds, the command line will begin the process of downloading and installing the package. Once finished, you will see a message similar to Figure 7-1.

```
Collecting Pygame
  Downloading pygame-2.5.1-cp311-cp311-win_amd64.whl (10.6 MB)
                                     10.6/10.6 MB 50.4 MB/s eta 0:00:00
Installing collected packages: Pygame
Successfully installed Pygame-2.5.1
```

Figure 7-1. *Congratulations! You have now installed your first Python package*

Creating Your Own Module

Using pre-existing built-in modules and packages is a great way to make your programs more efficient and less prone to errors. Another tool you can use to save you time and lots of keyboard head-banging (a lot of that occurs when you are looking for programming errors late in the night or listening to *Metallica*) is to create your very own modules that you can use over and over again.

The first part of creating our module is to create a function that we can call or reference from within another program. For this exercise, we will need two Python files. We will start by creating the actual module that will be used by our main program.

Create a file called ourFirstModule.py and enter in the following code:

```
# Define your function using def
def firstFunction():
    print("This is our first function!")
```

Save the file and try to run it. While you can see that the program does indeed execute, nothing really seems to happen. This is because we have only defined what our function is going to do, but we have not invoked it, called it, or told it to do anything yet.

To actually use this function, we have to call it from another file.

Create another file named testingModule.py and enter in the following code:

```
# We first have to import our module
# We import our module by using the name of the file, minus the .py
extension
import ourFirstModule
# Now we call the function to use it
ourFirstModule.firstFunction()
```

When you run this file, you should see the following result:

```
This is our first function!
```

Congratulations, you have created your first module and successfully called it from within another program!

Of course, modules can have more than one function within them, so let's add a few more functions and practice calling them in our file. Open back up your ourFirstModule.py file and edit the code so it looks like this:

```
# Define your function
def firstFunction():
    print("This is our first function!")
# Define a second function
def secondFunction():
    print("Look, a second function!")
# Define a variable
a = 2+3
```

Next, we need to edit our testingModule.py file to make use of our newly defined functions and variables. Modify the code so it resembles the following:

```
# We first have to import our module
# We import our module by using the name of the file, minus the .py extension
import ourFirstModule
```

```
# Now we call the function to use it
ourFirstModule.firstFunction()
# Calling our second function
ourFirstModule.secondFunction()
# Calling and printing a variable within our module
print("The value of a is: ",ourFirstModule.a)
```

In addition to calling not one, but two functions, this code also prints out the value of our variable named a. We achieve this using the code `print(ourFirstModule.a)`. The part `ourFirstModule` references the `ourFirstModule.py` file and tells Python where to pull the function from, while the `.a` tells it what variable to print. If our variable were named `lastName`, for example, it would look like this instead: `print(ourFirstModule.lastName)`.

Finally, as with any code that we create, we always want to be sure to document our work. Earlier, we used `.__doc__` and `help()` to print out the documentation for modules. Now, we will use multi-line commenting (or three sets of ") to create our own documentation.

Open up your `ourFirstModule.py` file and modify the code for the first function – `firstFunction()` – by adding the following comments to it:

```
# Define your function
def firstFunction():
    """ This is the documentation - or docstring - for firstFunction()
We can put examples of use here or just document what the function is for
That way future programmers - or ourselves later on - can read the
"helpfile" for our firstFunction and know what it was intended for
    """
print("This is our first function!")
```

Everything between the first indented set of """ and the closing set of """ is considered a comment or documentation, as discussed in a previous chapter.

Now, open up your `testingModule.py` file, and let's add the following code to it, in order to print out the documentation:

```
# print the helpfile for firstFunction()
help(ourFirstModule)
```

You can place this code anywhere in the file, but I chose to place it directly beneath the print( ) function that prints out firstFunction.

Run the program and you should see the following results:

```
This is our first function!
Help on module ourFirstModule:
NAME
    ourFirstModule - # Define your function
FUNCTIONS
    firstFunction()
        This is the documentation - or docstring - for firstFunction()

We can put examples of use here or just document what the function is for
        That way future programmers - or ourselves later on - can read the
        "helpfile" for our firstFunction and know what it was intended for
        secondFunction()
DATA
    a = 5
Look, a second function!
The value of a is: 5
```

Common Built-In Functions

Python has many great built-in functions, and we have covered a great many in this book so far. But just like items in a trusty utility belt, you can never have too many tools on hand. Sure, a can of shark repellent might seem ridiculous, but wait till you get into a battle with Guy-That-Can-Hold-His-Breath-and-Oh-Yeah-Also-Speak-To-Sharks Man. Now how silly do you think shark repellent is?

There are nearly 70 built-in functions, most of which you will use in your life as a programmer. For now, we are going to discuss a few of the more common ones that we have skipped thus far. We will tackle them by category, beginning with string functions.

String Functions

String functions, as you can probably guess, are functions that work on strings. We have already covered a few, including `str.upper()` and `str.lower()`, which convert strings to upper- and lowercase, respectively.

In addition to actually making a string uppercase or lowercase, you can also perform a check to see what case a string's content actually is. For example, maybe you want to know whether a user has typed in all capital letters. To check, you could use the following code:

```
# Create a string of all uppercase letters
testString = "I AM YELLING!"
print("Is the user yelling?")
# Check to see if the value of testString consists of all uppercase letters
print(testString.isupper())
```

In this case, we use the string function known as str.isupper() to check that the string contains uppercase letters. If you were to run the this code, you would get a boolean response (True or False):

```
Is the user yelling?
True
```

Note that if any character at all in the string is lowercase, it would return a `False` value instead, as the function is checking to see if the entire string contains uppercase letters.

If we wanted to check to see if the case was lower, we would use the string function str.islower( ), like so:

```
# Create a string of all uppercase letters
testString = "I AM YELLING!"
print("Is the user yelling?")
# Check to see if the value of testString consists of all uppercase letters
print(testString.islower())
```

Which, of course – in this instance – would return a `False`.

There are times when we might want to check what type of characters the user typed in. For example, if the user was filling out a form and we wanted to know their first and last name, we would not want them to input a numeric value – not unless they were robots, aliens, or a cool rapper mind you.

To check if a string only contains letters (and no numbers), you would use str. isalpha():

```
# Create a string to check if the variable only contains letters
firstName = "James8"
# Check to see if the value of firstName contains any numbers
print("Does your name contain any letters?")
if firstName.isalpha() == False:
    print("What are you, a robot?")
```

Since the value of the string firstName does not just contain letters (it has a number in it), then the if returns a False value, causing the print() function to print out its text:

```
Does your name contain any numbers?
What are you, a robot?
```

If firstName *only* contained alphabetic characters (A–Z and a–z), the if would have returned True, and nothing would have printed.

We can also check if the values are only numeric or contain just numbers. For example, maybe we want to make sure someone is not entering letters into a social security or phone number field. To check for number-only values in a string, we use the function str.isnumeric():

```
# Create a string to check if the variable only contains numbers
userIQ = "2000"
# Check to see if the value if userIQ contains only numbers and no letters
if userIQ.isnumeric() == False:
    print("Numbers only please!")
else:
    print("Congrats, you know the difference between a number and a letter!")
```

Again, we check to see if the result of the evaluation of whether userIQ contains only numbers is True or False. Since userIQ only contains numbers – and no letters – the result is True, and we get the result:

```
Congrats, you know the difference between a number and a letter!
```

We can also check to see if our strings contain only spaces – also known as whitespaces. To do that, we use the function `str.isspace()`:

```
# Check to see if the value of UserIQ contains all spaces or whitespace
characters
if userIQ.isspace() == True:
    print("Please enter a value other than a bunch of spaces you boob!")
```

Since `userIQ` does not contain all spaces, nothing happens. If it were full of only spaces, Python would have executed the print() function we defined.

Another useful string function we can use is `len()`, which lets us count the number of characters in a string. You may be asking yourself, "Why in the world would I want to do that?" The answer is simple: you may want to limit the number of characters in a variable, such as a password, or make sure it has enough characters.

Or, maybe, you have OCD (obsessive-compulsive disorder) like me, and feel the need to count everything. I consider it one of my many, many superpowers....

To count the number of characters in a string, you could use code similar to this:

```
# Create a variable to count the number of characters it holds using len()
testPassword - "MyPasswordIsPassword!"
print(len(testPassword))
```

When you run this code, you will get the result:

21

Number Functions

Now that we have learned a few new string functions, let's move on to working with numbers. We previously examined several functions that helped us work with numbers, as well as operators that let us perform nifty mathematical equations without hurting our brains (too much, anyway).

To make our brains ever more gooder at numbers (don't tell your English teacher I wrote that!), let us take a gander at some more functions that will up our programming skills and make us look like proverbial rocket scientists.

Sometimes when we work with numbers, we will be asked to tell our bosses which number is higher than all of the other ones. To find out which number is the max in a series of numbers, we use max().

```
# Create a list containing a group of numbers
studentGrades = [100, 90, 80, 70, 60, 50, 0]
# Use max() to find the highest number in the studentGrades list
print("What is the highest grade in the studentGrades list?")
print:("Answer :")
print(max(studentGrades))
```

If we were to run this code, it would result in:

```
What is the highest grade in the studentGrades list?
100
```

Because 100 is the highest value in our list studentGrades. If we wanted to find out the minimum value of a list of numbers, we would use min():

```
# Create a list containing a group of numbers
studentGrades = [100, 90, 80, 70, 60, 50, 0]
# Use max() to find the highest number in the studentGrades list
print("What is the highest grade in the studentGrades list?")
print:("Answer :")
print(max(studentGrades))
# Use min() to find the lowest number in the studentGrades list
print("What is the lowest grade in the studentGrades list?")
print:("Answer :")
print(min(studentGrades))
```

Once run, this code outputs:

```
What is the highest grade in the studentGrades list?
100
What is the lowest grade in the studentGrades list?
0
```

We could also use min() and max() without creating a list. To use them as stand-alones, you would type:

```
print(min(100, 90, 80, 70, 60, 50, 0))
print(max(100, 90, 80, 70, 60, 50, 0))
```

Note   You can also use min() and max() on strings – for example, using min on the alphabet, listed from a to z, would return "a," while using max() would return "z."

Another common practice is to sum up all of the numbers in a given list. Maybe you need to calculate your company's total payroll or hours worked. To do so, you use the sum() function. Let's sum it up with the following code:

```
# Create another list containing more numbers, representing payroll
totalPayroll = [500, 600, 200, 400, 1000]
# Use sum() to calculate the sum of the numbers in a list
print("How much did we pay employees this week?")
print("The total payroll was: ")
print(sum(totalPayroll))
```

The output of this example would be:

```
How much did we pay employees this week?
The total payroll was:
2700
```

Practice Your New Functions

We have added a lot of new functions to your superhero programming utility belt. Now is the time to practice what you learned to sharpen your skills. In the following you will find a list of new string functions we learned and a list of new number/math functions we toyed around with in this chapter.

Feel free to input this code on your own and figure out new and exciting ways to use these simple, yet powerful, functions.

String Function Examples

```
# Create a string of all uppercase letters
testString = "I am YELLING!"
# Create a string to check if the variable only contains letters
firstName = "James8"
# Create a string to check if the variable only contains numbers
userIQ = "2000"
# Create a variable to count the number of characters it holds using len()
testPassword = "MyPasswordIsPassword!"
# A series of functions are tested below
print("Is the user yelling?")
# Check to see if the value of testString consists of all uppercase letters
print(testString.isupper())
# Check to see if the value of firstName contains any numbers
print("Does your name contain any numbers?")
if firstName.isalpha() == False:
    print("What are you, a robot?")
# Check to see if the value if userIQ contains only numbers and no letters
if userIQ.isnumeric() == False:
    print("Numbers only please!")
else:
    print("Congrats, you know the difference between a number and a
    letter!")
# Check to see if the value of UserIQ contains all spaces or whitespace
characters
if userIQ.isspace() == True:
    print("Please enter a value other than a bunch of spaces you boob!")
# Count the number of characters in a password
print("Let's see how many characters are in testPassword!")
print("I count: ")
print(len(testPassword))
```

Number Function Examples

```
# Create a list containing a group of numbers
studentGrades = [100, 90, 80, 70, 60, 50, 0]
# Create another list containing more numbers, representing payroll
totalPayroll = [500, 600, 200, 400, 1000]
# Use max() to find the highest number in the studentGrades list
print("What is the highest grade in the studentGrades list?")
print:("Answer :")
print(max(studentGrades))
# Use min() to find the lowest number in the studentGrades list
print("What is the lowest grade in the studentGrades list?")
print:("Answer :")
print(min(studentGrades))
# Use min() and max() without defining a list
print(min(100, 90, 80, 70, 60, 50, 0))
print(max(100, 90, 80, 70, 60, 50, 0))
# Use sum() to calculate the sum of the numbers in a list
print("How much did we pay employees this week?")
print("The total payroll was: ")
print(sum(totalPayroll))
```

In This Episode!

This episode was spectacular! It was amazing! It was astonishing! It was spider…well, let's just say it was incredible and leave it at that (hey, those big comic book companies don't own those words!).

You really took a great leap forward in your programming powers this chapter, learning how to create your very own modules and functions. You topped that off by learning a few more built-in functions and even gained the ability to use one of Python's most powerful components – community-created packages.

We covered a lot, so, as always, here is a summary of some of the great things we added to your superpower kit in this chapter!

- There are three types of modules: built-ins, packages, and custom-created.

- Built-ins come pre-installed in Python, packages are created by third-party suppliers/the Python community, and custom-created are the ones you create yourself.

- help( ) and .__doc__ help print a module's documentation or help file:

- Example: help(time) and print(time.__doc__)

- help("modules") lists all of the available modules your Python install currently has to offer.

- import imports the module into your program.

- Example: import time

  You can install a package using pip on the command line:

  ```
  python -m pip install <name of module>
  ```

  def is used to define a function.

  Example:

  ```
  def firstFunction():
              print("Hello!")
  ```

- str.upper( ) and str.lower( ) convert a string to upper- and lowercase, respectively.

- str.isalpha, str.isnumeric, and str.isspace( ) all check to see if the correct data type is being used.

- len( ) counts the number of characters in a string.

- min( ) and max( ) find the minimum and maximum value in a list of numbers or string values.

- sum( ) calculates the sum of values contained within a list.

## CHAPTER 8

Using Classes and Objects

Up to this point, we have covered some pretty standard programming language features and practices. This chapter will continue this tradition; however, the subject matter may be a little tougher to grasp at first glance. Don't worry though – you have come this far, and we have watched you morph from stumbling sidekick to full-on, beastly hero.

Your parents would be proud – or they would be – if they had survived the attack of the Ooze People from Planet Gorgon. Moving on….

This chapter will focus on a concept known as OOP – or *object-oriented programming*. You will be learning about things called classes and objects, constructors, superclasses, subclasses, and a powerful tool known as inheritance. We will then use these new, powerful concepts and methods to make a version of the program we created back in Chapter 6.

That's right – just when you thought we couldn't improve upon the good ole' Superhero Generator 3000, yours truly pulled the rug out from under you and blew your mind! I hope you are wearing a helmet because I'm not cleaning up all those brains!

What Is OOP?

Truth be told, Python is, in fact, an object-oriented programming language. Not everyone uses it as such, and not everyone is a fan of – or truly grasps – the true power of OOP.

Some would argue that writing in an OOP manner makes Python, well, less Python; that is, they feel that using the methods, classes, and objects that are at the core of object-oriented programming makes Python less readable and user-friendly.

There may be some merit to that argument, but overall, what a programmer loses in readability, they make up for in efficiency, error reduction, and, frankly, good programming habits. Besides, if you follow the practice of good code documentation (as we have discussed time and again), your code will be *very* readable, as you will clearly state your intention in every section of your program.

© James R. Payne 2024
J. R. Payne, *Python for Teenagers*, https://doi.org/10.1007/978-1-4842-9988-3_8

Object-oriented programming (OOP) is all about creating reusable code. Remember how we discussed the benefits of function and modules? Those same rules apply to using OOP practices. It is perfect for more complicated or long programs, as it lets you reuse snippets of code and keep everything in a nice, tight, easily accessible bundle.

Up until this point, we have *mostly* relied on something known as procedural programming. Procedural code is essentially lines of code that appear – and are mostly used – in sequential order. In this chapter, we will change all of that!

The core concept of OOP programming – a concept that exists in many other programming languages by the way – involves things known as *classes* and *objects*.

What Are Classes (And Will I Be Graded?)

Don't worry – I know the word "class" frightens you and reminds you of long lectures on the joys of mathematics or the telling of riveting tales of the economic systems of the early Etruscan peoples. In Python, classes are much more interesting; however, though, in truth, there is much joy to be found in a nice slice of pi.

Crickets

But I digress.

A class can best be described as the DNA for an object; better yet, you can think of it as a blueprint of an object or even as a template. Think of a class in this way: if you were going to build a car, you wouldn't just randomly hammer some metal and rubber tires together and hope for the best. If you did, your car would not get too far or look that great!

Instead, you would create a blueprint – or a class – that would contain certain details or features that you would want your car to have. Further – since us hero programmers are all about efficiency – we would want to create a blueprint (class) that we could use when we constructed *any* car. That way, when we went to make another model of vehicle, we wouldn't have to draw up plans all over again.

If we created a class for a car, for instance, we might want to say that every car has four tires, a windshield, doors, an engine, and so forth. These would all be common things that every car would have. The color, paint, number of doors, size of tires, and so forth might differ, but those basic features would exist on every car.

So, to summarize, a class is basically a blueprint that lets us create multiple objects that all have the same basic features. Instead of having to code or define those features each time we create a new object, we simply call an instance of our class and blammo – all of the work is already done.

If this concept doesn't fully click in your brain just yet, don't worry – it will start to be crystal clear when we begin to use it in actual code. For now, just be aware of the basic concept:

Classes. Are. Blueprints.

What Are Objects

If classes are the blueprints, then objects are, well, the objects we create from them! In programming terms, when we create an object, we are creating an *instance* of the class.

Objects can be used to represent a whole slew of things in a program. As stated, you could use them to create a vehicle, for example. Or they could represent a dog breed or a type of employee.

Of course, this is a superhero programming book, so what better way to introduce the concept of classes and objects – and how to use them – than to create our own blueprint (class) of a superhero (object)?

Creating Our First Class

Creating a class is a relatively simple thing to do. It is, in fact, very similar to creating a function. When we create a class – as is the case with functions – it is known as *defining a class*. We do so using the `class` keyword:

```
class Superhero():
...(write some code)
....(more code here)
```

This example shows how to create a class named Superhero. Note the naming convention for classes is to capitalize the first letter of the beginning word. If there are two or more words in the name, you would capitalize the first letter of each word. For instance, if you wanted to create a class to represent an "American Superhero," you would use:

```
class AmericanSuperhero():
        ...(write some code)
        ...(write some more code)
```

Of course, these classes do not technically do anything. For them to be useful and perform their function, we need to add code to them that tells them what to do or that helps define the objects that we will be creating from them.

When we add a function to a class, the function is known as a method. Methods must be indented beneath the class that they belong to.

```
class Superhero():
    def fly(self):
        print("Look at me, I'm so fly!")
```

This code creates a class named Superhero with a method named fly, which prints out the text "Look at me, I'm so fly!"

When we define a method, we do so using def, followed by the name of the method. Methods contain *arguments*, encapsulated in parentheses. Every method of a class must contain the self argument at the very least; they can contain any number of other arguments as well (more on this soon!).

self is used to reference the instance of the object you create. Again, this will make more sense as we actually create our classes and put them to work.

Also note that the code beneath the method definition must be indented in relation to the method it belongs to as well.

We can place any number of methods within a single class and can add all sorts of code to them as well, including variables and so forth.

For instance, if we wanted to add two methods to our Superhero class – one that lets him fly, the other that lets him eat a lot of hot dogs – we could just define our class this way:

```
class Superhero():
    def fly(self):
        print("Look at me, I'm so fly!")
    def hotDog(self):
        print("I sure do like hot dogs!")
```

If we were to run this code, nothing would happen, as all we are doing is defining our Superhero class. To actually use the class, we have to create an instance – or an object – of the class.

Creating Our First Object

Now that we have a basic blueprint of a superhero created via our Superhero class, we can create our first hero, or, more aptly put, our first hero object.

In order to create an object (or an instance of a class), we must initialize – or create – a copy of the class, similar to creating a variable and giving it a value:

```
HotDogMan = Superhero()
```

Creating an object is just that simple. Now, the object HotDogMan has all of the traits of our Superhero class. The instance/object of the Superhero class gets stored in HotDogMan, including all of the attributes and methods that we defined when we created the class.

To see this in action, we can call the two methods that we defined in the Superhero class, which are now part of the HotDogMan object. To *call* means to execute or run part of some code:

```
HotDogMan.fly()
HotDogMan.hotDog()
```

The first line of this code tells Python to access the HotDogMan object and look for a method named fly, then, once found, execute it. The second line does the same thing, only it looks for the method hotDog and runs that portion of code.

To better understand everything we have covered so far, let's create a new file named SampleClassandObject.py and add the following code to it (Note: this code is specifically the code we have discussed so far in this chapter, collected into one file):

```
class Superhero():
      def fly(self):
            print("Look at me, I'm so fly!")
      def hotDog(self):
            print("I sure do like hot dogs!")
HotDogMan = Superhero()
HotDogMan.fly()
HotDogMan.hotDog()
```

When we run this code, we get the following result:

```
Look at me, I'm so fly!
I sure do like hot dogs!
```

This is all well and good, but, in reality, these examples do not show the true power that classes and objects – and object-oriented programming – have to offer. Now that we understand the basic concept of classes and objects, let's use them in a more practical and real-world manner.

Improving the Superhero Generator 3000!

If you recall back in Chapter 6, we created a program that randomly generated a superhero. Specifically, we randomly generated a superhero name, a power, and some statistics. To do so, we had the user run the program and answer a few simple questions before displaying the results.

We created that program in a very sequential order; that is, the code we wrote was read by the Python interpreter – and any programmers who view it – line by line. While the program performed (flawlessly, I might add!), what would happen if we wanted to create a second, or thousandth, superhero? To do that, in the program's current state, the user would have to run the program over and over again.

Not very efficient.

We could have always created a loop to continue the superhero choosing process if the user requested more than one hero or we could have just kept adding more code to allow for more superheroes, but, again, we want to create as few lines of code as possible to make our programs run better and reduce the possibility of errors.

Think of it this way: our old Superhero Generator 3000 program was a system that hand-built each and every superhero. If we used classes and objects instead, we would have a high-tech factory that could print out superheroes by the thousands and without having to worry as much about human error. Additionally, it would save tons of time because we wouldn't have to write so much code.

With all of this in mind, let's take a stab at recreating the Superhero Generator 3000, this time making use of classes and objects.

If you will recall, in our original version of the program, each hero had a set of statistics that defined their physical and mental characteristics. These included

- Brains: How smart the hero is

- Braun: How strong the hero is

- Stamina: How much energy the hero has

- Wisdom: How wise they are and how much real-life experience they have

- Constitution: How well their body can recover from injury and resist illnesses

- Dexterity: How acrobatic and nimble our hero is

- Speed: How fast the hero is

We can assign each of these attributes to a Superhero class, and that way, when we create an object from that class, any and all heroes we make will have the same set of statistics. We do this, because we know that every hero should have at least some brains, braun, dexterity, and so forth – these are all common traits of a standard hero and, therefore, will be part of our hero blueprint or template.

Let's create a new file named SuperheroClass.py and add the following code to it:

```
# Import the random module so we can randomly generate numbers
import random
# Create a Superhero class that will act as a template for any heroes
we create
class Superhero():
    # Initializing our class and setting its attributes
    def __init__(self):
        self.superName = " "
        self.power = " "
        self.braun = braun
        self.brains = brains
        self.stamina = stamina
        self.wisdom = wisdom
        self.constitution = constitution
        self.dexterity = dexterity
        self.speed = speed
# Adding random values to each stat using the random() module
braun = random.randint(1,20)
brains = random.randint(1,20)
stamina = random.randint(1,20)
wisdom = random.randint(1,20)
```

```
constitution = random.randint(1,20)
dexterity = random.randint(1,20)
speed = random.randint(1,20)
```

In this code, we are introduced to a new method, known as the `constructor` method. We use it to initialize any new data that belongs to the class. The `constructor` method is also called the __init__ method and is always the first method we create in a class when we need to add data to any variables up front.

If we have parameters, we place them in the parentheses of the __init__ method. Here, we set each `self` reference equal to each parameter. For example:

```
self.brains = brains
```

sets `self.brains` equal to `brains`. That way, later in the program when we create our objects, we can refer to the different parameters – which, in this case, represent our hero stats – and use them in our program.

Next, in this case, we want to create hero templates and we want each hero stat to be randomized, so we use the random() module on each parameter that will represent our hero stat. For example:

```
braun = random.randint(1,20)
```

adds a random value to `braun`, ranging from 1 to 20.

Again, classes, objects, and methods can be a difficult subject to grasp for a beginner, so be patient and be sure to follow along the code, even if things do not make 100% sense right off the bat; sometimes you need to see the code in action to fully grasp what it is intended to do.

Now that we have set up our initial Superhero class and decided what the template for any superheroes that we create are going to look like, let's go ahead and try to create an instance of the class (again, also known as creating an object). Then, we will print out the stats of our hero. Add the following code to your SuperheroClass.py file:

```
# Import the random module so we can randomly generate numbers
import random
# Create a Superhero class that will act as a template for any heroes we create
class Superhero():
    # Initializing our class and setting its attributes
    def __init__(self):
        self.superName = ""
```

```
        self.power = ""
        self.braun = braun
        self.brains = brains
        self.stamina = stamina
        self.wisdom = wisdom
        self.constitution = constitution
        self.dexterity = dexterity
        self.speed = speed
# Adding random values to each stat using the random() function
braun = random.randint(1,20)
brains = random.randint(1,20)
stamina = random.randint(1,20)
wisdom = random.randint(1,20)
constitution = random.randint(1,20)
dexterity = random.randint(1,20)
speed = random.randint(1,20)
print("Please enter your super hero name: ")
# Creating the Superhero object
hero = Superhero()
# Assigning a value to superName using the user's input
hero.superName = input('>')
# We print out the result of the created object, including its parameters
print("Your name is %s." % (hero.superName))
print("Your new stats are:")
print("")
print("Brains: ", hero.brains)
print("Braun: ", hero.braun)
print("Stamina: ", hero.stamina)
print("Wisdom: ", hero.wisdom)
print("Constitution: ", hero.constitution)
print("Dexterity: ", hero.dexterity)
print("Speed ", hero.speed)
print("")
```

In this version of our program, we ask the user to enter their own name for the superhero vs. randomly generating one as we did in our original Superhero Generator 3000 program. Don't fret – we will randomize that value soon enough. For now, we want to keep things simple, as we let the user enter their own name, using the input() function. The input() function's value is placed in the hero object's superName parameter. This is all achieved in the line:

```
hero.superName = input('>')
```

You may have noticed that we used input() a little different here than before. The '>' in the parentheses simply places a > prompt on the user's screen so they know where to type.

Next, we printed out the randomly generated values of each parameter of the hero object using, for example, line's like this:

```
print("Brains: ", hero.brains)
```

Then, hero.brains portion of that line tells Python to print the value stored in the hero objects brains parameter – similar to the way a variable works.

If you run that program, you will get a result like this – keeping in mind your values will be different because they are randomly generated:

```
Please enter your superhero name:
>SuperPowerAwesomeManofAction
Your name is SuperPowerAwesomeManofAction.
Your new stats are:
Brains:  10
Braun:  10
Stamina:  5
Wisdom:  17
Constitution:  1
Dexterity:  19
Speed  15
```

Perfect so far! Now, let's add the code to randomly generate the hero's name and superpower. For this part, we are going to add the lines:

```
# Creating a list of possible super powers
superPowers = ['Flying', 'Super Strength', 'Telepathy', 'Super Speed', 'Can
Eat a Lot of Hot Dogs', 'Good At Skipping Rope']
# Randomly choosing a super power from the superPowers list
# and assigning it to the variable power
power = random.choice(superPowers)
# Creating lists of possible first and last names
superFirstName = ['Wonder','Whatta','Rabid','Incredible', 'Astonishing',
'Decent', 'Stupendous', 'Above-average', 'That Guy', 'Improbably']
superLastName = ['Boy', 'Man', 'Dingo', 'Beefcake', 'Girl', 'Woman', 'Guy',
'Hero', 'Max', 'Dream', 'Macho Man','Stallion']
# Randomizing Super Hero Name
# We do this by choosing one name from each of our two name lists
# And adding it to the variable superName
superName = random.choice(superFirstName)+ " " +random.choice(superLastName)
```

Right below where we defined our superhero stats. Since we are now randomly generating the superhero's name, we no longer need to ask the user for their input, so we remove the lines:

```
print("Please enter your super hero name: ")
```

as well as

```
# Assigning a value to superName using the user's input
hero.superName = input('>')
```

We no longer need those, since we are now randomly generating our superName based off of the superFirstName and superLastName lists, just as we did in the original version of our program.

So now, all together, your code should match the following; if it does not, review this section again and change your code to match mine:

```
# Import the random module so we can randomly generate numbers
import random
# Create a Superhero class that will act as a template for any heroes we create
```

```python
class Superhero():
    # Initializing our class and setting its attributes
    def __init__(self):
        self.superName = superName
        self.power = power
        self.braun = braun
        self.brains = brains
        self.stamina = stamina
        self.wisdom = wisdom
        self.constitution = constitution
        self.dexterity = dexterity
        self.speed = speed
# Adding random values to each stat using the random() function
braun = random.randint(1,20)
brains = random.randint(1,20)
stamina = random.randint(1,20)
wisdom = random.randint(1,20)
constitution = random.randint(1,20)
dexterity = random.randint(1,20)
speed = random.randint(1,20)
# Creating a list of possible super powers
superPowers = ['Flying', 'Super Strength', 'Telepathy', 'Super Speed', 'Can
Eat a Lot of Hot Dogs', 'Good At Skipping Rope']
# Randomly choosing a super power from the superPowers list
# and assigning it to the variable power
power = random.choice(superPowers)
# Creating lists of possible first and last names
superFirstName = ['Wonder','Whatta','Rabid','Incredible', 'Astonishing',
'Decent', 'Stupendous', 'Above-average', 'That Guy', 'Improbably']
superLastName = ['Boy', 'Man', 'Dingo', 'Beefcake', 'Girl', 'Woman', 'Guy',
'Hero', 'Max', 'Dream', 'Macho Man','Stallion']
# Randomizing Super Hero Name
# We do this by choosing one name from each of our two name lists
# And adding it to the variable superName
```

```
superName = random.choice(superFirstName)+ " " +random.
choice(superLastName)
# Creating the Superhero object
hero = Superhero()
# Assigning a value to superName using the user's input
# hero.superName = input('>')
# We print out the result of the created object, including its parameters
print("Your name is %s." % (hero.superName))
print("Your super power is: ", power)
print("Your new stats are:")
print("")
print("Brains: ", hero.brains)
print("Braun: ", hero.braun)
print("Stamina: ", hero.stamina)
print("Wisdom: ", hero.wisdom)
print("Constitution: ", hero.constitution)
print("Dexterity: ", hero.dexterity)
print("Speed ", hero.speed)
print("")
```

If you run this program now, you will get the following result (again, your value will be different as they are randomly generated):

```
Please enter your super hero name:
Your name is Incredible Dream.
Your super power is:  Good At Skipping Rope
Your new stats are:
Brains:  1
Braun:  1
Stamina:  5
Wisdom:  11
Constitution:  6
Dexterity:  9
Speed  13
```

So now, at this point, our program works almost the same as the original version of the Superhero Generator 3000, only there are fewer lines of code and fewer chances for an error to occur. Some of the prompts are different also – for instance, we have not yet asked the user if they want to create a hero, and we have not inserted our dramatic pause effects while the values are being generated. However, the bare bones are in place, and in this next section, we will add in some of the old bells and whistles, as well as some new, really cool features that showcase the *true* power of classes and objects!

Inheritance, Subclasses, and More!

One of the great things about classes is that you can use them to create other classes and, by way of a thing called `inheritance`, pass their attributes along to the newly recreated class, without having to use a bunch of lengthy code. It's similar to how your parents pass their genetic code down to you, only in Python, we get to say what exactly a class inherits.

When we create a class based off of another class, we call this newly created class a `subclass`. By default, these subclasses inherit the methods and parameters of the class they are created from – which, by the way, are known as parent classes or superclasses.

As with all things code, sometimes it is best to demonstrate how this idea works through an actual program.

So far, the Superhero Generator 3000 only lets us create regular old superheroes. However, as you well know, not all heroes are created equally. For instance, Superman is technically just an alien from another planet that can see through clothes and eats sunlight (like a buff plant) to get strong. Batman, meanwhile, has no powers at all; or rather, his superpowers consist of having boat loads of money, an awesome car, and a butler with some far-fetched computer programming skills. I mean, really? My parents can't figure out how to text, and here Alfred is, using the world's most powerful supercomputer.

But I digress.

To make our program a little more realistic, we are going to introduce a new attribute to our superheroes: superhero type. For each type that we create, we are going to give them a bonus of some sort. For now, let's focus on creating two subclasses to represent our new "types" of heroes. One will be for superheroes that are robots and the other for superheroes that are mutated.

Here is how that would look in code:

```
# Creating a subclass of Superhero named Mutate
# Mutate heroes will get a +10 bonus to their speed score.
class Mutate(Superhero):
    def __init__(self):
        Superhero.__init__(self)
        print("You created a Mutate!")
        self.speed = self.speed + 10
        self.superName = random.choice(superFirstName)+ " " +random.
        choice(superLastName)
# Creating a subclass of Superhero named Robot
# Robot heroes will get a + 10 bonus to their braun score.
class Robot(Superhero):
    def __init__(self):
        Superhero.__init__(self)
        print("You created a robot!")
        self.braun = self.braun + 10
        self.superName = random.choice(superFirstName)+ " " +random.
        choice(superLastName)
```

Here, we have created two new classes, which are both actually subclasses of our Superhero class. The way we achieve this is by putting the name of the parent class in the parentheses of the newly created class. For example, class Mutate(Superhero) tells the Python interpreter to create a class that is a child or subclass of Superhero and inherit its methods and parameters.

We then initialize our new subclass using def __init__(self) and re-initialize our Superhero class using Superhero.__init__(self), since we will be creating new objects based off of, technically, both the class and subclass.

Finally, we want to give our heroes a bonus based off of which type of hero they are. The mutate character will receive a bonus to speed, as shown in this line of code:

```
self.speed = self.speed + 10
```

While robots will get a bonus to braun, via this line of code:

```
self.braun = self.braun + 10
```

All other hero stats will remain the same, as they were generated in the Superhero class originally; if we wanted to modify their values again, we would have to do so explicitly in our newly created subclasses.

Now that we have created two new classes, we need to actually create an instance/ object based off of them to see them in action. The code to create an object based off of a subclass is the same as it is to create one based off of any class; if we wanted to create a new mutate hero and a new robot hero, we would do so using these lines of code:

```
hero2 = Robot()
hero3 = Mutate()
```

Let's create some code to print out the stats of a regular superhero, a robot, and a mutate:

```
# Creating the Superhero object
hero = Superhero()
# We print out the result of the created object, including its parameters
print("Your name is %s." % (hero.superName))
print("Your super power is: ", hero.power)
print("Your new stats are:")
print("")
print("Brains: ", hero.brains)
print("Braun: ", hero.braun)
print("Stamina: ", hero.stamina)
print("Wisdom: ", hero.wisdom)
print("Constitution: ", hero.constitution)
print("Dexterity: ", hero.dexterity)
print("Speed ", hero.speed)
print("")
# Creating a Mutate object
hero2 = Mutate()
print("Your name is %s." % (hero2.superName))
print("Your super power is: ", hero2.power)
print("Your new stats are:")
print("")
print("Brains: ", hero2.brains)
print("Braun: ", hero2.braun)
```

```
print("Stamina: ", hero2.stamina)
print("Wisdom: ", hero2.wisdom)
print("Constitution: ", hero2.constitution)
print("Dexterity: ", hero2.dexterity)
print("Speed ", hero2.speed)
print("")
# Create a Robot character
hero3 = Robot()
print("Your name is %s." % (hero3.superName))
print("Your super power is: ", hero3.power)
print("Your new stats are:")
print("")
print("Brains: ", hero3.brains)
print("Braun: ", hero3.braun)
print("Stamina: ", hero3.stamina)
print("Wisdom: ", hero3.wisdom)
print("Constitution: ", hero3.constitution)
print("Dexterity: ", hero3.dexterity)
print("Speed ", hero3.speed)
print("")
```

If you were to add all of this new code to your file (we will in a moment) and run it, your results would be similar to this:

```
Your name is Above-average Boy.
Your super power is:  Flying
Your new stats are:
Brains:  16
Braun:  4
Stamina:  4
Wisdom:  18
Constitution:  16
Dexterity:  12
Speed  2
You created a Mutate!
Your name is Above-average Boy.
```

```
Your super power is:  Flying
Your new stats are:
Brains:  16
Braun:  4
Stamina:  4
Wisdom:  18
Constitution:  16
Dexterity:  12
Speed  12
You created a robot!
Your name is Above-average Boy.
Your super power is:  Flying
Your new stats are:
Brains:  16
Braun:  14
Stamina:  4
Wisdom:  18
Constitution:  16
Dexterity:  12
Speed  2
```

Notice how the regular superhero has a speed of 2, as does the robot. Yet the mutate has a speed of 12. Likewise, both our regular heroes and our mutate have a braun of 4, while our robot has a braun of 14 – just as intended.

At this point if you add in the new code, your SuperheroClass.py file should resemble this – if it does not, please take the time to make sure it does:

```
# Import the random module so we can randomly generate numbers
import random
# Create a Superhero class that will act as a template for any heroes
we create
class Superhero():
    # Initializing our class and setting its attributes
    def __init__(self):
        self.superName = superName
        self.power = power
```

```
        self.braun = braun
        self.brains = brains
        self.stamina = stamina
        self.wisdom = wisdom
        self.constitution = constitution
        self.dexterity = dexterity
        self.speed = speed
# Adding random values to each stat using the random() function
braun = random.randint(1,20)
brains = random.randint(1,20)
stamina = random.randint(1,20)
wisdom = random.randint(1,20)
constitution = random.randint(1,20)
dexterity = random.randint(1,20)
speed = random.randint(1,20)
# Creating a list of possible super powers
superPowers = ['Flying', 'Super Strength', 'Telepathy', 'Super Speed',
'Can Eat a Lot of Hot Dogs', 'Good At Skipping Rope']
# Randomly choosing a super power from the superPowers list
# and assigning it to the variable power
power = random.choice(superPowers)
# Creating lists of possible first and last names
superFirstName = ['Wonder','Whatta','Rabid','Incredible', 'Astonishing',
'Decent', 'Stupendous', 'Above-average', 'That Guy', 'Improbably']
superLastName = ['Boy', 'Man', 'Dingo', 'Beefcake', 'Girl', 'Woman', 'Guy',
'Hero', 'Max', 'Dream', 'Macho Man','Stallion']
# Randomizing Super Hero Name
# We do this by choosing one name from each of our two name lists
# And adding it to the variable superName
superName = random.choice(superFirstName)+ " " +random.
choice(superLastName)
# Creating a subclass of Superhero named Mutate
# Mutate heroes will get a +10 bonus to their speed score.
class Mutate(Superhero):
    def __init__(self):
```

```
        Superhero.__init__(self)
        print("You created a Mutate!")
        self.speed = self.speed + 10
        self.superName = random.choice(superFirstName)+ " " +random.
choice(superLastName)
# Creating a subclass of Superhero named Robot
# Robot heroes will get a + 10 bonus to their braun score.
class Robot(Superhero):
    def __init__(self):
        Superhero.__init__(self)
        print("You created a robot!")
        self.braun = self.braun + 10
        self.superName = random.choice(superFirstName)+ " " +random.
choice(superLastName)
# Creating the Superhero object
hero = Superhero()
# We print out the result of the created object, including its parameters
print("Your name is %s." % (hero.superName))
print("Your super power is: ", hero.power)
print("Your new stats are:")
print("")
print("Brains: ", hero.brains)
print("Braun: ", hero.braun)
print("Stamina: ", hero.stamina)
print("Wisdom: ", hero.wisdom)
print("Constitution: ", hero.constitution)
print("Dexterity: ", hero.dexterity)
print("Speed ", hero.speed)
print("")
# Creating a Mutate object
hero2 = Mutate()
print("Your name is %s." % (hero2.superName))
print("Your super power is: ", hero2.power)
print("Your new stats are:")
print("")
```

```
print("Brains: ", hero2.brains)
print("Braun: ", hero2.braun)
print("Stamina: ", hero2.stamina)
print("Wisdom: ", hero2.wisdom)
print("Constitution: ", hero2.constitution)
print("Dexterity: ", hero2.dexterity)
print("Speed ", hero2.speed)
print("")
# Create a Robot character
hero3 = Robot()
print("Your name is %s." % (hero3.superName))
print("Your super power is: ", hero3.power)
print("Your new stats are:")
print("")
print("Brains: ", hero3.brains)
print("Braun: ", hero3.braun)
print("Stamina: ", hero3.stamina)
print("Wisdom: ", hero3.wisdom)
print("Constitution: ", hero3.constitution)
print("Dexterity: ", hero3.dexterity)
print("Speed ", hero3.speed)
print("")
```

Adding the Bells and Whistles

The last thing we need to do now is add some bells and whistles to our program.
Remember, the goal of this chapter was to learn how to use object-oriented
programming to remake our Superhero Generator 3000 program with those principles;
our original version had some dramatic pauses and asked the user some questions.
Here, we are going to add all of these features back into our program and give them a
choice to choose a hero type.

We will be using principles we have learned throughout this book so far, including
if-elif-else statements, the random(), input(), and time() modules and, of course,
the OOP principles from this very chapter.

As an exercise, rather than re-walk you through every step of the code, I will highlight some of the main features of the code we are going to add now and then input the program in its entirety for you to peruse and code on your own.

For starters, we want to provide the users a choice, as we did in our original program – mainly, we are asking if they want to use the Superhero Generator 3000. If they choose "Y", the program continues; if not, the loop continues asking them if they want to continue:

```
# Introductory text
print("Are you ready to create a super hero with the Super Hero
Generator 3000?")
# Ask the user a question and prompt them for an answer
# input() 'listens' to what they type on their keyboard
# We then use upper() to change the users answer to all uppercase letters
print("Enter Y/N:")
answer = input()
answer = answer.upper())
# While loop to check for the answer "Y"
# This loop will continue while the value of answer IS NOT "Y"
# Only when the user types "Y" will the loop exit and the program continue
while answer != "Y":
    print("I'm sorry, but you have to choose Y to continue!")
    print("Choose Y/N:")
    answer = input()
    answer = (answer.upper())
print("Great, let's get started!")
```

Again, this is code from the original version of our program that we have simply added to our new version, so you should be familiar with its usage.

Next, we want to add some brand *new* code. The purpose of this new code will be to let the user choose the *type* of hero they want to create. We are giving them three options: regular, mutate, or robot.

```
# Letting the user choose which type of hero to create
print("Choose from the following hero options: ")
print("Press 1 for a Regular Superhero")
print("Press 2 for a Mutate Superhero")
```

```
print("Press 3 for a Robot Superhero")
answer2 = input()
```

This will be followed by an `if-elif-else` block that will check the value of the user's answer – which we stored in the variable `answer2` – and respond accordingly. For example, if the user chooses option 1, a regular superhero will be created; option 2, a mutate; and so forth.

Here is the block of code:

```
if answer2=='1':
    # Creating the Superhero object
    hero = Superhero()
    # We print out the result of the created object, including its
    parameters
    print("You created a regular super hero!")
    print("Generating stats, name, and super powers.")
    # Creating dramatic effect
    for i in range(1):
        print("...........")
        time.sleep(3)
        print("(nah...you wouldn't like THAT one...)")
    for i in range(2):
        print("...........")
        time.sleep(3)
    print("(almost there....)")
    print(" ")
    print("Your name is %s." % (hero.superName))
    print("Your super power is: ", hero.power)
    print("Your new stats are:")
    print("")
    print("Brains: ", hero.brains)
    print("Braun: ", hero.braun)
    print("Stamina: ", hero.stamina)
    print("Wisdom: ", hero.wisdom)
    print("Constitution: ", hero.constitution)
    print("Dexterity: ", hero.dexterity)
```

```
    print("Speed ", hero.speed)
    print("")
elif answer2=='2':
        # Creating a Mutate object
        hero2 = Mutate()
        print("Generating stats, name, and super powers.")
    # Creating dramatic effect
        for i in range(1):
            print("...........")
            time.sleep(3)
            print("(nah...you wouldn't like THAT one...)")
        for i in range(2):
            print("...........")
            time.sleep(3)
        print("Your name is %s." % (hero2.superName))
        print("Your super power is: ", hero2.power)
        print("Your new stats are:")
        print("")
        print("Brains: ", hero2.brains)
        print("Braun: ", hero2.braun)
        print("Stamina: ", hero2.stamina)
        print("Wisdom: ", hero2.wisdom)
        print("Constitution: ", hero2.constitution)
        print("Dexterity: ", hero2.dexterity)
        print("Speed ", hero2.speed)
        print("")
elif answer2=='3':
        # Create a Robot character
        hero3 = Robot()
        print("Generating stats, name, and super powers.")
        # Creating dramatic effect
        for i in range(1):
            print("...........")
            time.sleep(3)
        print("(nah...you wouldn't like THAT one...)")
```

```
        for i in range(2):
            print("...........")
            time.sleep(3)
        print("Your name is %s." % (hero3.superName))
        print("Your super power is: ", hero3.power)
        print("Your new stats are:")
        print("")
        print("Brains: ", hero3.brains)
        print("Braun: ", hero3.braun)
        print("Stamina: ", hero3.stamina)
        print("Wisdom: ", hero3.wisdom)
        print("Constitution: ", hero3.constitution)
        print("Dexterity: ", hero3.dexterity)
        print("Speed ", hero3.speed)
        print("")
else:

print("You did not choose the proper answer! Program will now self-
destruct!")
```

Finally, we also need to import time or our dramatic effects won't work! We do that at the very top of our code, underneath our import random statement.

The New and Improved Superhero Generator 3000 Code!

Now that we have all of our pieces coded, let's make sure they are all in order. Compare your code to the following code and make sure everything matches. Then, run the program several times trying out all of the options to see how the program works:

```
# Import the random module so we can randomly generate numbers
# Import time module for dramatic pausing effect
import random
import time
# Create a Superhero class that will act as a template for any heroes
we create
class Superhero():
    # Initializing our class and setting its attributes
```

```python
    def __init__(self):
        self.superName = superName
        self.power = power
        self.braun = braun
        self.brains = brains
        self.stamina = stamina
        self.wisdom = wisdom
        self.constitution = constitution
        self.dexterity = dexterity
        self.speed = speed
# Adding random values to each stat using the random() function
braun = random.randint(1,20)
brains = random.randint(1,20)
stamina = random.randint(1,20)
wisdom = random.randint(1,20)
constitution = random.randint(1,20)
dexterity = random.randint(1,20)
speed = random.randint(1,20)
# Creating a list of possible super powers
superPowers = ['Flying', 'Super Strength', 'Telepathy', 'Super Speed', 'Can
Eat a Lot of Hot Dogs', 'Good At Skipping Rope']
# Randomly choosing a super power from the superPowers list
# and assigning it to the variable power
power = random.choice(superPowers)
# Creating lists of possible first and last names
superFirstName = ['Wonder','Whatta','Rabid','Incredible', 'Astonishing',
'Decent', 'Stupendous', 'Above-average', 'That Guy', 'Improbably']
superLastName = ['Boy', 'Man', 'Dingo', 'Beefcake', 'Girl', 'Woman', 'Guy',
'Hero', 'Max', 'Dream', 'Macho Man','Stallion']
# Randomizing Super Hero Name
# We do this by choosing one name from each of our two name lists
# And adding it to the variable superName
superName = random.choice(superFirstName)+ " " +random.
choice(superLastName)
# Creating a subclass of Superhero named Mutate
```

```python
# Mutate heroes will get a +10 bonus to their speed score.
class Mutate(Superhero):
    def __init__(self):
        Superhero.__init__(self)
        print("You created a Mutate!")
        self.speed = self.speed + 10
# Creating a subclass of Superhero named Robot
# Robot heroes will get a + 10 bonus to their braun score.
class Robot(Superhero):
    def __init__(self):
        Superhero.__init__(self)
        print("You created a robot!")
        self.braun = self.braun + 10
# Introductory text
print("Are you ready to create a super hero with the Super Hero
Generator 3000?")
# Ask the user a question and prompt them for an answer
# input() 'listens' to what they type on their keyboard
# We then use upper() to change the users answer to all uppercase letters
print("Enter Y/N:")
answer = input()
answer = answer.upper()
# While loop to check for the answer "Y"
# This loop will continue while the value of answer IS NOT "Y"
# Only when the user types "Y" will the loop exit and the program continue
while answer != "Y":
    print("I'm sorry, but you have to choose Y to continue!")
    print("Choose Y/N:")
    answer = input()
    answer = answer.upper()
print("Great, let's get started!")
# Letting the user choose which type of hero to create
print("Choose from the following hero options: ")
print("Press 1 for a Regular Superhero")
print("Press 2 for a Mutate Superhero")
```

```
print("Press 3 for a Robot Superhero")
answer2 = input()
if answer2=='1':
    # Creating the Superhero object
    hero = Superhero()
    # We print out the result of the created object, including its
parameters
    print("You created a regular super hero!")
    print("Generating stats, name, and super powers.")
    # Creating dramatic effect
    for i in range(1):
        print("...........")
        time.sleep(3)
        print("(nah...you wouldn't like THAT one...)")
    for i in range(2):
        print("...........")
        time.sleep(3)
    print("(almost there....)")
    print(" ")
    print("Your name is %s." % (hero.superName))
    print("Your super power is: ", hero.power)
    print("Your new stats are:")
    print("")
    print("Brains: ", hero.brains)
    print("Braun: ", hero.braun)
    print("Stamina: ", hero.stamina)
    print("Wisdom: ", hero.wisdom)
    print("Constitution: ", hero.constitution)
    print("Dexterity: ", hero.dexterity)
    print("Speed ", hero.speed)
    print("")
elif answer2=='2':
        # Creating a Mutate object
        hero2 = Mutate()
        print("Generating stats, name, and super powers.")
```

```python
    # Creating dramatic effect
        for i in range(1):
            print("...........")
            time.sleep(3)
            print("(nah...you wouldn't like THAT one...)")
        for i in range(2):
            print("...........")
            time.sleep(3)
        print("Your name is %s." % (hero2.superName))
        print("Your super power is: ", hero2.power)
        print("Your new stats are:")
        print("")
        print("Brains: ", hero2.brains)
        print("Braun: ", hero2.braun)
        print("Stamina: ", hero2.stamina)
        print("Wisdom: ", hero2.wisdom)
        print("Constitution: ", hero2.constitution)
        print("Dexterity: ", hero2.dexterity)
        print("Speed ", hero2.speed)
        print("")
elif answer2=='3':
        # Create a Robot character
        hero3 = Robot()
        print("Generating stats, name, and super powers.")
        # Creating dramatic effect
        for i in range(1):
            print("...........")
            time.sleep(3)
        print("(nah...you wouldn't like THAT one...)")
        for i in range(2):
            print("...........")
            time.sleep(3)
        print("Your name is %s." % (hero3.superName))
        print("Your super power is: ", hero3.power)
        print("Your new stats are:")
```

```
        print("")
        print("Brains: ", hero3.brains)
        print("Braun: ", hero3.braun)
        print("Stamina: ", hero3.stamina)
        print("Wisdom: ", hero3.wisdom)
        print("Constitution: ", hero3.constitution)
        print("Dexterity: ", hero3.dexterity)
        print("Speed ", hero3.speed)
        print("")
else:

        print("You did not choose the proper answer! Program will now self-
        destruct!")
```

In This Episode!

We made some incredible leaps and bounds in this chapter, as we tackled what is, arguably, the most difficult concept to master of all the topics we discuss in this entire book. That's right – the rest is smooth sailing in comparison!

As a brief reminder/future cheat sheet, here is a summary of the things we covered in this chapter:

- OOP stands for object-oriented programming.

- Object-oriented programming is a concept where we practice creating code that can be reused in our programs.

- Procedural programming involves writing code that is designed to – for the most part – execute line by line or in a linear fashion.

- The core of OOP revolves around classes, objects, and methods.

- A class is like a blueprint or template.

- An object is an instance of a class. For instance, if a class is the blueprint for a home, the object is the actual house created from that blueprint.

- A function used within a class is known as a method.

- To define a class, we type

class Superhero:

```
...some code...
```

The def statement is used to define a method within a class. For example:

def Fly:

```
...code...
```

- __init__(self) is used to Initialize an object.

- self is used to reference a parameter when we create an instance of a class.

- We define an object by assigning it to a variable, like so:

```
hero = Superhero()
```

- Classes are hierarchal in nature; we can have a main class (the parent) and then a subclass (the child).

- Subclasses inherit the methods and parameters of the parent or superclass.

- To define a subclass, you use code such as:

```
class Mutate (Superhero)
```

## CHAPTER 9

Introducing Other Data Structures

Welcome back budding hero! Looks like you've had a long day of homework, chores, and, of course, fighting crime. Now all that is left to do is eat your vegetables, put away your dishes, and for the love of God, man, brush those teeth!

Of course, you could always brush your teeth really fast tonight, and that might buy you some time to put some more crime-fighting abilities into that programmer brain of yours! I mean, who needs teeth, after all, when you can just program yourself an app to chew your food for you?

Seriously though, go brush those teeth....

We are now over halfway through with this book, and you have learned a good, solid foundation for good programming practices and practical language skills that you will be able to take with you as you enter the workforce or venture out on your own and develop your own best-selling software.

Of course, there is always more to learn. Even after you finish reading this masterful Tome of Programming Knowledge, your journey will not be complete. Being a programmer is like being a student for life – you will always have to hone your skills and learn the newest and greatest technology.

In addition to language updates (did we mention that computer languages get updates pretty frequently?), at some point you will want to venture off into other programming languages and frameworks. That, however, is for another chapter in the near future.

This chapter, meanwhile, will be taking a look back. We discussed data structures earlier, learning how to work with variables and lists. While those are both powerful instruments we can use to store information, they are not the only data structures that we have available to us.

© James R. Payne 2024
J. R. Payne, *Python for Teenagers*, https://doi.org/10.1007/978-1-4842-9988-3_9

There are two more that we need to discuss: *tuples* and *dictionaries*. Those will be the topic of conversation for this episode. We will also look at some functions for working with these two storage units and incorporate them into some new programs.

So, you know what to do – no, not use your X-ray vision to spy on the answers to this week's math test.

Brush your teeth!

Then get back here and prepare to learn how to code like a hero. Some more.

More Data Structures

As stated, we have already looked at two data structures: lists and variables. We know that a data structure is a storage container that holds data or a piece/pieces of information. We can store information in these data structures, we can remove the data, and we can add different data into them. We can also take the data out, use it for part of a program (metaphorically), and place it back (it doesn't really ever leave the container).

A variable is able to hold one piece of data. That data can be a letter, a number or integer, a string of characters, a sentence, a paragraph, and so forth. Additionally, variables can also hold objects such as lists, which technically means they can hold more than "one" piece of data. A list, meanwhile, can hold multiple pieces of information. Think of a variable as a single file folder and list as a file cabinet.

To define a variable, you may recall, we use code such as:

```
a = "Hello"
b = 7
c = "Hello, I am being held prisoner in a variable!"
```

To define a list, we use this method:

```
employees = ['Big E.', 'Bloke Hogan', 'Alfredo the Butler']
priceList = [5, 10, 20, 30, 40, 50]
```

If we want to print from a variable, we would write something along the lines of:

```
print(a)
print("You have this many apples: ", b)
```

You can also use the formatter %s as a stand-in for your variable. For example, let's say you wanted to write the sentence, "You have X apples," where X is the value of variable b. If you typed this code:

```
print("You have %s apples!" , b)
```

You would get the following output when you run it:

```
You have 7 apples!
```

```
To print a list, we can use:
print(employees)
```

Or to print a single item from a list, we use its index (Remember: the first item in a list is located at index 0):

```
print(employees[1])
```

This would print out:

```
Bloke Hogan
```

Now that we have reviewed variables and lists and refreshed our memories about how data structures work a little, let's move on to learning all about the other two types of data structures that Python has to offer.

What Are Tuples?

Tuples, like lists and variables, are a type of data structure. Unlike variables and lists, however, tuples are considered *immutable*. This is just a fancy way of saying that you cannot change their value or modify them in the normal way.

Tuples are made up of ordered sequences of *items*. These items – or values – are defined in between parentheses and separated by commas. To define a tuple, you use code such as:

```
villains = ('Eyebrow Raiser', 'Angry Heckler', 'Not So Happy Man', 'The
Heck Raiser')
```

Just as with a list, we can print out the contents of our tuple using a simple print( ) function:

```
print(villains)
```

This would result in:

```
('Eyebrow Raiser', 'Angry Heckler', 'Not So Happy Man', 'The Heck Raiser')
```

Also similar to lists, the items in a tuple can be referenced by their index number. Items in a tuple begin at index 0. So, for instance, if we wanted to print the first item in our villains tuple, we would use:

```
print(villains[0])
```

Which would give us the horrible villain:

```
Eyebrow Raiser
```

If we wanted to use the villain tuple as part of a sentence, there are a number of ways we could do so:

```
# Defining our tuple
villains = ('Eyebrow Raiser', 'Angry Heckler', 'Not So Happy Man', 'The
Heck Raiser')
# Printing the items in a tuple
print(villains)
# Printing single items in a tuple
print(villains[0])
print(villains[1])
print(villains[2])
print(villains[3])
# Ways to append tuple items to sentences
print("The first villain is the sinister", villains[0])
print("The second villain is the terrifying " + villains[1])
```

Giving us:

```
('Eyebrow Raiser', 'Angry Heckler', 'Not So Happy Man', 'The Heck Raiser')
Eyebrow Raiser
Angry Heckler
Not So Happy Man
The Heck Raiser
The first villain is the sinister Eyebrow Raiser
The second villain is the terrifying Angry Heckler
```

Another way that we can use items in a tuple is by *slicing* them (note that we can also slice lists). When you slice a tuple, you are singling out a range of values that you wish to use. The format of this is `villains[0:3]`, as an example. If we run this code:

```
print(villains[0:3])
```

the output would be:

```
('Eyebrow Raiser', 'Angry Heckler', 'Not So Happy Man')
```

I know what you are thinking – the item at index 3 is `'The Heck Raiser'`, so why didn't that print out?

The answer is simple: when we slice, the first number *before* the colon tells Python where to start; the number *after* the colon tells it to end *before* that number.

If we were to write `print(villains[0:4])`, only then would it print out all four of our items, because Python searches for the item in index 4 – of which there are none – and prints the item before it.

Note that the starting number of the index does not have to be 0. If we wanted to skip printing the first item in our tuple, for instance, we could just use `print(villains[1:4])`, and it would start printing at the second item:

```
('Angry Heckler', 'Not So Happy Man', 'The Heck Raiser')
```

Another trick we can do with tuples is add them together. For instance, let's say you have a tuple containing sparkly, purple capes and another tuple full of polka-dotted capes. Maybe you are tired of having too many closets full of capes, so you wish to combine them. If so, you can always concatenate your tuples together to make a brand-new tuple. Consider this example:

```
# Creating a tuple of my purple capes
purpleCapes = ('Purple Frilly Cape', 'Purple Short Cape', 'Purple Cape with
Holes In It')
# Creating a tuple of my Polka Dot capes
polkaCapes = ('Black and White Polka Dot Cape', 'White and Beige Polka Dot
Cape', 'Blue Polka Dot Cape Missing the Blue Polka Dots')
# Concatenating - or adding - my two tuples of capes together into a new tuple
allMyCapes = (purpleCapes + polkaCapes)
# Printing out the values of the newly created tuple
print(allMyCapes)
```

This code combines the tuple `purpleCapes` with the items listed in `polkaCapes` and stores them in a newly created tuple called `allMyCapes`. If you run this snippet of code, you would get:

```
('Purple Frilly Cape', 'Purple Short Cape', 'Purple Cape with Holes In It',
'Black and White Polka Dot Cape', 'White and Beige Polka Dot Cape', 'Blue
Polka Dot Cape Missing the Blue Polka Dots')
```

Note that this does not change or affect the values of `purpleCapes` or `polkaCapes`; remember – you cannot change or modify the values in a tuple.

In addition to using the + or concatenation operator on tuples, you can also use the * or multiplication operator to repeat the values stored in a tuple:

```
print(allMyCapes[1] * 3)
```

This prints out the item located at index 1 in the `allMyCapes` tuple, three times, resulting in:

```
Purple Short CapePurple Short CapePurple Short Cape
```

Note that there are no spaces after the items listed in our tuple, so when we print them out, they are devoid of any whitespaces.

The Tuple Functions

Just as there are with lists, tuples, too, have a set of functions you can use to interact with the data stored within them. These functions are not exclusive to tuples, however, and can be used elsewhere in your Python code.

Two familiar tuple functions should be min() and max(); you may recall using them in a previous chapter. When using these two functions in a tuple, they perform their usual role – that is, they return the minimum and maximum valued item(s) in a tuple.

For example:

```
# Create a tuple containing a set of numbers
lowest_value = (1, 5, 10, 15, 20, 50, 100, 1000)
# Use the minimum function to return the lowest value item in the tuple
print(min(lowest_value))
```

This code would return:

1

Since it is, technically, the lowest value number in our tuple.

If we wanted the highest number, we would use the max() function:

```
# Create a tuple containing a set of numbers
highest_value = (1, 5, 10, 15, 20, 50, 100, 1000)
# Use the maximum function to return the highest value item in the tuple
print(max(highest_value))
```

which, as you could guess, would return: 1000.

Another useful tuple function is len(), which, as you may recall, returns the length of a string or the number of elements in a list. When used with a tuple, it returns the number of items contained with the tuple.

```
# Create a tuple with some items
super_hair = ('Super Stache', 'Macho Beard', 'Gargantuan Goat-tee',
'Villainous Toupee', 'Unfortunate Baldness')
# Print out the number of items in our tuple
print(len(super_hair))
```

This would return, 5, since there are five total items in our super_hair tuple.

Examples of uses for the len() function include scenarios where you need to know the number of employees in a company or how many villains you have locked away in the *Villainous Vault of Retired Super Bad Guys*. If you had a tuple containing these nefarious character's names, you could simply use the len() function on it and get a quick head count.

Of course, returning a count of villains in the Villainous Vault of Bad Guys is helpful if we want to get a quick look at how many inmates there are, but what if we wanted to see that list printed out in some sort of order – if only there was a function for that....

Oh wait, there is!

```
# A list of Villains Locked Away in the Villainous Vault of Bad Guys
villains = ('Naughty Man ', 'Skid Mark ', 'Mister Millenial ', 'Jack Hammer ',
'The Spelling Bee ', 'Drank All The Milk Man ', 'Wonder Wedgie ',
'Escape Goat')
# Print out a sorted list of our villains tuple
print(sorted(villains))
```

To print a sorted list of a tuple (or lists for that matter), we use the sorted() function, as shown in the preceding code. A few important things to note. First, the sorted result is returned in alphabetical order. Second – and most important – the sorted() function only returns a sorted output – it does not actually sort the data in our tuple. Remember, tuples are immutable and cannot be changed – even by a function as mighty as sorted()!

If we were to run the preceding code, our result would be:

```
['Drank All The Milk Man ', 'Escape Goat', 'Jack Hammer ', 'Mister Millenial ',
'Naughty Man ', 'Skid Mark ', 'The Spelling Bee ', 'Wonder Wedgie ']
```

Of course, we can sort numbers just as easily. Consider this code:

```
# A tuple of numbers we are going to sort
numbers_sort = (10, 20, 5, 2, 18)
# Sorting numbers in our tuple
print(sorted(numbers_sort))
```

Were we to run that, it would return the output:

```
[2, 5, 10, 18, 20]
```

While we are looking at a tuple full of numbers, let's examine another useful function – sum(). Like other functions showcased thus far, sum() should also be familiar to you. To refresh your memory, it is used to sum – or total – the numbers in a data structure.

Here is the code we would use to sum up the total of the items in a tuple:

```
# A tuple of numbers we are going to sum
numbers_sum = (10, 20, 5, 2, 18)
# Summing items in a tuple
print(sum(numbers_sum))
```

Running this gives us the total of the items in the numbers_sum tuple: 55.

Finally, we can also convert other data structures – such as lists and variables – to a tuple, using the tuple() function:

```
# A list we will convert to a tuple
villainList = ['Naughty Man ', 'Skid Mark ', 'Mister Millenial ', 'Jack
Hammer ', 'The Spelling Bee ', 'Drank All The Milk Man ', 'Wonder Wedgie ',
'Escape Goat']
# Using tuple() to convert villainList to a tuple
tuple(villainList)
# A string we will convert to a tuple
villain1 = "Mustached Menace!"
tuple(villain1)
print(villainList)
print(villain1)
```

More Fun with Tuples

Just when you thought our fun with the mighty tuple was over, you find out you hit the bonus round! Before we move on to our next type of data structure, there are a few more things we need to learn.

In our introduction to the tuple, we learned that tuples differ from lists in one very important way: tuples are immutable, and the data contained in them cannot be changed in any way, whereas lists can be manipulated, updated, and added to.

This makes tuples a powerful tool if you care about data integrity for your data structure. If you have a group of items that absolutely must not get changed, storing them in a tuple is the man (or woman) for the job.

That being said, there are some instances where you may want to delete or remove a tuple from your program. For instance, maybe you have a tuple storing all the different types of facial hair that heroes and villains can have. What would happen if, suddenly (hopefully), these facial adornments went out of style? To ensure the items in the tuple were never accessed again – and to keep our code as neat and efficient as possible – we have two options.

First, we could simply comment out all the code referencing our tuple using the # or "''" comment. That leaves the possibility, however, of someone uncommenting your code, which could lead to errors or – God forbid – a return of the trend of facial hair...oh no!

Another option is to delete or modify the code referencing the tuple and then to actually delete the tuple itself.

There is a way for us to delete an entire tuple; we cannot, however, delete the items within a tuple. Here is how you can delete a tuple:

```
# A tuple full of facial hair styles for villains and heroes
facial_hair = ('Super Stache', 'Macho Beard', 'Gargantuan Goat-tee', 'Face
Mullet',)
# Printing out facial hair
print(facial_hair)
# Using del to delete a tuple entirely
del facial_hair
# Printing out
print(facial_hair)
```

In this code snippet we first create the facial_hair tuple and assign it a bunch of items – one frightening one known as 'face mullet' (I have no idea what that even means).

Next, we print out the items in facial_hair to prove that creating the tuple did, indeed, work. After seeing the list of atrocities people are willing to grow on their face, we decide it's best to delete the `facial_hair` tuple and pretend it never existed. We use the `del` statement to do so, as in the line that says: `del facial_hair`.

Finally, to make sure that `facial_hair` has truly been deleted, we print it one more time. When we run this code, two things happen with regard to output. First, the items in `facial_hair` get printed out. Second, we receive an error message.

Why the message error? Because we deleted `facial_hair` after printing it the first time; when we go to print it the second time, the interpreter can no longer find it. That means we succeeded in ridding the world of crazy `facial_hair`!

Just another day in the life of a hero!

Here is the result you would see if you ran the program:

```
('Super Stache', 'Macho Beard', 'Gargantuan Goat-tee', 'Face Mullet')
Traceback (most recent call last):

File "C:/Users/James/AppData/Local/Programs/Python/Python311/TupleExamples.
py", line 8, in <module>
    print(facial_hair)
NameError: name 'facial_hair' is not defined
```

Sometimes when we use tuples to store data, we may need to know how many times a particular item appears in our data structure. For example, the word "Mississippi" has a notorious amount of 'i's in it. The same with the letter 's'. If we created a tuple containing that word, we could count the number of instances that both 'i' and 's' occurred in the word so that when people asked us to tell them something interesting, we could say, "Did you know that Mississippi has a bunch of s's and i's in it? True story, bro!"

To count the number of instances that an item occurs in a tuple, or to count the number of items that equals s, we use the `count()` method.

```
# Tuple containing all of the letters used to spell Missisisippi
state = ('M', "i", "s", "s", "i", "s", "i", "s", "i", "p", "p", "i")
# Note: You could, technically, also easily create the tuple using state
= tuple('Missisisippi') with the tuple() command, which automatically
converts a string into a tuple.
# Count the number of times "i" appears in our tuple and print out
the result
print("There are this many of the letter i in Missisisippi: ")
```

```
print(state.count('i'))
# Count the number of times "s" appears in Missisisippi
print("There are this many of the letter s in Missisisippi: ")
print(state.count('s'))
```

The characters in parentheses in the code state.count('i') tell Python to count the number of times 'i' appears in the state tuple.

If we run this sample code, we would get the following output:

```
There are this many of the letter i in Missisisippi
5
There are this many of the letter s in Missisisippi
4
```

We can also search for an item in our tuple using the keyword in (we can do this in lists as well). This keyword basically asks if value "x" is *in* the tuple:

```
# Tuple containing all of the letters used to spell Missisisippi
state = ('M', "i", "s", "s", "i", "s", "i", "s", "i", "p", "p", "i")
# Checking to see if "z" or "i" appears in our state tuple
print('z' in state)
print('i' in state)
```

The in keyword returns a Boolean (True or False) response when checking to see if an item is contained within a tuple. When we run this code, it returns the output:

```
False
True
```

because it first checks to see if there is a 'z' in the state tuple and finds none (False). Then it checks for an 'i' in the state tuple and of course finds one or more (True).

Tuple Examples

We went through a lot of ways to work with tuples so far in this chapter, so to make things convenient, below you can find a sample Python file containing all of the code written in this chapter pertaining to tuples thus far.

Feel free to modify this code and to see how changing items in defined tuples affects the code snippets and their results:

```
# Defining our tuple
villains = ('Eyebrow Raiser', 'Angry Heckler', 'Not So Happy Man', 'The
Heck Raiser')
# Printing the items in a tuple
print(villains)
# Printing single items in a tuple
print(villains[0])
print(villains[1])
print(villains[2])
print(villains[3])
# Ways to append tuple items to sentences
print("The first villain is the sinister", villains[0])
print("The second villain is the terrifying " + villains[1])
# Slicing starting at index 0 and ending before the item at index 3
print(villains[0:3])
# Slicing starting at index 1 and ending before the item at index 4
print(villains[1:4])
# Creating a tuple of my purple capes
purpleCapes = ('Purple Frilly Cape', 'Purple Short Cape', 'Purple Cape with
Holes In It')
# Creating a tuple of my Polka Dot capes
polkaCapes = ('Black and White Polka Dot Cape', 'White and Beige Polka Dot
Cape', 'Blue Polka Dot Cape Missing the Blue Polka Dots')
# Concatenating - or adding - my two tuples of capes together into a
new tuple
allMyCapes = (purpleCapes + polkaCapes)
# Printing out the values of the newly created tuple
print(allMyCapes)
```

```python
# Print the item listed at index 1, 3 times
print(allMyCapes[1] * 3)
# Create a tuple containing a set of numbers
lowest_value = (1, 5, 10, 15, 20, 50, 100, 1000)
# Use the minimum function to return the lowest value item in the tuple
print(min(lowest_value))
# Create a tuple containing a set of numbers
highest_value = (1, 5, 10, 15, 20, 50, 100, 1000)
# Use the maximum function to return the highest value item in the tuple
print(max(highest_value))
# Create a tuple with some items
super_hair = ('Super Stache', 'Macho Beard', 'Gargantuan Goat-tee',
'Villainous Toupee', 'Unfortunate Baldness')
# Print out the number of items in our tuple
print(len(super_hair))
# A tuple of Villains Locked Away in the Villainous Vault of Bad Guys
villains = ('Naughty Man ', 'Skid Mark ', 'Mister Millenial ', 'Jack Hammer
', 'The Spelling Bee ', 'Drank All The Milk Man ', 'Wonder Wedgie ',
'Escape Goat')
# Print out a sorted list of our villains tuple
print(sorted(villains))
# A tuple of numbers we are going to sort
numbers_sort = (10, 20, 5, 2, 18)
# Sorting numbers in our tuple
print(sorted(numbers_sort))
# A tuple of numbers we are going to sum
numbers_sum = (10, 20, 5, 2, 18)
# Summing items in a tuple
print(sum(numbers_sum))
# A list we will convert to a tuple
villainList = ['Naughty Man ', 'Skid Mark ', 'Mister Millenial ', 'Jack
Hammer ', 'The Spelling Bee ', 'Drank All The Milk Man ', 'Wonder Wedgie ',
'Escape Goat']
# Using tuple() to convert villainList to a tuple
tuple(villainList)
```

```
# A string we will convert to a tuple
villain1 = "Mustached Menace!"
tuple(villain1)
# A tuple full of facial hair styles for villains and heroes
facial_hair = ('Super Stache', 'Macho Beard', 'Gargantuan Goat-tee', 'Face
Mullet',)
# Printing out facial hair
print(facial_hair)
# Using del to delete a tuple entirely
del facial_hair
# Printing out facial_hair to show that it is now empty
# print(facial_hair)
# Tuple containing all of the letters used to spell Missisisippi
state = ('M', "i", "s", "s", "i", "s", "i", "s", "i", "p", "p", "i")
# Count the number of times "i" appears in our tuple and print out
the result
print("There are this many of the letter i in Missisisippi: ")
print(state.count('i'))
# Count the number of times "s" appears in Missisisippi
print("There are this many of the letter s in Missisisippi: ")
print(state.count('s'))
# Checking to see if "z" or "i" appears in our state tuple
print('z' in state)
print('i' in state)
# Looping through the previously created villainList tuple and printing out
each item
for var in villainList:
    print(var)
```

Working with Dictionaries

Python has another data structure known as a *dictionary*. Dictionaries differ from
lists, variables, and tuples in quite an interesting way. Whereas lists and tuples have
data items that are stored at a specific index – and therefore can be referenced at those
reference numbers (starting at index 0) – dictionaries rely on what is known as *mapping*.

Mapping is a way for Python to store data, in which Python maps keys to values. This is known as a key-value pair.

The keys are defined on the left side of the key-pair value and typically relate to or describe the value to their right. Keys are immutable and cannot be changed, while values are changeable and can be made up of any data type.

To define a dictionary, you give it a name and then enclose the data you are storing in the dictionary between two curly braces {}:

```
algebro = {'codename': 'Algebro', 'power': 'Mathemagics', 'real-name':
'Al. G. Bro.'}
```

In this instance, we can say that the algebro dictionary represents the nefarious villain, *Algebro, Master of Mathemagics*! As part of our super villain database, we keep track of all the not-so-friendly neighborhood villains. In our dictionary, we have a few pieces of information – namely, their codename, their power, and their real-name. We represent this data in our dictionary by naming our keys to match the data they will be paired with.

So, in this example, for instance, codename would be a key, and Algebro would be a value that belongs to that key. Together they would make one key-value pair in our algebro dictionary.

The other key-value pairs in the algebro dictionary are

- power : mathemagics

- real-name: Al. G. Bro

If we wanted to print out the dictionary, we would use:

```
# Create a dictionary name algebro and fill it with key-value pairs
algebro = {'codename': 'Algebro', 'power': 'Mathemagics', 'real-name':
'Al. G. Bro.'}
# Print out the algebro dictionary
print(algebro)
```

Resulting in the output:

```
{'codename': 'Algebro', 'power': 'Mathemagics', 'real-name': 'Al.
G. Bro.'}
```

The key-value pairs in a dictionary can also be called elements or data items and are unsorted. They can also be printed or called separately, as you would expect. Let's say we just wanted to know Algebro's real-name. To print just the value of a specific key within the dictionary, we would write:

```
print(algebro['real-name'])
```

Python would return the result:

```
Al. G. Bro.
```

Dictionary Methods

Dictionaries have several built-in methods that we can use to interact with keys and values. Let's say we wanted to see which keys were in a dictionary. To print just those out, we would use the dict.keys() method:

```
# Create a dictionary name algebro and fill it with key-value pairs
algebro = {'codename': 'Algebro', 'power': 'Mathemagics', 'real-name':
'Al. G. Bro.'}
# Print just the keys in the algebro dictionary
print(algebro.keys())
```

When run, this gives us the output:

```
dict_keys(['codename', 'power', 'real-name'])
```

If we wanted to access just the values of the algebro dictionary, we would use the dict.values() method, like so:

```
# Print just the values in the algebro dictionary
print(algebro.values())
```

Giving us:

```
dict_values(['Algebro', 'Mathemagics', 'Al. G. Bro.'])
```

But what if we wanted to print both the key and values? There is a method for that as well, known as the dict.items( ) method:

```
# Print the key-value pairs
print(algebro.items())
```

The output?

```
dict_items([('codename', 'Algebro'), ('power', 'Mathemagics'), ('real-name', 'Al. G. Bro.')])
```

Using dictionary methods in this manner is great for when we need to compare data or check to see what data is within a dictionary. We can also compare our keys and their related data to other dictionaries. For example, Algebro the villain may appear in a several `different` dictionaries. One might store information about his superpowers and secret identity, while another dictionary may contain his high school records and the grades he got in P.E. (trust me, Algebro the Mathemagician was *terrible* at high school sports!).

Finally, there is another way to print out the data items in a dictionary – we can simply iterate (or loop) through the dictionary, printing out information at each iteration. Remember the `for` loop? It will come in handy here:

```
# Using a for loop to iterate through and print out our dictionary
for key, value in algebro.items():
    print("The key is: ", key, " and the value is: ", value)
```

This helpful code snippet results in a much friendlier output:

```
The key is:  codename  and the value is:  Algebro
The key is:  power  and the value is:  Mathemagics
The key is:  real-name  and the value is:  Al. G. Bro.
```

More Fun with Dictionaries

Unlike tuples, dictionary values – though not keys – can be modified. Let's say we wanted to add an *age* to our Algebro villain. To do so, we could simply use code such as:

```
# Create a dictionary name algebro and fill it with key-value pairs
algebro = {'codename': 'Algebro', 'power': 'Mathemagics', 'real-name': 'Al.
G. Bro.'}
# Add the key 'age' to the dictionary 'algebro' and assign it the
value '42'
algebro['age'] = 42
# Print out algebro to show the newly added key-value pair
print(algebro)
```

When running this code, we get the result:

```
{'codename': 'Algebro', 'power': 'Mathemagics', 'real-name': 'Al. G. Bro.',
'age': '42'}
```

We can see here that our new key-value pair of 'age' and '42' has been added.

The problem you may notice here is that age is not a static number; that is, it changes over time. Every time our villain Algebro has a birthday, we are going to have to update this key-value pair.

No worries, as it is just as simple to modify the value for a key as it is to add a new one:

```
# Updating a the value for our 'age' key
algebro['age'] = 43
# Printing the algebro dictionary to see the updated value of the 'age' key
print(algebro)
```

Now if we were to print the value of age, it would equal: 43.

Another way that we can update a dictionary value is using the dict.update() method. For example, we could alternatively add a new key known as villainType and give it a paired value of mutate using the dict.update() method, like so:

```
# Create a dictionary name algebro and fill it with key-value pairs
algebro = {'codename': 'Algebro', 'power': 'Mathemagics', 'real-name':
'Al. G. Bro.'}
# Using dict.update() to add a key-pair value to our 'algebro' dictionary
# Note the use of curly braces {}, mixed with parentheses ()
```

```
algebro.update({'villainType': 'mutate'})
# Printing out the results
print(algebro)
```

Now if you run this code, the output would be:

```
{'codename': 'Algebro', 'power': 'Mathemagics', 'real-name': 'Al. G. Bro.',
'age': 43, 'villainType': 'mutate'}
```

Note the addition of the key-value pair villainType mutate. Also notice that you can also use this method to update any existing key-value pairs in the dictionary, using the same code.

Using the del keyword – which we have seen before – we can remove a key-value pair from a dictionary. For instance, if, for some reason, Algebro lost his superpower, we could delete the entire key-value pair like this:

```
# Using the del keyword to delete a key-value pair
del algebro['power']
# Printing algebro to verify that we properly removed the key-value pair
print(algebro)
```

This gives us:

```
{'codename': 'Algebro', 'real-name': 'Al. G. Bro.', 'age': 43,
'villainType': 'mutate'}
```

Verifying that we did, in fact, successfully delete the key power and its related value.

Additionally, if we wanted to delete the entire dictionary, we could use del for that too:

```
# Deleting the algebro dictionary using the del keyword
del algebro
# Printing the deleted algebro, which results in an error
# This occurs because algebro no longer exists
print(algebro)
```

If you run that code, you will get an error message, because you are now trying to print the algebro dictionary, which we have previously deleted:

```
Traceback (most recent call last):

File "C:/Users/James/AppData/Local/Programs/Python/Python11/
DictionaryExamples.py", line 58, in <module>
    print(algebro)
NameError: name 'algebro' is not defined
```

Finally, there may come a time when you wish to remove all of the items or key-value pairs in a dictionary, yet *not* delete the dictionary itself. For that, we use the dict.clear( ) method:

```
# Create a dictionary name algebro and fill it with key-value pairs
algebro = {'codename': 'Algebro', 'power': 'Mathemagics', 'real-name': 'Al.
G. Bro.'}
algebro.clear()
print(algebro)
```

If you run this snippet of code, you would get the output:

```
{}
```

Or, basically, an empty dictionary. Alternatively, you could achieve the same effect by simply typing: algebro = {}.

Other Dictionary Methods

All told, there are roughly 26 dictionary methods that you have at your disposal; space does not permit me to cover all of them in this book; however, I urge you to branch out and research them on your own. Experiment with them and use your newfound powers wisely!

Some of these methods you have used already on lists and tuples; these include things like sum( ), min( ), max( ), sorted( ), and so on.

Here's a list of these other dictionary methods: go forth and experiment wildly!

- dict.clear( ): Removes all of the items in a dictionary

- dict.copy( ): Returns a copy of a dictionary

- dict.fromkeys( ): Used to create a dictionary from a sequence

- dict.get( ): Returns the value of a specified key

- dict.items( ): Returns a view of the given dictionary's key/pair values

- dict.keys( ): Returns the keys in a dictionary as a view

- dict.popitem( ): Returns – and also removes – a dictionary element

- dict.pop( ): Returns – and removes – an element from a specified key

- dict.setdefault( ): Checks to see if a key is present and, if not, insets the key (with a value)

- dict.values( ): Returns all of the values in a dictionary as a view

- dict.update( ): Used to update a dictionary

Other methods you can use on a dictionary include

- any( ): Tests whether an element of an iterable is True

- all( ): If all elements of an iterable are True, this returns True

- dict( ): Used to create a dictionary

- enumerate( ): Creates or returns an enumerate object

- iter( ): Returns an iterator for a given object

- len( ): Returns the length of an object

- max( ): Returns the largest element

- min( ): Returns the smallest element

- sorted( ): Returns a sorted list

- sum( ): Sums all items

Example Dictionary Code

Here is a sample file with all of the code contained in this chapter. Feel free to make any changes and experiment (wildly) with the code. Notice any errors and try to modify it in interesting ways, using the knowledge you have gained thus far in the book.

Remember, have fun and be adventurous (how else would a superhero be, after all?):

```python
# Create a dictionary name algebro and fill it with key-value pairs
algebro = {'codename': 'Algebro', 'power': 'Mathemagics', 'real-name':
'Al. G. Bro.'}
# Print out the algebro dictionary
print(algebro)
# Print out just the real-name key's value
print(algebro['real-name'])
# Print just the keys in the algebro dictionary
print(algebro.keys())
# Print just the values in the algebro dictionary
print(algebro.values())
# Print the key-value pairs
print(algebro.items())
# Using a for loop to iterate through and print out our dictionary
for key, value in algebro.items():
    print("The key is: ", key, " and the value is: ", value)
# Add the key 'age' to the dictionary 'algebro' and assign it the
value '42'
algebro['age'] = '42'
# Print out algebro to show the newly added key-value pair
print(algebro)
# Updating a the value for our 'age' key
algebro['age'] = 43
# Printing the algebro dictionary to see the updated value of the 'age' key
print(algebro)
# Using dict.update() to add a key-pair value to our 'algebro' dictionary
# Note the use of curly braces {}, mixed with parentheses ()
algebro.update({'villainType': 'mutate'})
# Printing out the results
```

```
print(algebro)
# Using the del keyword to delete a key-value pair
del algebro['power']
# Printing algebro to verify that we properly removed the key-value pair
print(algebro)
###########################################################
# This section of code is commented out because it will cause
everything error
# Deleting the algebro dictionary using the del keyword
# del algebro
# Printing the deleted algebro, which results in an error
# This occurs because algebro no longer exists
#print(algebro)
#################################################
# Create a dictionary name algebro and fill it with key-value pairs
algebro = {'codename': 'Algebro', 'power': 'Mathemagics', 'real-name': 'Al.
G. Bro.'}
algebro.clear()
print(algebro)
```

In This Episode!

You should be very proud of yourself for having come this far! In this episode, we expanded your brain storage capacity by including two new data structures to your memory banks – the tuple and the dictionary!

We covered a lot, and so, as always, it is always a good idea to sum up the majority of the knowledge we learned in this chapter in a cute bullet list. So guess what? Here it is:

- Tuples and dictionaries are two additional forms of data structures that hold information, alongside variables and lists.

- Tuples are similar to lists with the exception that tuples are immutable; that is, their values cannot be changed or modified.

- Tuples are defined in this manner:

- villains = ('Eyebrow Raiser', 'Angry Heckler', 'Not So Happy Man', 'The Heck Raiser')

- We can print a tuple using print(villains).

- We print an item in a tuple using print(villains[0]), which would print the first item – or the item listed at index 0 – in our tuple.

- To print a range of items in a tuple, we use print(villains[0:3]), which would print the items located at indexes 0, 1, and 2; it ends printing prior to the item located at the second parameter (in this case, 3).

- Tuple functions include min( ), max( ), len( ), sorted( ), sum( ), and tuple( ).

- The del keyword can be used to delete an entire tuple.

- count( ) counts the number of instances something occurs in a tuple.

- We can use in to check if something appears inside of a tuple; it returns a Boolean True or False value.

- Dictionaries use mapping to store data.

- Dictionaries contain a key-value pair or group of key-value pairs, also known as elements or data items.

- Keys are defined on the left side of the colon, while values are defined on the right.

- Dictionaries are defined like so:

```
algebro = {'codename': 'Algebro', 'power': 'Mathemagics',
'real-name': 'Al. G. Bro.'}
```

- You can print a dictionary using print(algebro).

- You can print the value of a specific key using print(algebro['real-name']).

- Dictionary methods include dict.keys( ), dict.items( ), and dict.update( ).

- The del keyword can also be used to delete a dictionary.

- dict.clear( ) allows you to clear the elements from a dictionary without deleting the actual dictionary (just its keys and values pairs).

CHAPTER 10

Python Files

So far, we have worked primarily within one file; that is, all of our code has been saved in a single `.py` file and run from that same file. However, in the real world, a lot of our programs will be stored in multiple files. What's more, we are likely to save some of our favorite code snippets and functions in files for later use. It is just the way we programmers – which include you now – work.

There are many reasons why we would use multiple files of code. Some of those centers around efficiency and reducing errors in our code – remember our whole bit about saving parts of programs that handle common tasks for later reuse in other programs? We discussed that in-depth when we spoke about functions and modules.

We also have the option to save classes and objects, variables, lists of data, and just about any type of commonly used code we can think of. Basically, if you think you will use something in a program later on down the line and it will save you time and reduce user errors through input (i.e., you typing in code while you are tired from all that crime fighting), then do yourself a big favor, and make a copy of it in a separate file for later use.

Oh, and make sure you document it thoroughly, so you know what you saved that awesome code for!

Another reason we use code from multiple files has to do with the fact that – and this is true on larger projects – often we are not the only coder working on a program. We may only be handling a small piece of the overall application. For that reason alone, you may find yourself dealing with a plethora of files.

For example, if you are coding a superhero role-playing game, you may be overseeing the entire project. Your friend Paul Coderman might be responsible for handling the portion of code that deals with combat. Your other friend, Ralph Programmerdudeson, could be handling character creation. And your office nemesis (everyone needs one of those) might just be sitting in a corner glaring angrily at you all day while eating questionable quantities of fast food.

© James R. Payne 2024

J. R. Payne, *Python for Teenagers*, https://doi.org/10.1007/978-1-4842-9988-3_10

To pull the program together, you might call in a group of functions from Paul Coderman's files and slip in the character creation engine from your boy Ralph Programmerdudeson's folder full of code. Finally, your nemesis will add his dose of anger and vitriol. When combined, you will have all of the elements needed for a successful role-playing game.

Working with Files in Python

If you have made it this far in the book, we are going to take it for granted that you know what a file system is. If not, just think of all of those little folders on your computer desktop that store documents, Manga comics, video games, and your ample supply of selfies.

When we initially installed Python, we let it install in the default location. Depending upon your computer, operating system, and the way you have your hard drives set up, you likely have something very similar to mine. For instance, my instance of Python and IDLE are installed at

```
C:\Users\James\AppData\Local\Programs\Python\Python311
```

Yours could be a little different, such as

```
C:\Users\YourName\Programs\Python\Python311
```

and so forth.

Incidentally, all of the `.py` or Python files that I create using IDLE are automatically stored in this same location. In fact, when I run a program, it searches this folder first, looking for the files. If I were to call another file from a Python program I created, it would automatically search this folder and expect to find it in here as well.

Here is an example of my Python directory folder, showing all the files I have written so far for this book (see Figure 10-1).

Name	Date modified	Type	Size
~~BoolEanExamples~~	8/12/2023 12:41 PM	Python File	1 KB
ConditionalStatements	8/12/2023 10:51 AM	Python File	1 KB
Count10	8/13/2023 1:47 PM	Python File	1 KB
DictionaruExamples	8/27/2023 7:04 PM	Python File	2 KB
DoomsdayClock	8/13/2023 1:53 PM	Python File	1 KB
InfiniteLoop	8/13/2023 12:25 PM	Python File	1 KB
LearningText	7/30/2023 7:57 PM	Python File	1 KB
ListExample	7/30/2023 8:11 PM	Python File	1 KB
listTest	7/30/2023 8:10 PM	Python File	1 KB
LogicalOperatorsExample	8/12/2023 12:52 PM	Python File	1 KB
MathIsHard	8/12/2023 12:43 PM	Python File	1 KB
PowersWeaknesses	7/30/2023 8:13 PM	Python File	1 KB

Figure 10-1. *Example of a Python directory folder*

Because these files are all in what we will call our `root` directory, when I call them into one of my Python programs, I don't have to do anything special like change directories or look in other folders; all I have to do is name the file in the program and it imports it in – easy-peasey, mac-n-cheesey.

Be right back, I need to go eat Mac-N-Cheese now.

Okay, I'm back.

In real-life scenarios, it isn't always so simple. We usually keep our program files for each program in specific folders so we don't get confused or accidentally call the wrong file. You can imagine that, over the course of even a year, you might accumulate quite a number of files and you definitely need a way to organize your work.

For instance, if you were working on that superhero RPG, you might have a main folder called SuperheroRPG. Then, within that folder, you would have a set of folders that would hold files for each section of the game. Consider this folder structure, for instance:

- SuperheroRPG

  - CharacterCreationModules

  - BattleEngine

  - VillainProfiles

  - AreaFiles

- RandomEncounterFunctions

- ItemLists

- SuperPowerLists

- VillainsDictionaries

- HeroClasses

  - Mutate

  - Human

  - Robot

  - Magician

- SidekickProfiles

and so forth. Each of these folders would hold pieces of your program that carried out the functions of each of those portions of the program. The `BattleEngine` folder, for example, would hold the functions and code responsible for handling fight scenarios, damage results, and so on.

Since all of those files would be stored *outside* of the `root` folder, we would need to call the file into our main program from whichever directory that portion of code resided in.

If that seems confusing at the moment, that is okay; we are going to cover how to call a program from within another program – regardless of where it is located – in great detail in this chapter.

Now that you are familiar with folder structure and the basic concept that your Python files might be stored in different locations, the rest will be a piece of cake.

Mmmm…cake. Be right back, gotta eat some cake.

File Types

So far, we have worked pretty exclusively with .py files. In reality, we can write code in text or .txt files, which is what most programmers do, relying on programs such as Windows' Notepad or another, more impressive text editor known as Notepad++. We will discuss some tools you can use for coding in the last two chapters of this book; for now, know that what we have primarily been working with are .py files.

As you branch out in your programming and develop your own programs or start working for a corporation, you will start to involve other file types as well. The most common of these are .txt, HyperText Markup Language (HTML) (used to develop web pages), and comma-separated values (CSV) files – think spreadsheet data.

Of course, you will work with other language files too, like C or C++ files and JSON. This is known as extending Python and is a subject we cover briefly in Chapter 13.

For the examples in this chapter, we will mostly be working with .txt and .py files, but much of the theory works across the board.

Creating a Text File in Python Code

There are several ways we could approach the next portion of this book. For starters, we could simply open up a notepad or text editor program and create a new text file, then save it to the same directory that you have all of your other (currently) .py and Python programming files saved to. But that seems a little lazy. Instead, let's go with a different approach – let's create a new text file using some Python code.

We are going to learn a few new concepts in this section, so do not worry too much if things do not click right away; we will cover everything pretty thoroughly after we get the core concepts down. Additionally, be sure – as always – to read the commented code so that you know what each line is meant for.

Remember: our goal in this program is to create a new *text* file using Python. These are different than the .py or Python files we have been creating thus far. The trick here is that we will be creating a text file from within our Python file, so be sure you do not get confused on which file we are working on.

To start, we need to create a new Python file named FunWithFiles.py. Add the following code to it:

```
# This code is used to open a file
# However, since the file does not already exist
# Python instead creates it for us
newFile = open("CreatedFile.txt", 'w')
# This code is similar to a print() statement
# However, instead of writing text or output to a user's computer screen
# It writes it to a file instead
newFile.write("Look, we created a brand new file using Python code!")
# The close() function closes the file we are working on and saves it
```

```
# It is important to always close a file when we are finished with it
# To ensure we do not make any additions or mess up the file in anyway
newFile.close()
```

There are several things to note in this code. First, our intent here is to use code to create a new text or .txt file named CreatedFile.txt. We start off by making a variable named newFile and applying the open() function to it. Normally, we use open() to do exactly what you think it might do – open a file so that we can take some sort of action upon it. However, in this instance, since there is no file named CreatedFile.txt for Python to find, it goes ahead and assumes we wanted to create a new .txt file and does so. Note that, even if there was a file that existed with the same name, it would overwrite the existing file and leave it blank inside, so be careful when using this method!

In the line

```
open("CreatedFile.txt", 'w')
```

"CreatedFile.txt" is the name of the file we wish to open/create. The 'w' part is known as an *argument* and is one of several that we can use within the open() function.

In this instance, 'w' tells Python that you wish to open the file for *writing*; therefore, Python opens the file in *write mode*. This mode allows us to make changes or add things to the file in question.

Alternatively, we could have used the 'x' mode, which lets us create and write to a new file. However, it creates the file exclusively, meaning that if the file name already exists, it will fail and cause an error. To use that, we would simply change the code to:

```
open("CreatedFile.txt", 'x')
```

Next in our code, we wanted to add something to our newly created file; we didn't have to, of course – we could have just left it blank. However, we may as well have put something in it while we had it open.

The .write method in the line

```
newFile.write("Look, we created a brand new file using Python code!")
```

is used to store or write the text "Look, we created a brand new file using Python code!" into the newly created CreatedFile.txt file.

Finally, we always want to close any file we open or create once we are finished with it, to ensure it does not get damaged, changed, or affected in any way that we do not intend. To do that, we used the `close()` function, as in

```
newFile.close()
```

Reading Files in Python

In addition to creating files and writing to them, we can also read from them as well. Now that we have created our new file, `CreatedFile.txt`, let's create a program to read from it. Add the following code to your `FunWithFiles.py` file:

```
# Open the file CreatedFile.txt
read_me_seymour = open("CreatedFile.txt", 'r')
# Read the contents of the file
print(read_me_seymour.read())
CreatedFile.close()
```

Here, we used `open()` to open our previously created file, and we passed it the `'r'` or read argument/parameter. Then, we used the `print()` function with the *.read* method to print the text to the screen so we could see the contents of our file.

This works fine when we have a single line of text in a file, but what if we have multiple lines?

Change the code in the `FunWithFiles.py` file so that it matches this example:

```
# This code is used to open a file
# However, since the file does not already exist
# Python instead creates it for us
# Remember, if the file name already exists, it will overwrite the existing
one, erasing its contents in the process.
newFile = open("CreatedFile.txt", 'w')
# This code is similar to a print() statement
# However, instead of writing text or output to a user's computer screen
# It writes it to a file instead
newFile.write("Look, we created a brand new file using Python code!")
newFile.write("Here is a second line of text!")
# The close() function closes the file we are working on and saves it
# It is important to always close a file when we are finished with it
```

```
# To ensure we do not make any additions or mess up the file in anyway
newFile.close()
# Open the file CreatedFile.txt
read_me_seymour = open("CreatedFile.txt", 'r')
# Read the contents of the file
print(read_me_seymour.read())
```

All we added to our code was this line:

```
newFile.write("Here is a second line of text!")
```

When we run the file, we expect to see two lines of text, such as

```
Look, we created a brand new file using Python code!
Here is a second line of text!
```

However, that is not the case. Instead, we get the output:

```
Look, we created a brand new file using Python code!Here is a second line
of code!
```

But why is that?

There are two answers, both of which we will discuss. First, when we originally wrote text to our newly created file, we did not provide it any format; .write does not assume a return carriage or newline character (the equivalent of you pressing the Enter button after typing a sentence) at the end of the text.

In order to ensure our lines do not run together, therefore, we must be sure to add a \n *newline* character at the end of our text. Essentially, you want to modify the two .write statements so they appear like this:

```
newFile.write("Look, we created a brand new file using Python code!\n")
newFile.write("Here is a second line of text!\n")
```

Go ahead and change your FunWithFiles.py file so that it matches those changes. Now try running the program again. This time, you should have the result:

```
Look, we created a brand new file using Python code!
Here is a second line of text!
```

Using readline( ) and readlines( )

There will be times when you only want to read a specific line – or a few specific lines – in a text file. The `.read` method reads the entire contents of a file, so that will not work in this scenario. Instead, we need to use readline( ).

To see this in action, let's modify our code and change

```
print(read_me_seymour.read())
```

to

```
print(read_me_seymour.readline())
```

Now when you run the program, your result will be

```
Look, we created a brand new file using Python code!
```

This is because `readline()` only reads one line of text at a time. To read the next line of text in the file, you would simply add another instance of `readline()`. Go ahead and make sure your current copy of `FunWithFiles.py` matches this code:

```python
# This code is used to open a file
# However, since the file does not already exist
# Python instead creates it for us
newFile = open("CreatedFile.txt", 'w')
# This code is similar to a print() statement
# However, instead of writing text or output to a user's computer screen
# It writes it to a file instead
newFile.write("Look, we created a brand new file using Python code!\n")
newFile.write("Here is a second line of text!\n")
# The close() function closes the file we are working on and saves it
# It is important to always close a file when we are finished with it
# To ensure we do not make any additions or mess up the file in anyway
newFile.close()
# Open the file CreatedFile.txt
read_me_seymour = open("CreatedFile.txt", 'r')
# Read the contents of the file
# Read the first line in the txt file
print(read_me_seymour.readline())
```

```
# Read the second line in the txt file
print(read_me_seymour.readline())
# Close the file again
read_me_seymour.close()
```

In addition to readline( ), there is also a function known as readlines( ), which operates a little differently, despite appearing nearly identical. If we were to change our code (don't) to say `print(read_me_seymour.readlines())`, instead of printing out a line of text from the txt file we specify, it would print out a list of lines in the file. The result would be something like this:

```
['Look, we created a brand new file using Python code!\n', 'Here is a
second line of text!\n']
```

A Warning About Reading and Writing to Files

Before we progress any further, we should discuss how writing to files works. When you write to a file the first time, everything is fine. However, if we try to open a file and write to it a second time – using the 'w' parameter – you will actually be overwriting whatever currently exists in the file you are trying to write to.

For example, if you wrote the code

```
# This code is used to open a file
# However, since the file does not already exist
# Python instead creates it for us
newFile = open("CreatedFile.txt", 'w')
# This code is similar to a print() statement
# However, instead of writing text or output to a user's computer screen
# It writes it to a file instead
newFile.write("Look, we created a brand new file using Python code!\n")
newFile.write("Here is a second line of text!\n")
# Opening the File to add more text
addingToFile = open("CreatedFile.txt", 'w')
# Writing more text
addingToFile.write("This is new text.\n")
addingToFile.close()
```

and tried to print out the results, what do you think the result would be?

While you might expect it to be something along the lines of

```
Look, we created a brand new file using Python code!
Here is a second line of text!
This is new text.
```

that would be false. In reality, the second time that we open the file and start to write to it, we overwrite any text that already exists and insert new lines of text instead. The real answer, in this scenario, would be

```
This is new text.
```

So, the moral of the story here is simple: always be aware of what mode you are in when you work with files.

Appending to Files

To solve the dilemma of how to write to a file without overwriting any existing text in the file, we simply switch from the 'w' parameter to the 'a' – or append – parameter.

Let's say we wanted to add another line of text to our file FunWithFiles.py. All we would need to do is re-open the file enter into append mode. Let's modify our program so it matches the following:

```
# This code is used to open a file
# However, since the file does not already exist
# Python instead creates it for us
newFile = open("CreatedFile.txt", 'w')
# This code is similar to a print() statement
# However, instead of writing text or output to a user's computer screen
# It writes it to a file instead
newFile.write("Look, we created a brand new file using Python code!\n")
newFile.write("Here is a second line of text!\n")
# The close() function closes the file we are working on and saves it
# It is important to always close a file when we are finished with it
# To ensure we do not make any additions or mess up the file in anyway
```

```
newFile.close()
# Open the file CreatedFile.txt
read_me_seymour = open("CreatedFile.txt", 'r')
print("THE ORIGINAL TEXT IN THE FILE")
print(read_me_seymour.readline())
print(read_me_seymour.readline())
# Closing the file
read_me_seymour.close()
# Opening the file again to write some text to it
addingToFile = open("CreatedFile.txt", 'a')
# Adding some text to the file in append mode
addingToFile.write("This is new text.")
# Closing the file
addingToFile.close()
# Opening the file yet again, to read it
# Now that we have appended a line
print("THE TEXT IN THE FILE AFTER WE APPEND")
appendedFile = open("CreatedFile.txt", 'r')
# This is another way we can print from a file
# Here we are using a for loop
# And using the keywords in and line to print each line
# In the text file
for line in appendedFile:
    print(line)
# Closing the file again
appendedFile.close()
```

We made quite a few additions this go-around. Thanks to solid documentation practices, however, it should be fairly obvious what changes were made and what they did.

Despite that being the case, however, let's discuss some of the code that was added. First, a brief overview of the code and its purpose. The intent of the code was to

- Create a new txt file

- Write two lines of text to the file

- Open the file in read mode to read the file

- Print out the lines in the file

- Open the file in append mode

- Append a new line of text to the file

- Print out the contents of the modified file

In between each of these steps, we also closed the file. So, for each instance of opening to either read, write, or append, we always wanted to be certain we practiced good coding and closed our file. This may not have been the most efficient way to code the file, but for our purposes here – which is simply to learn the basic language, coding principles, and theory – this works best.

Finally, you may have noticed that we snuck in a little for loop near the end of our code. This is just another way that we can print out the lines in a text file.

Working with Directories

As we discussed earlier, so far, we have only worked within the directory that we originally installed Python. In this section, we are going to learn how to open files from other folders or directories on your computer.

Before we do that, however, let's look at a simple way to figure out exactly which directory we are currently in. Create a new Python called WorkingWithDirectories.py, and type in this code:

```
# Import the module os
# This is used to work with operating system information
import os
# Use the getcwd() method of the os module
# To see what directory we are in
os.getcwd()
```

When you run this code, you will get a result similar to mine; it will be different, because our computer systems and setups are different, but it should appear something like this:

```
C:\Users\James\AppData\Local\Programs\Python\Python311
```

This is important information to have on hand, as we may have files in different directories. If we try to open a file in our current directory and it does not exist, we will either end up with an error or will accidentally create a new version of the file. This, of course, would make things confusing if we had multiple copies of a file in different directories.

Now that we know our current directory, we *could* change to another directory and open a file from there. I say "could" because before we actually try it, we need to create a new directory to change to. If you remember, at the start of this chapter, I showed you what my current Python directory looked like. That image was a little misleading, as it did not include all of the directories or folders that I had. Here is what mine really looks like (see Figure 10-2).

Name	Date modified	Type	Size
Tools	7/10/2023 7:56 PM	File folder	
tcl	7/10/2023 7:56 PM	File folder	
Scripts	7/10/2023 7:56 PM	File folder	
libs	7/10/2023 7:56 PM	File folder	
Lib	7/10/2023 7:56 PM	File folder	
include	7/10/2023 7:56 PM	File folder	
Doc	7/10/2023 7:56 PM	File folder	
DLLs	7/10/2023 7:56 PM	File folder	
NEWS	6/7/2023 6:04 AM	Text Document	1,459 KB
LICENSE	6/7/2023 6:02 AM	Text Document	32 KB
WorkingWithDirectories	8/27/2023 8:17 PM	Python File	0 KB
WonderBoyTheme	7/30/2023 8:05 PM	Python File	1 KB
WonderBoyPassword	8/13/2023 12:31 PM	Python File	1 KB
VariableTest	7/23/2023 7:56 PM	Python File	1 KB
VariableChange	7/23/2023 7:59 PM	Python File	1 KB
UncleElself	8/12/2023 12:49 PM	Python File	2 KB
TupleExamples	8/27/2023 6:48 PM	Python File	4 KB
tests	8/27/2023 7:02 PM	Python File	1 KB

Figure 10-2. *View of my real Python directory, showing files and folders*

If you have been following along with this book and creating the files as suggested, yours will look similar, minus a file or two.

Let's go ahead and create a new directory that we will call newDirectory using the mkdir() method of os. Add this code to your WorkingWithDirectories.py file:

```
# Create a new directory or folder
os.mkdir("newDirectory")
```

Now, run the file, which will create a new folder called newDirectory. If you open up your Python directory folder, you should see it added in the list.

Now, the next part is important! We are now going to comment out the code we just added before we change directories. We do this, because if we don't, we will receive an error message. Why? Because Python won't create a directory if it already exists. And since we just created it – well, you get the picture!

Modify your code so it matches mine and then run the program.

Note   Make sure that ("C:/Users/James/AppData/Local/Programs/Python/Python311/newDirectory") matches your directory and not mine; you can use the value returned in the first example of this section where we first learned how to use os.getcwd(). If not, you will get an error. Also, make sure to change your \'s to /'s in your directory path, or you will also receive an error.

Here is the code:

```
# Import the module os
# This is used to work with operating system information
import os
# Use the getcwd() method of the os module
# To see what directory we are in
os.getcwd()
# Create a new directory or folder
# We commented this out because we created the directory earlier
# If we don't, Python will try to create it again
# Causing an error
# os.mkdir("newDirectory")
# Using the chdir() method to change directories
os.chdir("C:/Users/James/AppData/Local/Programs/Python/Python311/
newDirectory")
print(os.getcwd())
```

Warning! If you received an error message, the reason is most likely because the directory you tried to change to is incorrect. If you wrote your code to match mine exactly, this is definitely the case. Remember, our directories are different, so you have to insert your directory. For example:

```
os.chdir("C:/Users/James/AppData/Local/Programs/Python/Python311/
newDirectory")
```

This is how I change my directory; yours might be more like:

```
os.chdir("C:/Users/YourName/Programs/Python/Python311/newDirectory")
```

It should match whatever the `os.getcwd()` example returned in our first example of this section, plus the addition of `/newDirectory`.

In addition, remember to change your backslashes to forward slashes. For instance, my original directory was

```
C:\Users\James\AppData\Local\Programs\Python\Python311
```

but when we write it in code, it should be

```
C:/Users/YourName/Programs/Python/Python311/
```

Once your code is sorted out and you run it, you will receive a similar output to this:
C:\Users\James\AppData\Local\Programs\Python\Python311\newDirectory

showing the directory that you switched to. So long as the last section says \ `newDirectory,` we know that the code worked.

Now that we know how to create a new directory and how to change to a different directory, let's switch back to our original directory, so that we can continue working on the code we have created thus far in the book.

To switch back, we just use the chdir() method again, this time pointing it back to our original directory. Remember, use your original directory in place of what I write for mine:

```
# Using the chdir() method to change directories
print("Changing to the newDirectory folder: ")
os.chdir("C:/Users/James/AppData/Local/Programs/Python/Python311/
newDirectory")
# Print out the current directory to verify it changed
print(os.getcwd())
# Switching back to the original directory
# Remember to use your own directory, not mine!
os.chdir("C:/Users/James/AppData/Local/Programs/Python/Python311")
```

212

```
# Verifying that we are back to the original directory
print("Back to the original directory: " )
print(os.getcwd())
```

Here, we have added a few `print()` functions to show what stage of the directory switch we are in. We also added a final directory change to get back to our original directory. The result, when run, should be similar to

```
Changing to the newDirectory folder:
C:\Users\James\AppData\Local\Programs\Python\Python311\newDirectory
Back to the original directory:
C:\Users\James\AppData\Local\Programs\Python\Python311
```

One last thing before we wrap up our discussion on creating directories and changing back and forth between them. To avoid any future confusion, let's go ahead and delete the newDirectory folder. We could do so by simply opening up the Python folder and clicking the folder and choosing delete. However, we are programmers now, and, as programmers are known to do, we should use code to do the hard work for us!

To delete a directory, just add this code to the file:

```
# Deleting the newDirectory directory
# Using the rmdir() method
os.rmdir('newDirectory')
```

Once you run that code, if you look in your Python folder, you will see that the newDirectory folder no longer exists. Note that we did not need to use the full path for Python to find the directory. This is because the folder exists in the current root folder that we have directed Python to search in (i.e., `C:\Users\James\AppData\Local\Programs\Python\Python311`). This also holds true when using mkdir and chdir if you are changing folders into "newDirectory."

Bonus Round!

We learned a lot about working with files and navigating directories in this chapter, but there are still a few things we need to learn how to do. I don't want to overwhelm you with too much information, so I am going to make this special super-secret-bonus-round short and sweet.

We learned how to delete directories in the last section, but what about deleting files? Deleting files is very simple; all we do is use the remove() method, as shown here:

```
# import os
import os
# Remove a file use the remove() method
os.remove('test.txt')
```

This code would remove the file test.txt from the *current* directory. If the file were located in a directory other than the current one, we could either switch to that directory and then use remove( ), or we could just give the file path and name to the remove( ) method, like so:

```
# import os
import os
# Remove a file use the remove() method
# If the file existed in the newDirectory folder
os.remove('C:\Users\James\AppData\Local\Programs\Python\Python311\
newDirectory\test.txt')
```

where the directory would equal the directory path where the file existed.

Finally, there may come a time when you wish to change the name of a file. We can do this using another method, rename():

```
# import os
import os
# Rename the file using the rename() method
# Rename requires two arguments
# The current filename and the new filename
os.rename('test.txt', 'newTest.txt')
```

This code would take the file test.txt in our current directory and rename it to newTest.txt.

FunWithFiles.py Code

Here is a compiled copy of all of the code from our FunWithFile.py file. Feel free to change this code and experiment with it, running it frequently to see the results of your changes!

```python
# This code is used to open a file
# However, since the file does not already exist
# Python instead creates it for us
newFile = open("CreatedFile.txt", 'w')
# This code is similar to a print() statement
# However, instead of writing text or output to a user's computer screen
# It writes it to a file instead
newFile.write("Look, we created a brand new file using Python code!\n")
newFile.write("Here is a second line of text!\n")
# The close() function closes the file we are working on and saves it
# It is important to always close a file when we are finished with it
# To ensure we do not make any additions or mess up the file in anyway
newFile.close()
# Open the file CreatedFile.txt
read_me_seymour = open("CreatedFile.txt", 'r')
print("THE ORIGINAL TEXT IN THE FILE")
print(read_me_seymour.readline())
print(read_me_seymour.readline())
# Closing the file
read_me_seymour.close()
# Opening the file again to write some text to it
addingToFile = open("CreatedFile.txt", 'a')
# Adding some text to the file in append mode
addingToFile.write("This is new text.")
# Closing the file
addingToFile.close()
# Opening the file yet again, to read it
# Now that we have appended a line
print("THE TEXT IN THE FILE AFTER WE APPEND")
appendedFile = open("CreatedFile.txt", 'r')
# This is another way we can print from a file
# Here we are using a for loop
# And using the keywords in and line to print each line
# In the text file
```

```
for line in appendedFile:
    print(line)
# Closing the file again
appendedFile.close()
```

WorkingWithDirectories.py

Here is the complete code from the WorkingWithDirectories.py file. Note that some of the code is commented out, as using it more than once will result in an error. This relates specifically to when we create and delete new directories – if we try to create a directory that already exists, it will cause an error.

Once again, feel free to experiment with this code and, above all, have fun. After all, breaking code – and then fixing it – is how we become truly powerful coding superheroes!

```
# Import the module os
# This is used to work with operating system information
import os
# Use the getcwd() method of the os module
# To see what directory we are in
os.getcwd()
# Create a new directory or folder
# We commented this out because we created the directory earlier
# If we don't, Python will try to create it again
# Causing an error
# os.mkdir("newDirectory")
# Using the chdir() method to change directories
print("Changing to the newDirectory folder: ")
os.chdir("C:/Users/James/AppData/Local/Programs/Python/Python311/
newDirectory")
# Print out the current directory to verify it changed
print(os.getcwd())
# Switching back to the original directory
# Remember to use your own directory, not mine!
os.chdir("C:/Users/James/AppData/Local/Programs/Python/Python311")
# Verifying that we are back to the original directory
```

```
print("Back to the original directory: " )
print(os.getcwd())
# Deleting the newDirectory directory
# Using the rmdir() method
os.rmdir('newDirectory')
```

In This Episode!

You were truly bold in this adventure, young hero! You learned enough to make EnormoBrain the Wise, Yet Evil jealous. You should see that guy's forehead by the way – it's huge!

As bright and gifted as you are, however, it is always a good idea to have a little refresher on what you learned. So, without further ado – and before EnormoBrain comes to steal your glory – here is this episode's summary:

- Python is capable of handling many file types, including .py, .txt, .html, .c, CSV, and JSON.

- open( ) is used to open a file; you can also create a file with open( ) provided a file of the same name does not already exist.

- An example of using open( ): open("CreatedFile.txt", 'w').

- The 'w' parameter is used to open a file in write mode.

- The 'x' parameter is used to open a file in creation/write mode.

- The .write method lets us add text to a file.

- An example of using the .write method: newFile.write("Here is some text.").

- Always be certain to close a file using the close( ) function when you are finished using it.

- An example of using close( ): newFile.close( ).

- The argument 'r' is used to open a file for reading.

- The .read( ) method reads all of the text in a file.

- An example of using the .read( ) method: print(readMe.read( )).

- We use readline( ) to read a single line of a file.

- An example of readline( ): print(readMe.readline( )).

- The append argument – 'a' – should be used to write to an existing file. Using 'w' will overwrite the contents of an existing file.

- To work with directories, we must import os.

- We use getcwd( ) to see what our current directory is.

- An example of using getcwd( ): os.getcwd( ).

- We use mkdir( ) to create a new directory. For example: os.mkdir("newDirectory").

- We use chdir( ) to change directories. For example: os.chdir ("C:/Users/YourName/").

- We can remove or delete a directory using rmdir( ). For example: os.rmdir("newDirectory").

- We can delete files using os.remove( ). For example: os.remove ('test.txt').

- We can rename files using os.rename( ). For example: os.rename('test.txt', 'newTest.txt').

CHAPTER 11

Python for Gaming

It is only appropriate that we have a chapter where we discuss creating video games in Python – after all, it is that very interest that got me started programming all those years ago when I was a kid. Things have progressed a lot since then; at the time, PC games were text-based with the only images consisting of really poor-quality graphics or, worse, made out of ASCII characters.

Even the sounds were very basic: think single-tone digital boops, beep, and borps. And animations? Well, they technically existed – for a good example of a really high-tech PC game of my era, check out a YouTube video for games such as *Where in the World Is Carmen Sandiego?* and, my favorite, *The Oregon Trail*.

Go ahead, I'll wait. Finished laughing? Good, let's continue.

That isn't to say that better-quality video games were not around. Atari had been around for ages at this point, and the Nintendo Entertainment System (NES), Sega, and Commodore were all available. I even owned a Nintendo and marveled at the high-tech 8-bit graphics and cutting-edge sound.

And while those games were great – some of them still stand up to this very day and are more fun than a lot of the games I run on my PS5 – those console games lacked one thing my PC games had; I was able to hack them and, more importantly, create my own versions on a computer.

Now things are different. If you want, you can purchase a developer console for major consoles and, given the right resources and skills, start developing your own games. Whether those games will ever see the light of day in any game stores or not, who can say, but the point is, you can, technically, create console games these days.

Back then, at my age at the time, you couldn't.

Video games are a great way to learn computer programming skills. Given a complex enough video game and you can really flex your coder muscles. You get to use code in ways that you might not normally think of using them, and you really need to plan out your code for a game before you write one – that part is very crucial, especially if you create a game with a storyline behind it.

© James R. Payne 2024

J. R. Payne, *Python for Teenagers*, https://doi.org/10.1007/978-1-4842-9988-3_11

More important to me, however, is the passion that video games can instill in a person. I am hoping that if nothing else in this book really gets your imagination cooking or excites you about programming, creating your own games will.

Even if you have no desire to create games and are more interested in security, desktop applications, data science, or working with web frameworks, I still encourage you to follow along in this chapter. While there will not be a ton of in-depth coding involved, we do cover some concepts that can be used outside of games, such as working with sounds, images, and even animations.

And besides, every hero needs to learn as much about their powers as they can. I mean, they say Superman can leap tall buildings, but how often do you see him do it?

Still, one day something might happen where he can't fly any longer (maybe he loses his pilot license), and then how will he ever get to the top of a building to stop that giant ape with the big brain from throwing that really cool – but totally evil – rooftop party in downtown Metropolis?

Python for Gaming

Python, admittedly, is not the first language that comes to mind when you think of video game programming. That being said, it is used in some of the largest games out there – Battlefield being a great example of a game that is on PC and consoles that uses some Python.

If you really want to be a game developer, you will want to learn as much as you can about C++ and JAVA. Those are the two top languages used for most games right now. Others, such as C# (which extends with Python) for Unity, are also used, but really, you will want to focus on C++, especially if you wish to pursue console and PC gaming alike.

If you plan on programming web-based games, then you will need HTML5, CSS3, JavaScript, and SQL (a database language).

There are, of course, a multitude of languages you can develop games in, but those listed here are the heavy hitters.

That being said, Python is a pretty good choice if you are looking to learn the core concepts and even create your own games – whether for fun, to share with friends, or as part of your portfolio. Python is much easier to learn than C++, and if you made it this far into the book, you already have a pretty good handle on coding basics.

Python also has the very handy `pygame` module, which we installed earlier in the book, which is really a collection of a bunch of different modules that let you create your own games and animations in Python.

Since this is a Python book, we will be focusing on how to create games with Python; but I wouldn't want you to neglect the fact that you should add other languages to your repertoire once you have mastered using Python.

Types of Games You Can Code in Python

There really is no limit on the *types* of games you can create with Python – at least in theory. You can make role-playing games (RPG), first-person shooters (FPS), platformers, puzzle games, and so on. These games can be text-based, a mixture of simple graphics, sounds, and text, animated, 2D side scrollers (think games like Contra on the NES), and even 3D games.

If you want to branch out to making 3D games, you will need to learn some additional technologies, such as Panda3D (`www.panda3d.org/`). We won't be diving that far into game development here but be aware that the option does exist.

While Python helps you make great games, really resource-intensive games – games that require a lot of memory and processing power – are better served being created with C++, which gives you greater access to processing and graphic hardware.

To really see what types of games you can develop in Python – and specifically which type you can program using the `pygame` module that we will be covering in this chapter – visit the official Pygame website's project library, and browse the plethora of games hosted there: `www.pygame.org/tags/all`.

You can view games developed by Python programmers by type, libraries used, and more. It is a great place to get some ideas and inspiration, as well as play some games and have a lot of fun!

Pygame Introduction

We installed the `pygame` module already if you have been following along in this book, but don't worry – we will go over installing it again in case you skipped over that part or want to learn how to do so again.

First, however, we should talk a little bit about Pygame's history and what, exactly, it is.

While we refer to pygame as a module, in reality, it is a set of modules created specifically for video game development. Developed by Pete Shinners, the first version was released back in October 2000. The module(s) was made using a mixture of Python, C, and Assembly.

In addition to games on PCs, Pygame can also be used to develop games for Android devices using a subset known as PGS4A; you can learn more about programming games for mobile developments with this specific subset by visiting http://pygame.renpy.org/.

Installing Pygame

As discussed, we have already installed the pygame module. For clarity's sake, however, here is how to install it again, just in case you do not feel like flipping back a few chapters to Chapter 7.

To install a module – and pygame in particular – open up your command or CMD window and enter the following at the command prompt:

```
python -m pip install Pygame
```

If you do not already have pygame installed, you will see the download and installation process of the package begin after a few moments in the CMD window. The message will look similar to Figure 11-1.

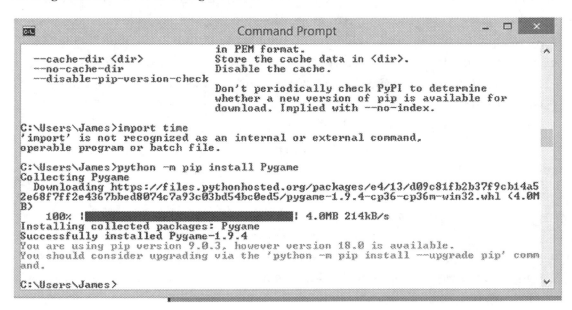

Figure 11-1.   *Installing pygame*

It is just that simple!

Setting Up the Pygame Bare Bones for a Game

The first thing we need is a structure to create our Pygames in. For that, we could use a bare-bones engine – for lack of a better word, that looks something like this:

```
import pygame
from pygame.locals import *
import sys
# Initialize all of the Pygame modules so we can use them later on
pygame.init()
# Create the game screen and set it to 800 x 600 pixels
screen = pygame.display.set_mode((800, 600))
# Create a loop that will keep the game running
# Until the user decides to quit
while True:
# Get feedback from the player in the form of events
    for event in pygame.event.get():
        # If the player clicks the red 'x', it is considered a quit event
        if event.type == QUIT:
            pygame.quit()
            sys.exit()
```

This is a very bare-bones version of a game using the pygame module. While there is no technically playable game in this code, it does create a system for us to build our games on. The code works in the following manner.

After importing the modules we will need – pygame and sys - we also import all of the extra modules contained within pygame. Importing pygame should be enough, but sometimes – depending on your system – all of the modules bundled with pygame won't load, so we use:

```
from pygame.locals import *
```

to make sure we import everything as a precaution.

Now that our modules are loaded, we need to initialize all of the pygame modules. We do so using the code: pygame.init().

So far in our programs, we have run code using IDLE and displayed the results in the Python Shell. When we write games using Pygame, however, since we are dealing with graphics, we need to create an actual screen to display our programs on. We use `.display.set_mode()` to create a window or screen. This line:screen = pygame.display. set_mode((800, 600))

creates a screen or window that is 800 x 600 pixels in width and height. It is to this screen that we will later paint – or `blit` – our images, graphics, and text to.

The final piece of this code – and something you will need to create for all of your games – is known as the game loop. This structure's purpose is fairly simple: receive input from the user in the form or mouse-clicks and keyboard/key presses, which are known as *events*.

When we create an interactive game, we need a way for the user to tell the game that they are finished playing and to exit out. The game loop also serves this purpose.

The `while` loop that starts with `while True` starts the game loop. The program then waits for the user to take an action – to create an event. Right now, all we have the game set to look for is a `QUIT` event.

A `QUIT` event means that the user has closed the window using the red X in the right-hand corner of the window. Once this happens, we use two vital functions that, again, all Pygames must have: `pygame.quit()` and `sys.exit()`. These two events end Pygame and exit the game, respectively. You must have both together; if not, your window will freeze or hang.

If you were to run this program right now, a window would pop up with a black background. Nothing else would occur. When you clicked on the red X, the window would close and the program would end.

Adding to Our Game Skeleton

Now that our Pygame game skeleton is in place, we can add a little pizzazz to it, if we wanted to spice things up a little. After all, we are superheroes, and what are heroes without a little bit of flair?

For starters, let's create a new file called `pygameExample.py`. Add the following code to it:

```
import pygame
from pygame.locals import *
import sys
```

```python
# Creating a tuple to hold the RGB (Red, Green Blue) values
# So that we can paint our screen blue later
colorBLUE = (0, 0, 255)
# Initialize all of the Pygame modules so we can use them later on
pygame.init()
# Create the game screen and set it to 800 x 600 pixels
screen = pygame.display.set_mode((800, 600), 0, 32)
# Set a caption to our window
pygame.display.set_caption("Super Sidekick: Sophie the Bulldog!")
# Draw a blue background onto our screen/window
screen.fill(colorBLUE)
# Draw the now blue window to the screen
pygame.display.update()
# Create a variable to hold the value of whether
# The game should end or not
running = True
# Create a loop that will keep the game running
# Until the user decides to quit
# When they do, it will change the value of running
# To False, ending the game
while True:
# Get feedback from the player in the form of events
    for event in pygame.event.get():
        # If the player clicks the red 'x', it is considered a quit event
        if event.type == QUIT:
            pygame.quit()
            sys.exit()
```

This code is similar to the example I showed you earlier. I did add a few more lines to the code, with the intent of sprucing up the window and making it look a little better.

The first piece of code I added was:

```python
colorBLUE = (0, 0, 255)
```

As the comments suggest, this is a tuple, whose values represent the RGB (red, green, blue) values that we will use to color our screen later on. We have to pass these values into our screen object/variable as a tuple value, as this is the data type that it accepts.

The theory behind RGB values is this: Using a combination of red, green, and blue, you can make any color visible to the human eye. In our case, the first value of 0 means there will be zero red in our color. The second value 0 means there will be zero green in our color. Finally, the third value 255 is the maximum amount of blue that we can add. If we were to use (0,0,0) instead, as an example, we would end up with the color black, which is a lack of any colors at all. On the flip side, (255,255,255) would equal white, as white is a combination of all colors.

Next, we want to add a title or caption to the window that we created, and we do so by using .display.set_caption(), as in this line:

```
pygame.display.set_caption("Super Sidekick: Sophie the Bulldog!")
```

This code will create a caption that looks like this, located at the top of the window, as shown in Figure 11-2.

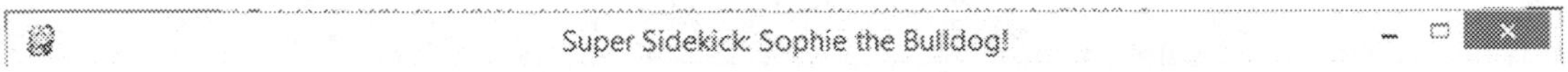

Figure 11-2. *Example of a window caption*

After that, we want to actually fill the background/screen with the color blue. To do this, we used .fill():

```
screen.fill(colorBLUE)
```

Note that this does not actually add anything to the window just yet. Before the blue background is actually drawn, we need to update the display using .display.update():

```
pygame.display.update()
```

Now when we save our program and run it, a blue screen will pop up, different than the black one from before, complete with a caption/title for our program! Go ahead and try it; just remember to click the red X to quit the program.

Adding Images and Sprites in Pygame

Now that we know how to format our game window and set up a basic game loop, the next thing we want to do is learn how to work with images. After all, the whole purpose of using the pygame module is so that we can create video games, right?

When we discuss images in two-dimensional – or 2D – video games, we refer to them as a sprite. This is a simplistic view of what a sprite is, but for our purposes it will work just fine.

A sprite in video games usually refers to characters, enemies, or images that represent players. Sprites are also objects in a game, such as bullets, trees, rocks, and so forth.

These sprites can be static – not moving – or animated. In this section, we are going to simply discuss a static sprite. You may have noticed that our window caption/title read: Super Sidekick: Sophie the Bulldog; this was no accident!

Plenty of superheroes have animal sidekicks. Fear of being sued and losing my vast wealth and collection of slightly vintage mopeds prevent me from naming any, but trust me, there are a whole slew of them.

Why should you and I be any different? Don't we deserve a sidekick animal as well? Mine happens to be a bulldog named Sophie, whose superpower is to burp, sleep, bite my toes, and snore really loud.

For this portion of our code, I am going to add an image of Sophie the Bulldog to our game window. If you want, you can follow along. Better yet, if you have an image of your animal – or any animal you would like to be your sidekick – go ahead and save the image in the same folder that your pygameExample.py file is located; if you don't, your program won't be able to find it.

A final note: be sure that you use the name of your file vs. what I type in the program. For example, the image I am using is named, "SophieTheBullDog.jpg"; yours might be named something different.

Add the following code to your pygameExample.py file, right beneath the section where you used screen.fill and right before you used pygame.display.update():

```
sidekick = pygame.Rect(100,100, 200, 200)
sophie = pygame.image.load('SophieTheBullDog.jpg')
thumbnail_sophie = pygame.transform.scale(sophie, (200,200))
screen.blit(thumbnail_sophie, sidekick)
```

I'll post the full, updated code after I explain this portion, so you can compare your file to mine.

The first thing we have to do is create another surface to blit – or paint – our image on top of. We achieve this in the line: sidekick = pygame.Rect(100,100, 200, 200).

This line of code creates a rectangle window that is located at the 100 by 100 *XY coordinate* of your screen and is 200 x 200 pixels (height and width).

XY coordinates relate to the position an object appears on your screen. The surfaces that we create in Pygame are made of pixels, with each pixel residing on a grid that relates to its XY position. The very top, left corner of a window is located in XY position (0, 0). Therefore, when we draw our rectangle at position (100, 100), what we are essentially saying is that it will be located at the 100th pixel across and the 100th pixel down.

If that bit is confusing, don't worry too much; it will make sense once you run the program in a few minutes.

The next line of code:

```
sophie = pygame.image.load('SophieTheBullDog.jpg')
```

stores the image named `'SophieTheBullDog.jpg'` in the variable `sophie`. Again, your image name will be different than mine, so simply replace my image name with yours.

Since my `'SophieTheBullDog.jpg'` image is pretty large – it measures in at 1400 x 1400 – it would be too large to display at its current size in the game window, let alone in the rectangle surface that we created for it. Therefore, we need to shrink it down to size.

We do this using `.transform.scale()`, which transforms an image by scaling it to a size that we give it.

Our line:

```
thumbnail_sophie = pygame.transform.scale(sophie, (200,200))
```

shrinks the image to 200 x 200 pixels, which is the exact same size as the `sidekick` object rectangle surface we created; if we scaled it larger than the surface, we would not be able to see the entire image, so always make sure the dimensions or size of the image matches the surface you created to display it upon.

Finally, the last step will be to actually paint – or `blit`, remember – the resized image to the `sidekick` rectangle surface we created. To do this, we typed:

```
screen.blit(thumbnail_sophie, sidekick)
```

The first argument in the parentheses ( ) is the name of the object we want to `blit`; the second argument is the object (which includes its location) that we want to `blit` the image onto.

Here is how the final code should look; modify your code so it looks like mine, being sure to change the name of your image to whatever your image is named. Also be certain to move your image into the same folder as your pygameExample.py file, or, again, it will not work:

```python
import pygame
from pygame.locals import *
import sys
# Creating a tuple to hold the RGB (Red, Green Blue) values
# So that we can paint our screen blue later
colorBLUE = (0, 0, 255)
# Initialize all of the Pygame modules so we can use them later on
pygame.init()
# Create the game screen and set it to 800 x 600 pixels
screen = pygame.display.set_mode((800, 600), 0, 32)
# Set a caption to our window
pygame.display.set_caption("Super Sidekick: Sophie the Bulldog!")
# Draw a blue background onto our screen/window
screen.fill(colorBLUE)
# Create a surface to hold our image
sidekick = pygame.Rect(100,100, 200, 200)
# create an object to load our image into
sophie = pygame.image.load('SophieTheBullDog.jpg')
# Resize our image so it fits the surface we are going to
# blit or paint our image onto
thumbnail_sophie = pygame.transform.scale(sophie, (200,200))
# blit or paint the image to the screen
screen.blit(thumbnail_sophie, sidekick)
# Draw the now blue window to the screen
pygame.display.update()
# Create a variable to hold the value of whether
# The game should end or not
running = True
# Create a loop that will keep the game running
# Until the user decides to quit
# When they do, it will change the value of running
```

```
# To False, ending the game
while True:
# Get feedback from the player in the form of events
    for event in pygame.event.get():
        # If the player clicks the red 'x', it is considered a quit event
        if event.type == QUIT:
            pygame.quit()
            sys.exit()
```

Save the code and run it. Your result will look different than mine, because I am using a different image than you, but your result should appear similar to Figure 11-3.

Figure 11-3. *Adding an image to the Pygame game window*

Before we move on, be sure to change the XY coordinates of the sidekick rectangle surface so that you can see how XY coordinates work. For example, change the line:

```
sidekick = pygame.Rect(100,100, 200, 200)
```

to

```
sidekick = pygame.Rect(200,200, 200, 200)
```

and so on.

Adding Text to Our Pygame Game Window

Adding images to our game is great, but what about text? We can add text as well, which is exactly what we will be doing in this section.

Adding text to your Pygame game window is a similar process to adding images; that is, you have to first create a surface to draw them onto. Then you dictate where that surface will appear on the window before you blit the text to it.

Add the following code to the pygameExample.py file, right below where we used our screen.fill(colorBLUE) code:

```
# Prepare our font for text
myFont = pygame.font.SysFont('None', 40)
# Create a text object
firstText = myFont.render("Sophie The Bulldog", True, colorRED, colorBLUE)
# Create the surface to write our text onto and its position
firstTextRect = firstText.get_rect()
firstTextRect.left = 100
firstTextRect.top = 75
# blit our text to the window
screen.blit(firstText, firstTextRect)
```

We are also going to define a new color, colorRED, to use with our text. Place this text under where you defined colorBLUE:

```
colorRED = (255, 0, 0)
```

I will display the code with current edits for you to compare after I explain these latest editions.

To start, we created an object to store our font, which we will apply to our text object once we create it. We do this in the line:

```
myFont = pygame.font.SysFont('None', 40)
```

The arguments for `pygame.font.SysFont()` are `'None'` and 40. The first argument tells Pygame what font to use. We could have used a font name such as `'Arial'`, but I chose to allow Pygame to use its default system font by choosing `'None'`. The argument 40 tells Pygame what size of font to use when rendering (or drawing) our text.

Next, we actually create our text object:

```
firstText = myFont.render("Sophie The Bulldog", True, colorRED, colorBLUE)
```

`myFont.render()`, in this example, has four arguments. The first is what text we actually want to print to the screen. The second argument – `True` – tells Pygame whether you want your text to be anti-aliased or not. This means whether you want it to be smooth or not; `True` means smooth; `False` means not smooth.

The third parameter (`colorRED`) is the color that we want the text to be, which is based off of our color tuple that we declared at the beginning of the program. The fourth and last argument is what color the background of our text should be. I set it to `colorBLUE` so that it would match and blend in with the color of our window.

Next, we define our surface, which is a rectangle, that we will print our text object onto. Then we set the position of where the surface will be, similar to how we decided where our image was going to appear.

`firstTextRect.left = 100` tells Pygame to draw the rectangle surface 100 pixels from the left of the screen. `firstTextRect.top = 75` tells Pygame to draw the rectangle surface 75 pixels down from the top of the screen.

It is important that we keep in mind where our image that we drew earlier is in relation to where we place our text.

For example, as you may recall, our image was place at 100 pixels down and 100 pixels from the left.

By setting our text surface at 100 pixels from the left, also, we are ensuring it is aligned properly with our image. We set the top of our text at 75, so that it sits just above our image.

Finally, we use `screen.blit(firstText, firstTextRect)` to paint our text to the screen.

Here is how my image looks after applying the new code – yours should look similar to Figure 11-4.

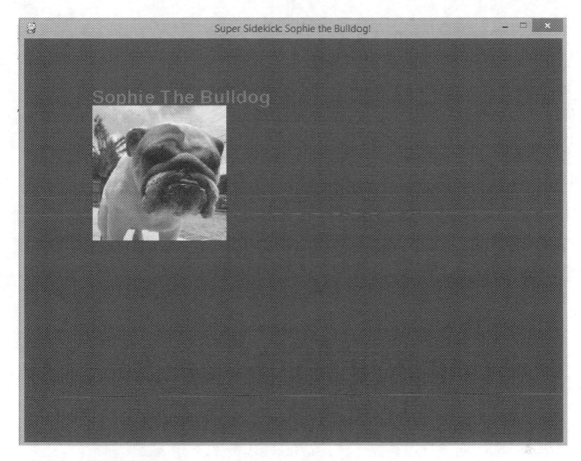

Figure 11-4. *Adding text to our Pygame game window*

Here is the current version of the code after adding our image and text. Make sure that your code matches mine:

```
import pygame
from pygame.locals import *
import sys
# Creating a tuple to hold the RGB (Red, Green Blue) values
# So that we can paint our screen blue later
# And our text red
colorBLUE = (0, 0, 255)
colorRED = (255, 0, 0)
# Initialize all of the Pygame modules so we can use them later on
pygame.init()
```

```python
# Create the game screen and set it to 800 x 600 pixels
screen = pygame.display.set_mode((800, 600), 0, 32)
# Set a caption to our window
pygame.display.set_caption("Super Sidekick: Sophie the Bulldog!")
# Draw a blue background onto our screen/window
screen.fill(colorBLUE)
# Prepare our font for text
myFont = pygame.font.SysFont('None', 40)
# Create a text object
firstText = myFont.render("Sophie The Bulldog", True, colorRED, colorBLUE)
# Create the surface to write our text onto and its position
firstTextRect = firstText.get_rect()
firstTextRect.left = 100
firstTextRect.top = 75
# blit our text to the window
screen.blit(firstText, firstTextRect)
# Create a surface to hold our image
sidekick = pygame.Rect(100,100, 200, 200)
# create an object to load our image into
sophie = pygame.image.load('SophieTheBullDog.jpg')
# Resize our image so it fits the surface we are going to
# blit or paint our image onto
thumbnail_sophie = pygame.transform.scale(sophie, (200,200))
# blit or paint the image to the screen
screen.blit(thumbnail_sophie, sidekick)
# Draw the now blue window to the screen
pygame.display.update()
# Create a variable to hold the value of whether
# The game should end or not
running = True
# Create a loop that will keep the game running
# Until the user decides to quit
# When they do, it will change the value of running
# To False, ending the game
while True:
```

```
# Get feedback from the player in the form of events
    for event in pygame.event.get():
        # If the player clicks the red 'x', it is considered a quit event
        if event.type == QUIT:
            pygame.quit()
            sys.exit()
```

Drawing Shapes in Pygame

Inserting images and sprites in your Pygame games is a great way to add scenery, characters, and items, but it is not your only option when it comes to graphics, nor is it always your best option. You also have the ability to draw shapes using some fairly simple code.

Let's start by adding a few more colors to our program. Underneath where we defined our previous colors, add the following bit of code:

```
colorPINK = (255,200,200)
colorGREEN = (0,255,0)
colorBLACK = (0,0,0)
colorWHITE = (255,255,255)
colorYELLOW = (255,255,0)
```

Next, we are going to draw our first few shapes. We will be drawing three circles – each different from the other in a unique way. Add the following code in your file, right before the `pygame.display.update()` line:

```
# Drawing a circle
pygame.draw.circle(screen, colorRED, (330, 475), 15, 1)
pygame.draw.circle(screen, colorYELLOW, (375, 475), 15, 15)
pygame.draw.circle(screen, colorPINK, (420, 475), 20, 10)
```

The `.draw.circle` method takes a few arguments. The first is what surface we want to draw our circle on; in this case, we draw it on `screen`, which is the name of the variable we created earlier to hold the surface object for our program.

The next argument is the color, which we defined using `colorRed`. Next, we tell Python at what pixel or XY coordinate we want the circle to be located at – in this case, where the center of the circle is.

The last two arguments dictate the radius of our circle – 15 in this example – and the thickness of the line.

The interesting thing to note here is that, were we to run the program after creating only the first circle, we would see a circle that was not filled with a color. This occurs because we set the last argument – the line thickness – to 1. If we wanted to entirely fill our circle with color, we would make the line thickness equal the radius.

We show an example of this, as a comparison, in the second circle we draw, which has a radius of 15 and a thickness, also, of 15.

Finally, we draw our third circle, and this time, we make the value of the circle's thickness half that of the circle's radius, just so we can see what happens. As a guess, I am going to say that our final circle will look like a donut. Let's see if I am right. Save the program and run it. You should see a result similar to Figure 11-5:

Your result should be similar to mine.

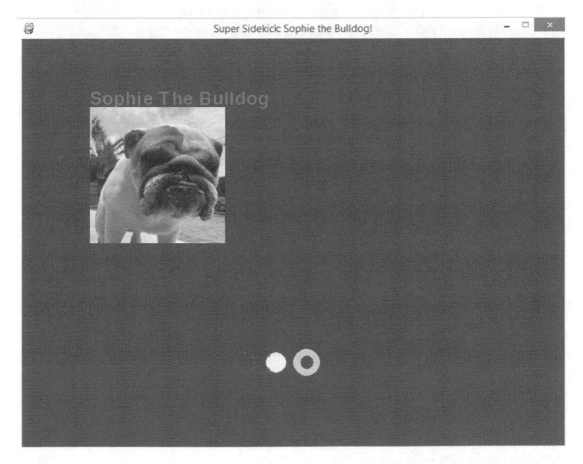

Figure 11-5. *Drawing shapes on our Pygame game window*

Here are some examples of different shapes you could draw (don't add them to your file just yet):

- Circles: pygame.draw.circles(surface, color, (x,y), radius, thickness)

  Example: pygame.draw.circle(screen, colorYELLOW, (375, 475), 15, 15)

- Rectangle: pygame.draw.rect(surface, color, (x,y,width,height), thickness)

  Example: pygame.draw.rect(screen, colorYELLOW, (455, 470, 20, 20), 4)

- Line: pygame.draw.line(surface, color, (X,Y Coordinates for the Beginning of the line),(X,Y Coordinates for the End of the Line), thickness)

  Example: pygame.draw.line(screen, colorRED, (300, 500), (500,500),1)

Go ahead and add the following lines of code to your file, just below where we placed the code to create our circles:

```
pygame.draw.rect(screen, colorYELLOW, (455, 470, 20, 20), 4)
pygame.draw.line(screen, colorRED, (300, 500), (500,500),1)
pygame.draw.line(screen, colorYELLOW, (300, 515), (500,515),1)
pygame.draw.line(screen, colorRED, (300, 530), (500,530),1)
```

If you run this code, your result will look similar to Figure 11-6.

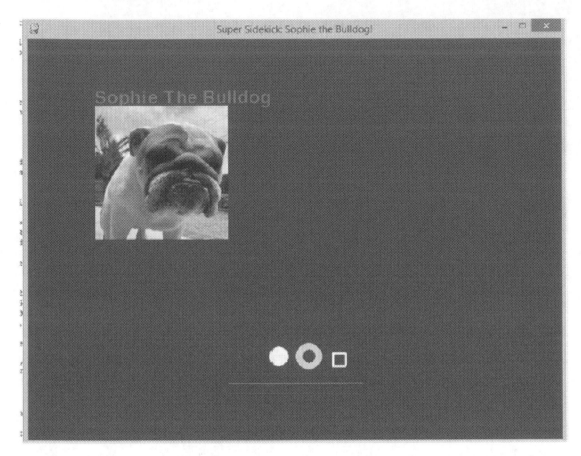

Figure 11-6. *Adding some lines to our Pygame game window*

Adding More Events

What good would a game be if it did not respond to a user? Further, what sort of program only allows users to quit by clicking the red 'X' in the top right-hand corner of the screen – that is not very intuitive, now is it?

Pygame programs are capable of responding to a vast array of events. These events can be anything from a click of the mouse, a scroll of the wheel, the press of an arrow on your keyboard, or a press of any key on a standard keyboard period, just to name a few.

Before we move away from our pygameExample.py file, let's add a few more events to program, just so that we have a better feel for how events operate.

If you have been following along, your pygameExample.py code should match the following; if it doesn't, take a moment to ensure that it does:

```
import pygame
from pygame.locals import *
import sys
import random
# Creating a tuple to hold the RGB (Red, Green Blue) values
# So that we can paint our screen blue later
# And our text red
colorBLUE = (0, 0, 255)
colorRED = (255, 0, 0)
colorPINK = (255,200,200)
colorGREEN = (0,255,0)
colorBLACK = (0,0,0)
colorWHITE = (255,255,255)
colorYELLOW = (255,255,0)
# Initialize all of the Pygame modules so we can use them later on
pygame.init()
# Create the game screen and set it to 800 x 600 pixels
screen = pygame.display.set_mode((800, 600), 0, 32)
# Set a caption to our window
pygame.display.set_caption("Super Sidekick: Sophie the Bulldog!")
# Draw a blue background onto our screen/window
screen.fill(colorBLUE)
# Prepare our font for text
myFont = pygame.font.SysFont('None', 40)
# Create a text object
firstText = myFont.render("Sophie The Bulldog", True, colorRED, colorBLUE)
# Create the surface to write our text onto and its position
firstTextRect = firstText.get_rect()
firstTextRect.left = 100
firstTextRect.top = 75
# blit our text to the window
screen.blit(firstText, firstTextRect)
# Create a surface to hold our image
```

```python
sidekick = pygame.Rect(100,100, 200, 200)
# create an object to load our image into
sophie = pygame.image.load('SophieTheBullDog.jpg')
# Resize our image so it fits the surface we are going to
# blit or paint our image onto
thumbnail_sophie = pygame.transform.scale(sophie, (200,200))
# blit or paint the image to the screen
screen.blit(thumbnail_sophie, sidekick)
# Drawing shapes
pygame.draw.circle(screen, colorRED, (330, 475), 15, 1)
pygame.draw.circle(screen, colorYELLOW, (375, 475), 15, 15)
pygame.draw.circle(screen, colorPINK, (420, 475), 20, 10)
pygame.draw.rect(screen, colorYELLOW, (455, 470, 20, 20), 4)
pygame.draw.line(screen, colorRED, (300, 500), (500,500),1)
pygame.draw.line(screen, colorYELLOW, (300, 515), (500,515),1)
pygame.draw.line(screen, colorRED, (300, 530), (500,530),1)
# Draw the now blue window to the screen
pygame.display.update()
# Create a variable to hold the value of whether
# The game should end or not
running = True
# Create a loop that will keep the game running
# Until the user decides to quit
# When they do, it will change the value of running
# To False, ending the game
while True:
# Get feedback from the player in the form of events
    for event in pygame.event.get():
        # If the player clicks the red 'x', it is considered a quit event
        if event.type == QUIT:
            pygame.quit()
            sys.exit()
```

The portion of the code we are going to be adding our events to is our game loop, which, to refresh your memory, is this portion of the code:

```
# Create a variable to hold the value of whether
# The game should end or not
running = True
# Create a loop that will keep the game running
# Until the user decides to quit
# When they do, it will change the value of running
# To False, ending the game
while True:
# Get feedback from the player in the form of events
    for event in pygame.event.get():
        # If the player clicks the red 'x', it is considered a quit event
        if event.type == QUIT:
            pygame.quit()
            sys.exit()
```

As game loops go, this is very simplistic. As stated, it only has one event. The first thing we want to do is add another way for the user to quit the application. We will use two methods for this. First, if the user presses 'q' on their keyboard, the application will close. Second, if the user presses the ESC key, the game will also close. Once our code is updated, the user will officially have three ways to quit our application.

Modify the game loop portion of the code so that it matches the following. Note: Be very mindful of proper indentation:

```
# Create a variable to hold the value of whether
# The game should end or not
running = True
# Create a loop that will keep the game running
# Until the user decides to quit
# When they do, it will change the value of running
# To False, ending the game
while True:
# Get feedback from the player in the form of events
    for event in pygame.event.get():
        # If the player clicks the red 'x', it is considered a quit event
```

```
    if event.type == QUIT:
        pygame.quit()
        sys.exit()
    if event.type == pygame.KEYDOWN:
        if event.key == pygame.K_q:
            pygame.quit()
            sys.exit()
    if event.type == pygame.KEYDOWN:
        if event.key == pygame.K_ESCAPE:
            pygame.quit()
            sys.exit()
```

Save the code and run your program several times. Be sure to press the 'q', click the red 'X', and press the ESC key as you re-run the program to make sure that each quit option works.

Note that, in our new code, we have two new event types. The first is pygame. KEYDOWN, which is used when we are waiting – or listening – for a user to press a key on their keyboard.

Indented below our pygame.KEYDOWN event type is event.key, which defines what *exact* key the program is listening for. Most letters and numbers on a keyboard are defined by typing pygame.K_ and then the letter or number.

For example, to listen for an 'a', you would use:

```
if event.type == pygame.KEYDOWN:
        if event.key == pygame.K_a:
                do something...
```

You can view a full list of keyboard constants by visiting: www.pygame.org/docs/ref/ key.html. In addition, here is a list of some of the more common keyboard constants you can listen for:

- Up arrow: K_UP

- Down arrow: K_DOWN

- Right arrow: K_RIGHT

- Left arrow: K_LEFT

- Space bar: K_SPACE

- Enter or return: K_RETURN

- Numbers: K_0, K_1, K_2, etc.

- Letters: K_a, K_b, K_c, K_d, etc.

Before we move on to our next section, let's add one more thing to our pygameExample.py file. Let's listen for another event – the keyboard character 'b'. When the user presses that button, the program will print out some text to the screen.

To achieve this, let's add the following to our game loop, right underneath our last if block:

```
if event.type == pygame.KEYDOWN:
        if event.key == pygame.K_b:
            barkText = myFont.render("Bark!", True, colorRED,
            colorBLUE)
            barkTextRect = barkText.get_rect()
            barkTextRect.left = 300
            barkTextRect.top = 175
            screen.blit(barkText, barkTextRect)
            pygame.display.update()
```

By now, you should have a pretty good understanding of what this code does. If not, that is okay – we will go through it step-by-step.

First, we listen for a KEYDOWN event type – that is, someone pressing a key down on their keyboard. Next, we tell Pygame what key we are listening for:

```
if event.key == pygame.K_b:
```

This line says that we are looking for the 'b' key to be pressed down. It is important to note the difference between a KEYDOWN event and a KEYUP event. As noted, a KEYDOWN event occurs when a user presses a given key on their keyboard; a KEYUP event occurs when they release that key. If a KEYUP event is not listened for, then nothing will happen once the user releases the key.

Next, we define what happens if the user presses the 'b' key. For starters, a text object name barkText is created. We set the arguments for the text object – what the text should say, if it is anti-aliased or not, the color of the text, and the color of the background of the text.

Next, in the line:

```
barkTextRect = barkText.get_rect()
```

We define the surface that our text will reside upon. From there, we indicated the position of the surface using:

```
barkTextRect.left = 300
barkTextRect.top = 175
```

Finally, we blit the text object and its surface onto the screen and update the display to show our newly created text.

If you save this code and run it, you will get a result similar to Figure 11-7, provided you press the 'b' key once the application loads:

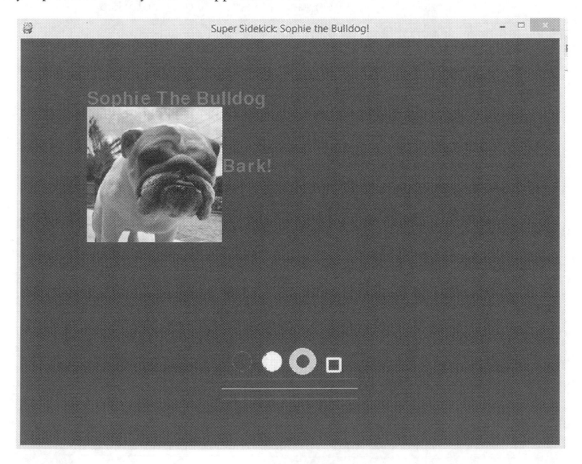

Figure 11-7. *Making "Sophie the Bulldog" bark*

That's right – Sophie the Bulldog barked! Apparently, she doesn't like those pesky circles, rectangles, and lines we drew earlier!

Since the "bark" text in our 'b' button event has been placed within our game loop, technically each time you press 'b', the text will reload to the screen. However, you will not be able to see this occur, as the replacement "bark" occurs instantly and is the same size, shape, and color.

There are a number of ways to make the text appear each time the user presses the 'b' key. One of the simplest is to use an illusion – something the insidious *Mathemagician* would no doubt be proud of!

To pull this illusion off, we are going to add another key press event. The key will still be 'b', but instead of a KEYDOWN event, we are going to add a KEYUP event.

The idea behind this next portion of code is simple: once the user releases the 'b' button, the "bark!" will disappear.

The reality is, we will simply be changing the color of the word "bark!" to the same exact color as the background, making it appear as if it disappeared, when, in fact, it will simply be hiding in the background.

When the user presses 'b' again, the color will change, once more, to red and become visible again. This cycle will continue each time the user presses 'b' until they exit out of the application.

Add this code right below where you defined your last KEYDOWN event, save it, and then run the program. Be sure to press the 'b' button a bunch of times until you get tired of seeing Sophie bark!

Note   Make certain you indent properly, so that your first if statement lines up with the previous if statement.

```
if event.type == pygame.KEYUP:
    if event.key == pygame.K_b:
        barkText = myFont.render("Bark!", True, colorBLUE,
        colorBLUE)
        barkTextRect = barkText.get_rect()
        barkTextRect.left = 300
        barkTextRect.top = 175
        screen.blit(barkText, barkTextRect)
        pygame.display.update()
```

If your code does not work, take time to make sure it matches the following code. Here is the complete code for pygameExample.py with all of our latest editions:

```
import pygame
from pygame.locals import *
import sys
import random
# Creating a tuple to hold the RGB (Red, Green Blue) values
# So that we can paint our screen blue later
# And our text red
colorBLUE = (0, 0, 255)
colorRED = (255, 0, 0)
colorPINK = (255,200,200)
colorGREEN = (0,255,0)
colorBLACK = (0,0,0)
colorWHITE = (255,255,255)
colorYELLOW = (255,255,0)
# Initialize all of the Pygame modules so we can use them later on
pygame.init()
# Create the game screen and set it to 800 x 600 pixels
screen = pygame.display.set_mode((800, 600), 0, 32)
# Set a caption to our window
pygame.display.set_caption("Super Sidekick: Sophie the Bulldog!")
# Draw a blue background onto our screen/window
screen.fill(colorBLUE)
# Prepare our font for text
myFont = pygame.font.SysFont('None', 40)
# Create a text object
firstText = myFont.render("Sophie The Bulldog", True, colorRED, colorBLUE)
# Create the surface to write our text onto and its position
firstTextRect = firstText.get_rect()
firstTextRect.left = 100
firstTextRect.top = 75
# blit our text to the window
screen.blit(firstText, firstTextRect)
# Create a surface to hold our image
```

```
sidekick = pygame.Rect(100,100, 200, 200)
# create an object to load our image into
sophie = pygame.image.load('SophieTheBullDog.jpg')
# Resize our image so it fits the surface we are going to
# blit or paint our image onto
thumbnail_sophie = pygame.transform.scale(sophie, (200,200))
# blit or paint the image to the screen
screen.blit(thumbnail_sophie, sidekick)
# Drawing shapes
pygame.draw.circle(screen, colorRED, (330, 475), 15, 1)
pygame.draw.circle(screen, colorYELLOW, (375, 475), 15, 15)
pygame.draw.circle(screen, colorPINK, (420, 475), 20, 10)
pygame.draw.rect(screen, colorYELLOW, (455, 470, 20, 20), 4)
pygame.draw.line(screen, colorRED, (300, 500), (500,500),1)
pygame.draw.line(screen, colorYELLOW, (300, 515), (500,515),1)
pygame.draw.line(screen, colorRED, (300, 530), (500,530),1)
# Draw the now blue window to the screen
pygame.display.update()
# Create a variable to hold the value of whether
# The game should end or not
running = True
# Create a loop that will keep the game running
# Until the user decides to quit
# When they do, it will change the value of running
# To False, ending the game
while True:
# Get feedback from the player in the form of events
    for event in pygame.event.get():
        # If the player clicks the red 'x', it is considered a quit event
        if event.type == QUIT:
            pygame.quit()
            sys.exit()
        if event.type == pygame.KEYDOWN:
            if event.key == pygame.K_q:
                pygame.quit()
```

```
                sys.exit()
        if event.type == pygame.KEYDOWN:
            if event.key == pygame.K_ESCAPE:
                pygame.quit()
                sys.exit()
        if event.type == pygame.KEYDOWN:
            if event.key == pygame.K_b:
                barkText = myFont.render("Bark!", True, colorRED,
                colorBLUE)
                barkTextRect = barkText.get_rect()
                barkTextRect.left = 300
                barkTextRect.top = 175
                screen.blit(barkText, barkTextRect)
                pygame.display.update()
        if event.type == pygame.KEYUP:
            if event.key == pygame.K_b:
                barkText = myFont.render("Bark!", True, colorBLUE,
                colorBLUE)
                barkTextRect = barkText.get_rect()
                barkTextRect.left = 300
                barkTextRect.top = 175
                screen.blit(barkText, barkTextRect)
                pygame.display.update()
```

In This Episode

Wow, what an exciting – if mind-boggling – chapter! If you made it through this chapter with only minor scrapes and bruises from gently banging your head on the desk, good job! The topics covered in this chapter were probably the most difficult to master; if nothing else, they were as equally complicated as classes and objects and are likely to be some of the most challenging things you ever have to wrap your brain around in Python.

Good job!

But don't rest on your laurels just yet. The next chapter continues our discussion on Pygame and dips into two more difficult – but powerful and rewarding – aspects of creating your own games: animation and collision detection. If you want to be a game developer or want a programming challenge, you definitely do not want to skip the next chapter!

Since this chapter and the next chapter go together and are such broad topics, we will be skipping the usual summary we perform at the end of each chapter; summing up the important talking points in bullet points does not do the topic justice.

Instead, practice the skills you learned in this chapter and the ones you will learn in the next chapter and re-read them as often as you need.

And, as always, experiment, experiment.

It literally is the name of the game!

CHAPTER 12

Animating Games

I see you came back for more punishment – good for you! The last chapter was pretty darned exciting, if I do say so myself. Not only did you get to learn some core game development theories and practices, but you also got to actually code some as well!

And, most importantly, you got to meet my bulldog Sophie. She's a good dog when she is sleeping and she makes an excellent pet sidekick. I mean sure, she tends to sleep through all of the action, but if you need someone to eat all the food and burp a lot, well, you couldn't ask for a better partner.

Last issue, we learned to draw shapes and insert images into our games. We also learned about game loops and creating events to allow the user to interact with our games.

This go-around, we learn two more crucial aspects of game development. The first is animation, which means having objects move around the screen. The second is known as *collision detection*, which is what happens when two or more objects touch or when an object touches the borders of your game window.

I won't bore you with a long introduction – oh, it's too late you say?

Let's get to it then smarty pants!

Creating Animations in Pygame

We have come a long way in learning some of the core concepts of game design and how to create our own games in Python using the pygame module. Thus far, we learned how to create our backgrounds, add images or sprites, insert text, and listen to – and more importantly, respond to – events such as key presses.

The real meat behind creating a visual, 2D game lies with animation, which is what we will discuss in this next section. As with all things Python, there are many ways to achieve animation in our pygames, but since this is a beginner's book, we are going to only look at the easiest methods.

© James R. Payne 2024
J. R. Payne, *Python for Teenagers*, https://doi.org/10.1007/978-1-4842-9988-3_12

Our last application, pygameExample.py, became a pretty large file. To avoid confusion and save some space, let's create a brand new file named pygameAnimations.py.

We will be recycling some of our code from pygameExample.py, so don't fret if some of the code looks a bit familiar. Remember: we always want to reuse our code whenever possible and appropriate. In particular, some of our color variables and the module import/initialization portions.

We will be making a bit of a change to the game structure itself, as well as the game loop. Since animations can be a little more complicated to work with, I wanted to key our file lean and straightforward to best explain how things work. Besides that, structures for animations tend to differ from static images and text.

Add the following code to your pygameAnimation.py file to set up the framework:

```
# import our modules
import pygame
from pygame.locals import *
import sys
import random
# Initialize our pygame modules
pygame.init()
# Create tuples for our colors
colorWHITE = (255,255,255)
colorBLACK = (0,0,0)
colorRED = (255,0,0)
# Create our main game window - last time we named it screen
# Let's give it a different name this time
gameWindow = pygame.display.set_mode((800,600))
# Set the caption/title for our animation
pygame.display.set_caption('Box Animator 5000')
```

Since we already wrote a version of this code in our previous application, there is no need to go over it again. Just know that it is the bare-bones code that sets up our screen, defines colors for us to use on our images and text, and imports and initializes our modules. We also changed the caption for our window to say "Box Animator 5000."

Next, we want to create a few more variables:

```
gameQuit = False
move_x = 300
move_y = 300
```

The first variable gameQuit will store the value that our game loop checks against to see if the program should end. So long as gameQuit does *not equal* True, the game will continue; once its value is changed to True, the game will end.

The next two variables – move_x and move_y – are used to set the initial position of the rectangle object that we are going to draw. We put these values in a variable instead of defining them directly in the rectangle's arguments because we are going to change the value of our object's XY coordinates later in the application.

move_x represents the object's X position, while move_y is used for its Y position.

Next up will be the game loop for our animated game. We have added a few newer events, which we will discuss in detail. Add the following to your code:

```
# Game Loop
while not gameQuit:
    for event in pygame.event.get():
        if event.type == pygame.QUIT:
            pygame.quit()
            sys.exit()
        # If the player presses 'q', it is considered a quit event
        if event.type == pygame.KEYDOWN:
            if event.key == pygame.K_q:
                pygame.quit()
                sys.exit()
        # If the player presses 'ESC', it is considered a quit event
        if event.type == pygame.KEYDOWN:
            if event.key == pygame.K_ESCAPE:
                pygame.quit()
                sys.exit()
        # If arrow key left is pressed, move the object left
        if event.type == pygame.KEYDOWN:
            if event.key == pygame.K_LEFT:
                move_x -= 10
        # If arrow key right is pressed, move the object right
```

```
        if event.key == pygame.K_RIGHT:
            move_x += 10
    # If arrow key up is pressed, move the object up
    if event.type == pygame.KEYDOWN:
        if event.key == pygame.K_UP:
            move_y -=10
    # If arrow key down is pressed, move the object down
        if event.key == pygame.K_DOWN:
            move_y +=10
```

Most of this game loop should be familiar. We have several events that cover a way for the user to quit – they can press either ESC or 'q', or click the red 'X'.

We then created key press events for the LEFT, RIGHT, UP, and DOWN arrows. If either of these buttons is pressed, the following occurs:

- If the LEFT key is pressed, the value of move_x is decreased by 10, moving the object to the left 10 pixels.

- If the RIGHT key is pressed, the value of move_x is increased by 10, moving the object to the right 10 pixels.

- If the UP key is pressed, the value of move_y is decreased by 10, moving the object up 10 pixels.

- If the DOWN key is pressed, the value of move_y is increased by 10, moving the object down 10 pixels.

Now that our game loop and events are in place, the last piece of business remaining is to create our window, fill it with a color, blit our shape, and update the display:

```
# Fill the gameWindow with the color white
gameWindow.fill(colorWHITE)
# Blit a black rectangle object
pygame.draw.rect(gameWindow, colorBLACK, [move_x,move_y,50,50])
# Update our screen
pygame.display.update()
```

There we have it – our first animated game! Go ahead and run the program and test it out. Be sure to press each of the arrow keys and then run it a few more times to test each of our "quit" events.

Your screen should look similar to Figure 12-1.

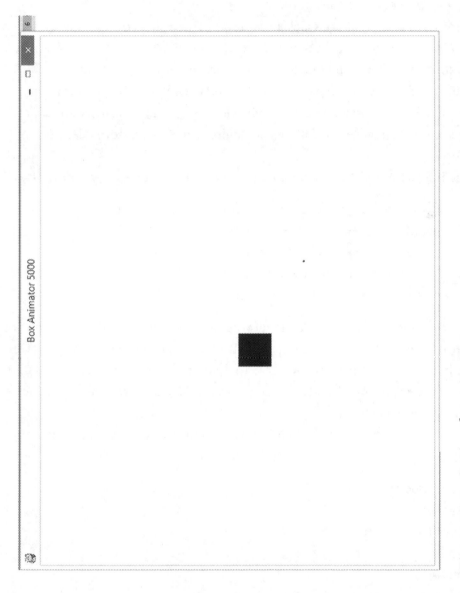

Figure 12-1. Testing the quit events

That is pretty cool, right? This type of animation logic can be applied to all sorts of games. For instance, you could make a racing game where a car has to move around the streets, a fighter game where the character moves across the board, and so forth.

Of course, right now our game is pretty boring, but the main concept to learn here was moving an object about the board.

As neat as this code is, it does lack a few things. One thing you may have noticed is that if you move the box too far in any direction, it will move off of the screen and eventually disappear. It will, technically, come back so long as you move it in the opposite direction, but you can see how this would cause problems in our game.

There are a few ways to fix this, which we will discuss in the next section. For now, however, let's add one more way for our rectangle to move – random teleportation! Talk about superpowers!

Add the following code snippet, right at the bottom of the rest of your events:

```
# if 't' is pressed, randomly teleport the object
if event.type == pygame.KEYDOWN:
    if event.key == pygame.K_t:
        move_y = int(random.randint(1,600))
        move_x = int(random.randint(1,600))
```

Astute observers may have noticed that we imported `random` at the beginning of our program; here is why. We want to randomly generate the XY coordinates of our rectangle object when the user presses 't'. To do that, we use `random.randint()`, as in the preceding example. We provide it a range of 1 and 600 pixels to ensure that it never completely disappears off of the screen.

By now, your code should look like this; if not, or if your code isn't working, make sure everything matches and that your indentation is set up correctly:

```
# import our modules
import pygame
from pygame.locals import *
import sys
import random
# Initialize our pygame modules
pygame.init()
# Create tuples for our colors
colorWHITE = (255,255,255)
```

```
colorBLACK = (0,0,0)
colorRED = (255,0,0)
# Create our main game window - last time we named it screen
# Let's give it a different name this time
gameWindow = pygame.display.set_mode((800,600))
# Set the caption/title for our animation
pygame.display.set_caption('Box Animator 5000')
gameQuit = False
move_x = 300
move_y = 300
# Game Loop
while not gameQuit:
    for event in pygame.event.get():
        if event.type == pygame.QUIT:
            gameQuit = True
            pygame.qui()
            sys.exit()
        # If the player presses 'q', it is considered a quit event
        if event.type == pygame.KEYDOWN:
            if event.key == pygame.K_q:
                pygame.quit()
                sys.exit()
        # If the player presses 'ESC', it is considered a quit event
        if event.type == pygame.KEYDOWN:
            if event.key == pygame.K_ESCAPE:
                pygame.quit()
                sys.exit()
        # If arrow key left is pressed, move the object left
        if event.type == pygame.KEYDOWN:
            if event.key == pygame.K_LEFT:
                move_x -= 10
        # If arrow key right is pressed, move the object right
            if event.key == pygame.K_RIGHT:
                move_x += 10
        # If arrow key up is pressed, move the object up
```

```
    if event.type == pygame.KEYDOWN:
        if event.key == pygame.K_UP:
            move_y -=10
    # If arrow key down is pressed, move the object down
        if event.key == pygame.K_DOWN:
            move_y +=10
    # if 't' is pressed, randomly teleport the object
    if event.type == pygame.KEYDOWN:
        if event.key == pygame.K_t:
            move_y = int(random.randint(1,600))
            move_x = int(random.randint(1,600))
# Fill the gameWindow with the color white
gameWindow.fill(colorWHITE)
# Blit a black rectangle object
pygame.draw.rect(gameWindow, colorBLACK, [move_x,move_y,50,50])
# Update our screen
pygame.display.update()
```

Run the code and teleport till your brain explodes!

Collision Detection: Bouncing Off the Walls

As we create more objects in our games, we inevitably run into the problem of handling how objects behave when they come into contact with each other. For example, if we have two rectangles animated to move to the center of the window, at some point, their paths will cross.

We can ignore this contact and in some instances this may be the best option. More likely than not though, we want to have our objects detect this collision and react a certain way.

Collision detection is the art of programming objects to be "aware" of when they bump up against another object and then react appropriately. In some instances, we may want our object to simply cease moving in that direction. In others, we may want them to bounce back a few steps, as if they ran into a strong force field.

Collisions can happen for other reasons as well. For instance, you may have created a maze that a character must get through. If we do not set up collision detection, the character may simply float straight through our walls. The same goes for doors.

In fact, even if you don't have walls or doors, or any other objects at all on the screen, setting up collision detection is a good idea. Why? We touched upon this topic very briefly when we animated our rectangle; objects we create that are capable of movement can – and will – move beyond the boundary of the screen we define.

While a window does not inherently have a wall boundary, they do, in fact, have a boundary. The height and width of the window is the boundary, in these cases. For instance, let's say we have a window that is 800 x 600 pixels. We could set the boundaries of our app along the sides, top, and bottom of this window, making our object bounce off of them if it crosses the line.

Finally, another form of collision we may want to be aware of is intentional collision. Think of a game where you are shooting bullets at the enemy. Every time those bullets hit their target – or collide – we would want them to do things like deal damage, score points, or trigger some sort of reaction.

In the most basic of terms, a collision occurs whenever two or more objects come into contact with one another – intentionally or not.

Collision Detection: Detecting the Window Boundaries

When we create our pygame applications, we need to keep the boundaries of our window in mind. For the most part, we will want our objects to stay within the width and height of our window or game screen. There are occasions where this won't be the case, but for our purposes, we are going to focus on what to do when we want to ensure our objects stay within view of the player.

For our next section of code, we are going to check to make sure that our rectangle object does not move beyond the width or height of our window. To do this, we have to check where our rectangle is as it moves around the board and have our program respond if the rectangle touches the borders.

To achieve this, we are going to use a series of `if` statements, which we will place below our game loop and event listeners and right before we create our `gameWindow.fill(colorWHITE)`.

Add the following code, being sure to indent properly:

```
# Check to see if we collide with the right screen end
    if move_x > 750:
        move_x -= 50
        pygame.display.set_caption('Right Collision')
    if move_x < 1:
        move_x += 50
    # Check to see if we collide with the left screen end
        pygame.display.set_caption('Left Collision')
    # Check to see if we collide with the bottom of the screen
    if move_y > 550:
        move_y -= 50
        pygame.display.set_caption('Bottom Collision')
    # Check to see if we collide with the top of the screen
    if move_y < 1:
        move_y += 50
        pygame.display.set_caption('Top Collision')
```

For such a small amount of code, it certainly does a lot. Let's walk through the steps.

Our first if statement states that *if* our rectangle object is located at a space of 750 pixels or greater, then move our rectangle object back 50 pixels in the opposite direction, creating a bounce effect. This is achieved by subtracting 50 (-=50) from the move_x variable, which, as you will recall, represents the X coordinate of our rectangle object.

You may have noticed that we did not have the program check to see if our object was located at a pixel coordinate of higher than 800 X. Why is that, you may ask? Simple: we always have to keep in mind the size of the object we are detecting collision for. We must subtract its size – in this case, 50 – from the highest coordinate value. Therefore, if our rectangle is 50 pixels, and our screen is 800 pixels across, in order to allow our rectangle to touch the border and not go beyond it, we have to check for an X coordinate of 750 or greater.

The next part of our code works on the X coordinate again. This time, we are checking for collision with the left side of the screen. Here, we want to check for values of less than 1 (remember: the border on the left side of the screen is located at X coordinate 0); once more, if we hit this "wall," the rectangle bounces 50 pixels in the opposite direction.

We continue this logic for the Y coordinates as well, checking for the top and bottom collisions of our window. Again, if a collision is detected, our rectangle will bounce in the opposite direction 50 pixels – this time up or down accordingly.

Finally, just to add a little more flair to the program, each if check will also change the window's caption if a detection occurs, alerting you to which direction – up, down, left, or right – the collision happened.

There you have it – our first collision detection feature!

Go ahead and save the program and test it out, being sure to bounce into each wall to make sure the program works properly. If it does not, make sure that it matches the following completed program code:

```
# import our modules
import pygame
from pygame.locals import *
import sys
import random
# Initialize our pygame modules
pygame.init()
# Create tuples for our colors
colorWHITE = (255,255,255)
colorBLACK = (0,0,0)
colorRED = (255,0,0)
# Create our main game window - last time we named it screen
# Let's give it a different name this time
gameWindow = pygame.display.set_mode((800,600))
# Set the caption/title for our animation
pygame.display.set_caption('Box Animator 5000')
gameQuit = False
move_x = 300
move_y = 300
# Game Loop
while not gameQuit:
    for event in pygame.event.get():
        if event.type == pygame.QUIT:
            gameQuit = True
            pygame.qui()
```

```python
        sys.exit()
    # If the player presses 'q', it is considered a quit event
    if event.type == pygame.KEYDOWN:
        if event.key == pygame.K_q:
            pygame.quit()
            sys.exit()
    # If the player presses 'ESC', it is considered a quit event
    if event.type == pygame.KEYDOWN:
        if event.key == pygame.K_ESCAPE:
            pygame.quit()
            sys.exit()
    # If arrow key left is pressed, move the object left
    if event.type == pygame.KEYDOWN:
        if event.key == pygame.K_LEFT:
            move_x -= 10
    # If arrow key right is pressed, move the object right
        if event.key == pygame.K_RIGHT:
            move_x += 10
    # If arrow key up is pressed, move the object up
    if event.type == pygame.KEYDOWN:
        if event.key == pygame.K_UP:
            move_y -=10
    # If arrow key down is pressed, move the object down
        if event.key == pygame.K_DOWN:
            move_y +=10
    # if 't' is pressed, randomly teleport the object
    if event.type == pygame.KEYDOWN:
        if event.key == pygame.K_t:
            move_y = int(random.randint(1,600))
            move_x = int(random.randint(1,600))
    # Check to see if we collide with the right screen end
    if move_x > 750:
        move_x -= 50
        pygame.display.set_caption('Right Collision')
    if move_x < 1:
```

```
            move_x += 50
        # Check to see if we collide with the left screen end
            pygame.display.set_caption('Left Collision')
        # Check to see if we collide with the bottom of the screen
        if move_y > 550:
            move_y -= 50
            pygame.display.set_caption('Bottom Collision')
        # Check to see if we collide with the top of the screen
        if move_y < 1:
            move_y += 50
            pygame.display.set_caption('Top Collision')
    # Fill the gameWindow with the color white
    gameWindow.fill(colorWHITE)
    # Blit a black rectangle object
    pygame.draw.rect(gameWindow, colorBLACK, [move_x,move_y,50,50])
    # Update our screen
    pygame.display.update()
```

Colliding Two Objects

Now that we have set up our border detection, we can move on to another important type of collision detection – detecting when two objects collide with one another. As stated prior, there are many reasons why you may want to check for collision between multiple objects. In addition to seeing if two characters have come into contact or if a weapon has hit its target, collision detection is useful for determining where an object is in perceived space.

For example, if you have a game where a character has to leap on top of objects – as you do in a platform game – how would your game know whether the character was standing on a patch of grass or atop a box? You can use collision detection – or hit detection – for just such a purpose.

In our next example, we are going to create a brand new Python file called objectCollisionExample.py. We will be borrowing some of the code from our pygameAnimations.py program. Instead of walking you through each section of code, I am going to start by pasting the entire program, then stepping through the new additions and modifications we made to our old code.

Take a moment to create your new file and copy the following code into it. Be sure to read the comments to see if you can figure out the purpose of the program and how it works before I explain it. As always, be sure to indent your code properly or you will receive errors:

```python
# import our modules
import pygame
from pygame.locals import *
import sys
# Initialize our pygame modules
pygame.init()
# Create tuples for our colors
colorWHITE = (255,255,255)
colorBLACK = (0,0,0)
colorRED = (255,0,0)
# Create our main game window - last time we named it screen
# Let's give it a different name this time
gameWindow = pygame.display.set_mode((800,600))
# Set the caption/title for our animation
pygame.display.set_caption('Colliding Objects')
gameQuit = False
# Create two variables that will store sprite rectangle objects
rect1 = pygame.sprite.Sprite()
rect1.rect = pygame.Rect(300,300,50,50)
rect2 = pygame.sprite.Sprite()
rect2.rect = pygame.Rect(100,100, 100,150)
# Game Loop
while not gameQuit:
    for event in pygame.event.get():
        if event.type == pygame.QUIT:
            gameQuit = True
            pygame.quit()
            sys.exit()
        # If the player presses 'q', it is considered a quit event
        if event.type == pygame.KEYDOWN:
            if event.key == pygame.K_q:
```

```
        pygame.quit()
        sys.exit()
# If the player presses 'ESC', it is considered a quit event
if event.type == pygame.KEYDOWN:
    if event.key == pygame.K_ESCAPE:
        pygame.quit()
        sys.exit()
# If arrow key left is pressed, move the object left
if event.type == pygame.KEYDOWN:
    if event.key == pygame.K_LEFT:
        rect1.rect.x = rect1.rect.x - 10
# If arrow key right is pressed, move the object right
    if event.key == pygame.K_RIGHT:
        rect1.rect.x = rect1.rect.x +10
# If arrow key up is pressed, move the object up
if event.type == pygame.KEYDOWN:
    if event.key == pygame.K_UP:
        rect1.rect.y = rect1.rect.y -10
# If arrow key down is pressed, move the object down
    if event.key == pygame.K_DOWN:
        rect1.rect.y = rect1.rect.y +10
# Check for collision between our two rect objects
# using collide_rect
# If a collision is detected, we relocate rect1
# by changing its y and x coordinates
if pygame.sprite.collide_rect(rect1, rect2):
    rect1.rect.y = 400
    rect1.rect.x = 400
# Check to see if we collide with the right screen end
# If it does, we move rect1 back to X coordinate 740
if rect1.rect.x > 750:
    rect1.rect.x = 740
    pygame.display.set_caption('Right Collision')
if rect1.rect.x < 1:
    rect1.rect.x = 51
```

```
    # Check to see if we collide with the left screen end
        pygame.display.set_caption('Left Collision')
    # Check to see if we collide with the bottom of the screen
    if rect1.rect.y > 550:
        rect1.rect.y = 540
        pygame.display.set_caption('Bottom Collision')
    # Check to see if we collide with the top of the screen
    if rect1.rect.y < 1:
        rect1.rect.y = 50
        pygame.display.set_caption('Top Collision')
# Fill the gameWindow with the color white
gameWindow.fill(colorWHITE)
# Blit our rectangle objects
pygame.draw.rect(gameWindow, colorBLACK, rect1)
pygame.draw.rect(gameWindow, colorRED, rect2)
# Update our screen
pygame.display.update()
```

This code works like the previous program in most ways; we create a rectangle object – this time inserted into a sprite – that we are going to move around the window using arrow keys. If the rectangle touches any of the window's edges or boundaries, the rectangle will bounce a few pixels off of the "wall."

In addition to this, we created a second rectangle object – rect2 – that is static and does not move around the board. We also set up code to check to see if rect1 bumps into rect2; if so, then we change the value of rect1's X and Y coordinates – just as if it had hit a wall.

The main difference in this code vs. the previous hit detection example has to do with the way we create our rectangle object. Instead of simply using .rect and blitting our rectangle, this time we want to actually create a variable to hold our rectangle object(s).

Further, we make these rectangles sprites, so that we can access some of the built-in functions that come with pygame.sprite.Sprite(). There are many built-in functions that accompany the pygame.sprite module, and unfortunately we do not have space in this book to cover them all. However, we will be touching upon a very important one whose purpose is to aid in collision detection.

By storing our rectangle objects in variables and making them sprites, we gain the ability to change their XY coordinates by directly accessing those attributes.

For example, in the code of the program, you may see something similar to `rect1.rect.x = 100`. This code basically says you want to take the variable named `rect1`, access the `rect` object stored in it, and change its x value to 100.

This part of our code:

```
rect1 = pygame.sprite.Sprite()
rect1.rect = pygame.Rect(300,300,50,50)
rect2 = pygame.sprite.Sprite()
rect2.rect = pygame.Rect(100,100, 100,150)
```

is used to create our two rectangle objects – `rect1` and `rect2`. Be sure to note that when we use `pygame.Rect`, the "R" is capitalized vs. when we use it in `rect1.rect`. Failing to properly capitalize it will lead to errors.

The next change is how we define the way objects – rect1 in particular – move around the window.

Since our `rect` object is now a sprite, we have to access its parameters – such as its XY coordinates – differently. Now, to make the object move, we use this method:

```
# If arrow key left is pressed, move the object left
if event.type == pygame.KEYDOWN:
    if event.key == pygame.K_LEFT:
        rect1.rect.x = rect1.rect.x - 10
```

Notice how instead of using the .move_ip method, we now, instead, simply reassign the value of rect1.rect.x to a new value, as in this line:

```
rect1.rect.x = rect1.rect.x - 10
```

which says to take the current X coordinate value of `rect1` and subtract 10 from it.

We do this for each key press event for the four directional arrows and change the value of `rect1.rect.x` and `rect1.rect.y` depending upon which direction the user is moving the rectangle in.

Remember that the X value represents left and right movements, while the Y value represents up and down motion.

The next step is to use collision detection to see if `rect1` ever touches `rect2`. This is where defining our rectangle objects as sprites comes in handy. One of the built-in functions of a sprite object is `collide_rect`, which takes two arguments: the names of the two objects you wish to detect collision on.

We use this inside of an `if` statement so that we can check if the objects ever touch or come into contact with one another. If they do, we change the value of rect1's X and Y coordinates to 400 x 400, teleporting it far away from the `rect2` object. This is all accomplished with this simple code:

```
if pygame.sprite.collide_rect(rect1, rect2):
    rect1.rect.y = 400
    rect1.rect.x = 400
```

Finally, the last change we made to our code was the way we handle border collision with the game window. It is largely the same as before, except, again, instead of changing the values of `move_x` and `move_y` to change the coordinates or our rectangle, we access the rectangle's XY parameters directly.

If a wall collision is detected, we simply move the rectangle back a few spaces:

For example:

```
if rect1.rect.x > 750:
        rect1.rect.x = 740
        pygame.display.set_caption('Right Collision')
```

says that if rect1's X coordinate is greater than 750, move rect1 back to X coordinate 740 and then change the window caption to say "Right Collision."

Go ahead and test the program, making sure to check that the collision detection works for all four sides of the two objects by trying to move the rect1 object into the rect2 object from the top, bottom, left, and right sides.

Then test the collision detection for the window borders, being certain to check, again, the top, bottom, left, and right boundaries.

If the code does not work, re-read it and compare, making sure it matches.

And, as always, be mindful of indentation.

In This Episode!

You accomplished some truly amazing things in the past two chapters, and it is looking like you are building up to be an unstoppable hero! While we did not cover every gaming topic possible in these last two chapters – it would take a whole book (if not more) to do so properly – we did touch upon enough information for you to design a basic video game and, more importantly, get started doing your own research to create your own complex games.

Your homework? Get out there and create an interesting game or, at least, the skeleton of one. I look forward to playing it on the Playstation 402 or whatever system is around when you become a world-famous game developer!

CHAPTER 13

Error Handling

We are rapidly approaching the end of this book and our time adventuring together. Soon, you will be donning your cape on your own, battling evil doers without my assistance (in your imagination only, of course!), and writing code all by yourself.

Cue sad music.

For now, though, we are still a superhero duo! And while we have learned how to defeat many programmatic villains and overcome many different obstacles, there is a topic we still need to discuss: how to overcome our own failures.

Failure, you say? What sort of hero or coder fails?

Sadly, we all do. Or, to look at it a better way: fortunately, we all do.

Why fortunately? Because failure is one of the greatest ways to grow stronger and improve our skills and programming abilities.

Think about this: do you know why you build muscle when you lift weights? It is because you tear muscle that then has to heal. When you lift weights, at some point you hit a point where you can lift no longer – that is, you fail. That failure is exactly what a bodybuilder is looking for, because they know that only once your muscles fail can they begin to repair the damage and grow even stronger.

Your programming skills are exactly the same. The only way, in my view, to ever really understand code is to screw it up and have to figure out what you did wrong. Anyone can know the language – *understanding* the language, however, takes years of failing.

Note, this same logic does not apply to your algebra tests...don't fail those!

So far, when we have encountered an issue, we simply read our .py file, line by line, trying to figure out what went wrong. And to be honest, there haven't really been any failures – provided you have typed in my examples exactly as written.

Odds are, however, that you mistyped a word or two and that did cause your program to fail. What you did after that – if you have made it this far – is you scoured your code looking for the culprit, the misspelled word or indentation that caused the problem, and then fixed it.

© James R. Payne 2024
J. R. Payne, *Python for Teenagers*, https://doi.org/10.1007/978-1-4842-9988-3_13

If this happened, congratulations – you have officially tested and *debugged* a program, even if only in the most basic sense of the word.

Debugging is a new word for us. It means to identify and remove errors from our code.

Let's look at that definition again: identify and remove errors from our code.

The biggest part of the debugging process, to me, is finding the error. From there, we have to understand the error, and only then can we repair or remove the issue causing the error.

For small programs, we can go line by line trying to find the issue. For larger programs, we will want to use a program known as a debugger.

Finding Errors

Python is usually pretty good at telling us we screwed something up. For this section, let's go ahead and create a new file called Oops.py.

This file is going to be full of errors, and when you run your programs, expect to get yelled at by IDLE. When we type in our code, the mistakes in the code may be obvious to you, or it may not; either way, follow along and pretend you don't see the mistakes if you do; it will help you understand how to fix programs better.

Enter the following code into Oops.py:

```
print hello
```

For astute programmers, you may already see the problem; if so, kudos, but pretend you didn't. Go ahead and run the program and look what happens. Finished? Did you get an error message? You bet you did! It should read something like

```
Missing parentheses in call to 'print'. Did you mean print(...)?
```

This should have appeared as a pop-up message. As you can see, IDLE is pretty smart – it not only saw that there was a problem in your code, it offered you a suggestion on how to fix it.

A few things to note here. First, while IDLE does offer a suggestion here, it is actually incorrect. Since we did not enclose the text we wanted to print in quotation marks, IDLE assumes that we were really trying to print a variable and shows us how to print a variable named hello.

In this instance, that was not our intent, but still, it is nice of Python to point out our error and offer a possible solution.

What we really meant to do was print out the word "hello," which of course is as simple as typing print("Hello"). However, remember, we want our program to fail.

So, the lesson from this first mistake? Sometimes IDLE will give us an error message in a pop-up message and suggest where the error occurred and a possible solution – which may or may not be correct.

Now, let's modify the code in our file so that it matches this:

```
print("Hello)
```

Again, you may already see the problem – that we forgot to close our `print()` function with a second or closing quotation marks – but go ahead and run the program to see what happens.

Here, again, we get another pop-up. This time we get a different type of error – an unterminated string literal error. It should say

```
Unterminated string literal (detected at line 1)
```

Here, Python is basically telling us that we did not close the line properly, which we know we did not do. If we click the "OK" button on the pop-up, IDLE should take us back to our file and highlight the rest of the line in red – indicating that it thinks there is an error in this region. It may also place the cursor somewhere on the line where the error occurs instead.

We know the problem is that we simply forgot our second quotation mark. We are going to fix that, but this time, let's leave off the second parentheses instead and see what happens. Edit your code to match the following, and then run it again:

```
print("Hello"
```

This time, we get another error pop-up. This one is a Syntax Error that says:

```
'(' was never closed
```

Again, Python will place the cursor back on the line where the error occurred.

When we run our code, Python was looking for an end to the line of our code – which should have been a closed parenthesis. Instead, it found no close, so it skipped to the next line looking for more code. When it didn't find the closed parentheses there either, it decided we goofed up and highlighted the line to show us where it ran into the error.

This is important, because usually we think Python is showing us where the error is; in fact, Python is showing us where it errored (is that even a word?). Think of it as running off of the edge of a diving board; the first step off of the diving board is where you screwed up, but you probably don't realize it until the moment right before you belly-flop awkwardly and lose your trunks in front of your entire class.

Python is the same way.

On to the next error.

Now, let's modify the code so it matches this:

```
prant("Hello")
```

Save the file and run it. No pop-ups this time – we must be doing good!

Well, not quite.

This time, when the program tries to run in the Python Shell, we get the following result:

```
Traceback (most recent call last):
  File "C:/Users/James/AppData/Local/Programs/Python/Python311/Oops.py",
  line 1, in <module>
    prant("Hello")
NameError: name 'prant' is not defined. Did you mean: 'print'?
```

This type of error is known as a NameError. Let's examine each part of this output carefully.

The first line says:

Traceback (most recent call last):

This is Python telling you that it is tracing back the errors in your code, with the last call appearing first. We only have one error this go-around, but don't worry – we will have multiple in a moment.

Next, Python tells us some important information. It tells us the location of the file (yours will be different than mine) and what line it thinks the error is on. In this instance, it says line 1, or the first line of your code.

Next, it shows us the code where the specific error occurs: `prant("Hello")`.

Finally, it ends by telling us the type of error – `NameError` – and provides more details: the name "prant" is not defined.

When we see a message like that, it means that Python saw

```
prant()
```

and could not find it in its built-in list of functions. The reason? Because it doesn't exist – we misspelled `print()` and while we know that, Python has no way of knowing that.

Since Python does not find a built-in function named `prant()`, it assumes that we are trying to call a function we created named `prant()`. Since we did not make a function with that name, then Python concludes that we have typed a wrong name or failed to define a function of that name. It also, conveniently, suggests that perhaps we meant 'print.'

This is a very basic error and is pretty simple for us to trace – or track down – and fix. All we have to do is look at line 1, find the messed-up code, and change `prant("Hello")` to `print("Hello")`. Then, if we saved it, we could run it and all would be right in the world.

Of course, we don't need to bother doing that just yet, because we are still intentionally making mistakes in our code.

Let's see if we can make one more type of error before we move on. Modify your code once more so that it matches the following:

```python
a = 1
whilst a < 4:
    print(a)
    a = a + 1
```

What this code should do is assign the value of 1 to the variable 'a.' Then, we created a `while` loop that looked to iterate or repeat so long as the value of `'a'` was less than 4.

For each iteration through this loop, the value of `'a'` gets printed, and we also add +1 to the value of `'a'`. In theory, the output of this code would be

---

```
1
2
3
```

However, we made another typo in our code – can you spot it this time?

If you run the code, you will get a hint in the form of a pop-up box that reads

---

```
invalid syntax.
```

What, exactly, does that mean? It means that we spelled something wrong in our code. Again, we get the red highlight showing where our area is near.

The issue? We spelled *whilst* instead of `while`.

Let's fix the spelling of *whilst* but make another mistake in its place. Edit the code so that it matches this:

```
a = 1
while a < 4
    print(a)
    a = a + 1
```

Can you spot the error this time? Save the file and run the code. Again, we get a syntax error, even though we fixed the spelling of `while`. Every other word is spelled correctly as well, so what gives?

Syntax errors cover general typos – not just spelling mistakes. In this case, we forgot to add a colon `:` at the end of our while statement. The line should read

```
while a < 4:
```

If you add the colon at the end and save the file, it should run properly. Python also gave us a hint about this in the pop-up, which read: "expected ':'".

Types of Errors

In reality, there are only three main types of errors in Python: syntax errors, logic errors, and exceptions. We will cover each of these error types and how to handle them in this section. So, strap on your superhero safety goggles, and let's get ready to fix the problems of the world!

Well, okay – maybe just the problems in our code to start with.

Syntax Errors

We already discussed syntax errors a little in our preceding overview of errors. To refresh your memory, a syntax error occurs when Python is unable to understand or read a line of code.

Syntax errors are normally caused by something as simple as a typo; perhaps you misspelled a function or forgot to add a colon at the end of your statement. Think of them as grammar or spelling mistakes.

Of all the errors you receive, odds are that syntax errors will occur the most frequently. This is both good and bad; it's good because it means that, most often, your errors are simply a spelling or punctuation problem and not an issue with programming logic. It's bad because, well, they can be annoying to track down, especially after your eyes are blurry from typing code all day... and night.

The vast majority of syntax errors are fatal and will cause your code not to execute, which again is a blessing in disguise. While it may be annoying to have your code not work at all, it also ensures that you don't ship a piece of software that has a hidden problem in it.

If you run into a syntax error, note where the red line is highlighted in IDLE or note the line number where the error occurs and look for any problems with spelling, indentation, colon, quotation, and parentheses use, or invalid arguments within that line, the line before it, or the line after it.

Logical Errors

The most problematic of all errors are the dreaded logic errors. As the name suggests, these occur when there is a flaw in your programming logic. These types of errors can cause your program to behave in a funny manner or explode completely.

Part of what makes logical errors so frustrating is the fact that they don't always cause an obvious error. Sometimes, Python does not even catch the error, and you, yourself, may miss it. This is why it is so crucial to frequently test your code and provide documentation whenever possible.

There are several ways to uncover these types of errors, including using a debugging program, which we will cover later on in this chapter. The best way to deal with logical errors is to prevent them in the first place. We do this by planning our programs in advance and testing frequently. Using flowcharts can help you figure out how each section of your code should flow and is a helpful tool to avoid logical errors.

Of course, logical errors will still happen; it is all just part of being a programmer.

Here is an example of a logical error – see if you can figure out why this program will return a result that is not what was intended. Here's a hint: the intent of this program is to find the average of two numbers:

```
a = 10
b = 5
average = a + b / 2
print(average)
```

If you are not great at math, don't worry; when we write this program, we expect that the average of 10 and 5 would be 7.5; however, when we run this program, we get the result:

```
12.5
```

which is certainly not right. Why did this happen? Let's check our math to see if we did the calculation correctly.

If we were writing this equation on a piece of paper, we would write a + b / 2 – exactly as we see it. a + b equals 15, divided by 2 equals 7.5 right?

If you will recall from our discussion on math operators and numbers, math does not always work the same in Python as it does when using pen and paper. In Python, there is an order of precedence, meaning Python looks at an equation and determines which portion to solve first before moving on to the next section.

If this part is unclear, I encourage you to go back to the chapter dealing with operators and numbers and review it one more time. Come back when it makes sense.

In order to have Python perform the equation in the order that we want it to, we need to force the order of precedence using parentheses ( ). The real way to write this code, without getting a logical error, would be:

```
a = 10
b = 5
average = (a + b) / 2
print(average)
```

This time, if you ran the code, you would get

```
7.5
```

For those that are not mathematically inclined – or those that are sleep deprived – you may have completely missed the fact that this code was not behaving properly at all. Python did not send a warning or an error message at all, so we would have no real way of knowing there was a problem if we did not test the results and double-check to make sure they were right.

Now, imagine if this were part of a banking application and you could see how a simple logical error could ruin an entire system – and make a lot of people very sad!

Exceptions

Exceptions are a peculiar breed of error. There are several types of built-in exceptions, but they are too numerous to cover in this chapter. Instead, you can visit the Python. org's doc page on built-in exceptions located at `https://docs.python.org/3/library/exceptions.html#built-in-exceptions` to see the different types. I'll explain why that may be even more useful than you think in a moment.

For now, know that exceptions occur when Python understands your code but is unable to perform an action based off of it. For instance, maybe you are trying to connect to the Internet to scrape – or copy – some data from a website, but you are unable to connect. Or maybe you have a script that is trying to make use of an API that no longer exists at the address you give it.

Exceptions differ from syntax errors in a number of ways. One of those is the fact that they do not always cause an error. This is good and bad; it is good because your programs can sometimes still run with an exception; it is bad because, well, your programs can still sometimes run with an exception!

We don't want our code to run with errors!

The great thing about exceptions – if you want to look on the bright side – is that we can do something called *exception handling*. To handle an exception basically means that we anticipate the error may occur and then script a way to deal – or handle – them.

Let's say that we have a program that asks for a user's four-digit pin number. We want to ensure that the value is numeric in nature. We have set our variable to specifically hold an integer value. Let's start out with the base code:

```python
pin = int(input("Enter your pin number: "))
print("You entered pin: ", pin)
```

If you put that code in a file and run it, it will ask you for a pin number. Go ahead and try it out – you can add it into your `Oops.py` file if you like. To begin with, type in a four-digit number and press Enter. The program will spit out a response similar to

```
You entered pin: 1234
```

where 1234 would be whatever number you entered.

Now, run the program again, only this time, enter something like "abcd" when prompted and press Enter.

This go-around you will get the following output:

```
Traceback (most recent call last):
  File "C:/Users/James/AppData/Local/Programs/Python/Python311/Oops.py",
line 1, in <module>
    pin = int(input("Enter your pin number: "))
ValueError: invalid literal for int() with base 10: 'abcd'
```

Here, we are presented with an exception error of the type ValueError. This happens because the type of value Python was expecting to find in the variable `pin` was an integer; instead, you typed in a string.

One of the ways we can ensure that Python does not toss an error like this and force our program to not run properly is to handle the error in advance. Since we know that someone may enter the wrong data type into our variable, we can create code to catch the error when it happens and handle it.

Try typing in this code, replacing the other version of the code, then save your file and run it:

```
# Example of exception handling a ValueError
try:
    pin = int(input("Enter your pin number: "))
    print("You entered: ", pin)
except ValueError:
    print("You must only enter a numeric value.")
```

This is known as a try and except block in Python. Its specific purpose is to catch an exception and handle it. The code contained within the block is treated with kid gloves, in a sense; Python realizes that you intend to handle an error if it occurs, and if one exists (of the type you specify), it triggers your except statement.

Go ahead and run this program and enter in 'abcd' when prompted again to see how the code now functions. You should get a response like:

```
Enter your pin number: abcd
You must only enter a numeric value.
```

Once Python hits the except statement, it follows your instructions and then exits out of the program. In real life, we would want to enclose this code in a loop so that it would start again if there was an exception. For instance, you could use a simple while loop, like this:

```
# Example of exception handling a ValueError
repeat = 1
while repeat > 0:
    try:
        pin = int(input("Enter your pin number: "))
        print("You entered: ", pin)
        repeat = 0
    except ValueError:
        print("You must only enter a numeric value.")
        repeat = 1
```

The Try Except Else Block

Another thing you can do is create a Try Except Else block. The idea behind this would be that if there were no exceptions, the code would carry out a different set of instructions. For example:

```
# Example of exception handling a ValueError
# Using a Try Except Else block
# Enclosed in a while loop
repeat = 1
while repeat > 0:
```

```
    try:
        pin = int(input("Enter your pin number: "))
    except ValueError:
        print("You must only enter a numeric value.")
        repeat = 1
    else:
        print("You entered: ", pin)
        repeat = 0
```

This has the same result – and works similar – to the previous version of the program. The difference? It is a little cleaner and more readable. It basically reads as

```
Try this code. If it doesn't work:
Execute some code if an exception occurs.
Else if there are no exceptions, run this code.
```

Using Finally

There is one more thing we can add to our block – the finally clause. finally is useful when we want some code to run no matter what – even if there is an error.

```
# Example of exception handling a ValueError
# Using a Try Except Else Finally block
try:
    pin = int(input("Enter your pin number: "))
except ValueError:
    print("You must only enter a numeric value.")
else:
    print("You entered: ", pin)
finally:
    print("Are we done yet?")
```

To study this code a little better, we removed the while loop and the repeat variable/ code relating to repeat. Basically, what this code is saying is this:

```
Ask for a pin number that is an integer value.
If the pin number is not an integer,
Trigger the except statement.
```

```
Else print the value of the pin number.
Additionally, no matter what,
Trigger the finally clause.
```

The result of this code if you entered `'abcd'` and triggered the exception would be:

```
Enter your pin number: abcd
You must only enter a numeric value.
Are we done yet?
```

If you ran it again and entered `'1234'` as your pin, it would result in:

```
Enter your pin number: 1234
You entered:  1234
Are we done yet?
```

Either way, you will note, our `finally` clause triggered – as intended. This is a great way to have your program carry on if you have an exception error that you anticipated.

Creating Custom Exceptions

In addition to handling exceptions from the defined list of built-in exceptions, we can also create a custom exception as well. To do this, we use `raise`. Here is a quick example:

```
super_name = "Afraid-of-Spiders-Man"
villain = "spiders"
if villain == "spiders":
    raise Exception("Yeah, no thanks...my name says it all...villain
    should NOT equal spiders!")
```

Here we start off creating two variables. One holds the name of our superhero, `super_name`, while the other holds the type of villain our hero will encounter – `villain`.

Next, we perform an if check that checks to see if the value of `villain` is equal to `'spiders'` (after all, our hero is named Afraid of Spiders Man!). Since `villain` does, indeed, match `'spiders'`, we use `raise` to create an exception:

When I run the code, I get this error:

```
Traceback (most recent call last):
File "C:/Users/James/AppData/Local/Programs/Python/Python311/Oops.py", line
4, in <module>

raise Exception("Yeah, no thanks...my name says it all...villain should NOT
equal spiders!")
Exception: Yeah, no thanks...my name says it all...villain should NOT
equal spiders!
```

Note   You can ignore the line number in this example – I have other code in my file that makes the line number the error appears on different than yours would appear.

Here we see our exception error being raised, printing out some text that says:

```
Exception: Yeah, no thanks...my name says it all...villain should NOT
equal spiders!
```

In this example, I was trying to be funny, so I made the exception say a joke. In reality, when you create your own exceptions, you will have them say something more along the lines of

```
Exception: the villain variable contains a value that is not allowed -
spiders.
```

That way if someone enters the wrong value, we immediately know when we look at the exception what the problem is without having to trace down the issue.

Another type of custom exception we can create is an `AssertionError` exception. This type of exception starts off a program by asserting that a given condition is `True` or met. If so, then the program can continue running. If not, an AssertionError exception is thrown.

Consider this short snippet of code

```
assert 1 + 1 == 2, "One plus One does equal 2!"
assert 2 + 2 == 5, "2 + 2 does not equal five! Error in line 2!!"
```

Here we have two `assert` statements. If we run this program, nothing happens for line 1 of the program – this is because the equation 1 + 1 does, in fact, equal 2, so the assert condition test equals `True`.

When the second line of code tries to be executed, the `assert` test condition proves `False` (2 + 2 does not equal 5), and so the AssertionError is triggered, resulting in this output:

```
Traceback (most recent call last):

File "C:/Users/James/AppData/Local/Programs/Python/Python311/Oops.py", line
2, in <module>
    assert 2 + 2 == 5, "2 + 2 does not equal five! Error in line 2!!"
AssertionError: 2 + 2 does not equal five! Error in line 2!!
```

To make things convenient, I went ahead and added the line the error in our code was written in the output from the `assert`, along with the reason the AssertionError was raised.

Logging

Another tool at our disposal for finding errors in our code – especially for longer programs – is to use `logging`. There are several ways to do this, but the easiest is probably by importing the `logging` module.

One method programmers use to reduce errors in their code is to use `print()` to verify everything is working as it should. For example, let's say that I have a group of stats – as we do in our Superhero Generator 3000 application – that are randomly generated.

I could just trust that my code is working right and assume that the stats are being randomly generated properly, but that might not be the smartest thing to do. To make sure I have coded everything properly, I might want to have the numbers randomly generate, then – temporarily – insert some code to print out the results of those stats. Once I am satisfied that the random number generation is working properly, I can remove all of the `print()` and continue with my code.

For example, I might write this code to start with

```
import random
brains = 0
braun = 0
stamina = 0
wisdom = 0
power = 0
constitution = 0
dexterity = 0
speed = 0
brains = random.randint(1,20)
braun = random.randint(1,20)
stamina = random.randint(1,20)
wisdom = random.randint(1,20)
constitution = random.randint(1,20)
dexterity = random.randint(1,20)
speed = random.randint(1,20)
```

Then, realizing that I need to check that all of the values are randomizing properly, I might go back and edit my code to add these print() functions:

```
import random
brains = 0
braun = 0
stamina = 0
wisdom = 0
power = 0
constitution = 0
dexterity = 0
speed = 0
brains = random.randint(1,20)
print("Brains: ", brains)
braun = random.randint(1,20)
print("Braun: ", braun)
stamina = random.randint(1,20)
print("Stamina: ", stamina)
```

```
wisdom = random.randint(1,20)
print("Wisdom: ", wisdom)
constitution = random.randint(1,20)
print("Constitution: ", constitution)
dexterity = random.randint(1,20)
print("Dexterity: ", dexterity)
speed = random.randint(1,20)
print("Speed: ", speed)
```

Then what I could do is run the program once, to see if values are being stored in my variables, giving me the result:

```
Brains:   19
Braun:   19
Stamina:   2
Wisdom:   11
Constitution:   14
Dexterity:   12
Speed:   6
```

Then, satisfied that values are being added, I would run one more test to make sure the values are being randomized each time the program runs. The test is simple: if the values are different the second time around, it works. The results?

```
Brains:   20
Braun:   2
Stamina:   14
Wisdom:   18
Constitution:   6
Dexterity:   19
Speed:   3
```

Since the values are different for each stat in both of my test runs, I can assume my use of random is correct. I no longer need my print() functions. I can either comment them out or remove them completely.

Since this is a simple piece of code, I will go ahead and remove the `print()` functions so that my code is more readable.

Instead of cluttering up my file with a bunch of print( ) functions, I could, instead, use logging to monitor the file and write the results to a separate text file.

Another benefit of logging is that we get to keep a record of events and errors that happen in our code for a later date, in case a new bug pops up or we need to review the log.

It is important to note that logging is about more than just monitoring for warnings and errors; it is also useful for monitoring triggered events as well.

In fact, the `logging` module has its own set of "level of importance" ratings you can use when logging. They are

Critical: Used for critical errors that can cause a program to have serious problems or not run at all.

Error: For serious, non-critical problems

Warning: Used for when something unexpected has – or could – happen

Info: Used as confirmation that your code is working as intended – similar to our use of the `print()` statement

Debug: Helpful for diagnosing any issues and providing information that may be helpful in the debugging process

In truth, logging and the use of the logging module in particular are beyond the scope of this book. It would take an entire chapter to explain its usage properly, and while I encourage a beginner to learn logging, it simply does not fit in our curriculum.

That being said, set aside some time to read the official Python documentation on logging and the `logging` module. Also, look at some tutorials on the Internet and in other, more advanced books, and start to dabble with logging as you create more complex programs.

Stick your toe in, and, when you are comfortable, dive on in!

Debugging Tools in Python

We spoke a lot about fixing errors in your code, testing your code, and how to perform exception handling. We also talked about logging and the basic concept of using the `logging` module to track errors and events in a log file.

Another trick up our superhero sleeves we can use to solve coding problems is a tool known as a *debugger*. There are many debuggers for Python available to choose from, each with their own strengths and weaknesses. Some cover specific areas of Python, choosing to specialize, while others are general-purpose debugging tools with similar features to other debugging programs.

Python, in fact, has its own debugging tool, known as pdb.

Technically, pdb is a module that you can import and use. The module lets you step into your programs and check them line by line to see if they are working properly.

Remember our example earlier of using print( ) statements to check that our stats random values were being assigned properly? Using the pdb debugger module, you could achieve the same result without having to write all of those print( ) statements.

You can learn more about the Python debugger pdb module at the Python's documentation website – just make sure the version of the documentation you are viewing matches the version of Python you have installed on your computer. Here is a link to Python 3.11, for example:

```
https://docs.python.org/3.11/library/pdb.html
```

As with logging, you should study debugging and begin learning the basics now, and then as you create more complex programs, get more comfortable using whichever you end up choosing. For now, I would stick with pdb.

One Final Tip for Handling Errors

If I haven't said this before, I wanted to leave you with one final tip for finding and dealing with errors in your code: use comments.

What, exactly, does that mean though?

The concept is simple enough: if you suspect a section of code is causing you a problem, use a comment (#) to make the line of code invisible to Python, and then run your code and see if the problem still exists. If it doesn't, you have found your problem; if the problem persists, move on to the next section of code.

For more complicated constructs like if blocks, use multi-line comments ("""") to comment out the whole section. For example:

```
"""
IF
code
```

```
code
code
"""
```

would comment out the code in between the triple quotation marks (*"""*).

This is a common practice used by coders of all levels. Just don't forget to uncomment your code after you check and/or fix it!

In This Episode!

Can you believe we have come this far? Only one chapter left till we conclude our superhero adventure together!

Super! Outstanding! Stupendous! Amazing! Spectacular!

Boom! Pow! Bam! Sock-O!

This chapter was all about errors: finding them, fixing them, logging them, and debugging them. Here are some highlights of these topics that you can review at your leisure.

And then, it is off to the final chapter!

- The three types of errors in Python are syntax errors, logic errors, and exceptions.

- Syntax errors are similar to a spelling error or grammar error; they are usually fatal and will cause your code not to execute.

- Logical errors occur when there is a flaw in your programming logic. They do not always cause a noticeable error and frequently cause programs to behave oddly vs. breaking.

- Exceptions do not always cause an error, and oftentimes programs can still run despite throwing an exception.

- There are many types of built-in exceptions, including ValueError and NameError.

- In addition to built-in exceptions, we can also create our own exceptions using raise and assert.

- Try-except-else-finally blocks give you more control over handling your errors by allowing you to dictate what happens if certain criteria – or error types – are encountered.

- Exception handling is the process of handling – or dealing with – exception errors.

- Logging allows you to track errors, warnings, debugging information, and events in your code. You can save these log files to a separate file for later use.

- You can use the logging module to assist in logging.

- There are many tools to help you debug – or find errors and fix them – available for Python.

- Python's built-in debugger is the module pdb.

- You can use single-line commenting and multi-line commenting to comment out blocks of code that may (or may not) be causing errors in your programs. You can then test your code to see if these commented-out portions were the culprit.

CHAPTER 14

Python Career

Well, young hero, it has been a long journey. We have overcome many foes – nefarious villains like Jack Hammer and the vile Algebro. We have read through this mystical tome and gained insight and wisdom that have allowed us to enhance our powers to heights previously unknown. We are talking Mount Everest types of heights.

Or, at the very least, the top of that really tall slide on the playground.

Regardless, when we first started this adventure together – and that is truly what it was, an adventure – you were a mere sidekick with a mustard stain on your super tights and a wrinkled cape. Your mask, though brightly colored, barely covered your face.

But look at you now! A full-blown hero, full of amazing powers. You can create your own programs, write video games, hack (ethically) computers, perform great feats of mathematics, randomly generate statistics, and so much more.

You have gone from fledgling hero to superhero; from student to... well, greater student.

But mostly, you have gone from reader to programmer. And that, my friend, was the purpose of this book.

And yet, even as you stand on this great precipice, comfortable in your tricked-out superhero lair and practicing your newfound powers and knowledge, you must never rest. The world is an ever-changing landscape, and so, too, is technology. Python, too, is an evolving beast, with no end in sight.

For that very reason, you must continue to practice the knowledge you already possess until it becomes like a second language. You need to dream in code! Then, go out, learn more of the language, and dream some more!

There is still a lot left of Python for you to discover and grow with. This book was just the tip of the iceberg. Practical, real-world experience that you cannot learn in a book awaits you. Updated versions of Python await you.

And, perhaps, other programming languages.

© James R. Payne 2024
J. R. Payne, *Python for Teenagers*, https://doi.org/10.1007/978-1-4842-9988-3_14

I encourage you to branch out and never be satisfied with your knowledge. Look at other languages. Consider learning some Perl, which is very similar to Python and should be easy for you to pick up. Ruby on Rails and PHP are great next languages as well, especially if you wish to branch out into web application programming.

C and C++ are a bit more difficult, but well worth the effort to learn, even if you just learn the basics. While you are at it, HTML, JavaScript, and JSON are all handy tools that you should add to your resume and skill set.

Speaking of resume, this final chapter serves one real purpose: to prepare you for the real world of programming. Whether you are 13 or 18, sooner or later you will need to decide what direction you wish to head in with regard to a career path; knowing what options are available to you now can help guide your learning path in the future.

For instance, if you decide you want to pursue game programming, continuing learning pygame and fooling around with Scratch will definitely help. Adding languages like C, JAVA, and C++ is a definite requirement – particularly C++.

In this chapter, we will look at all of the current – and future – career options to help you begin to think about what you want to do when you are an adult. We will also look at common interview questions, for those of you that already *are* adults and need to start paying those bills!

After all, you can't expect to make it on a superhero salary....

We will also refresh our memory on the best programming practices, so that we continue to write good code and keep our jobs once we get them. I can't stress the importance of good coding principles enough. The future of the world depends upon it!

Speaking of the future (yes, I am the Segue King!), we will look at the future of Python as a language. We will discuss its role in virtual reality (VR), augmented reality (AR), artificial intelligence (AI), and a whole slew of other abbreviations that make us sound hip and cool when we say them.

Finally, we will wrap up the chapter with a Python terms cheat sheet and answer some of the most frequently asked questions (FAQ) people have with regard to Python and programming in general.

It's been a long road – no reason to make it any longer. Strap on your superhero boots and lace 'em up! It's time to finish this journey.

Superhero style!

Working with Python

When you picked up this book, you may or may not have had a career path in mind and that is okay; many people go undecided about what they want to do when they are "grown-up" until they are, well, way past the point of being grown-up!

Whether you know what you want to be or not – or what profession you want to follow – one thing is for certain: you care about what that something is. That is evidenced by the fact that you invested in this book and, more importantly, yourself. You spent the time to read these pages and try out the code, and that is more than a lot of people your age have done so far. Good for you!

The next step is figuring out what you want to do with the knowledge you have gained. Most likely, you will want to continue on as a Python developer, regardless of the field or other languages and skills you may learn.

Some of what you do in your career will depend upon factors other than the ones you choose. People you meet, places you live, and available jobs will always factor in to where the road leads you. You might start out thinking you will be a video game programmer, intern at a video game development company as a game tester to gain some experience and veer off into that path. Who knows – that is part of the adventure of life!

That doesn't mean you can't aim for a certain goal and even stick to it. Just know that no matter how well-intentioned your plans are, sometimes you might find yourself somewhere other than you predicted, and that is okay.

All of that aside, it *is* good to have an idea of where you want to go. So, with that in mind, let's take a look at some possible career options as you develop into a part-time superhero, full-time programmer.

Career Paths for Python

The career paths listed in this section are not in any particular order; none is better than the others, although you may find pay rates are higher in some areas than others. We are not going to focus on that; I believe firmly in doing what you love. If you do that, success will follow.

This list is in no way conclusive; there are quite a few careers you can choose from, but these are the most common currently.

Beta Tester

Beta testers are the unsung heroes of the software developer world. They are the ones that test programs and software and figure out what works and what doesn't – both from a technical perspective and a user-experience perspective. In some instances, you may be asked to specifically test a certain feature or aspect of a program; in others, you may need to check everything.

Programming knowledge is important for this role but isn't the most important. I've beta tested many programs that I had no real experience for from a programming language perspective; I understood the concepts and how things worked and that served its purpose well.

Of course, if you know the language and can pinpoint exact issues in code, then all the better and you will likely have an easier time finding work.

Odds are, you have already beta tested software and maybe not fully realized it. If you are an avid video game player or a fan of mobile games, oftentimes you will get to try a beta version prior to it being released to the general population. While this isn't quite the same as having a paying gig, there can be benefits, such as free software and/or hardware.

Code Debugger/Bug Locator

This may sound similar to a beta tester, but it really is a little more involved in most instances. Your mission: locate wonky, bad code and report in on how to fix it – or fix it yourself, depending on the job.

If you are the type of person that likes to spend hours trying to solve the mystery of what is wrong with a program or like to take things apart, this may be a good career option for you; at the very least, it is a good skill to have, no matter where your career path takes you.

Keep in mind that you will be looking through *other* people's code and oftentimes *multiple* people's code. Hopefully those people document well and follow standard guidelines, but you never know what you are going to run into.

Still, this is a great way to stay at the top of your game and getting good at finding errors in programs will come in handy if you become a software developer or create your own applications.

Data Scientists

If you are good with statistics, numbers, and research, you may want to consider entering the field of data science. Python is huge in the world of data science, which is a mixture of statistics and machine learning techniques.

Thanks to its great library of mathematical and data visualization tools (such as matplotlib and NumPy), Python programmers lead the field in terms of data science careers. In this line of work, you will be using graphs and other tools to help organize, interpret, and display data sets for a broad range of industries and applications.

The algorithms you develop and your interpretation of data help an organization or business make critical decisions. You will need an analytical brain, good math skills, and, of course, a little programming know-how for this career path, but it promises to be a rewarding field for those that love figuring out what information really means!

Software Developer/Software Engineer

There are a ton of options when it comes to being a software developer. This is probably the role you think of first when you think of where you will fit in the grand scheme of things.

Software developers create a multitude of software, including productivity applications (like Microsoft Office) to music creation programs and pretty much anything you could think of. Just take a peek at the applications on your computer, and you will have a good idea of just how broad that spectrum really is.

If you do decide to be a software developer or software engineer, keep in mind that you will want to learn as much about Python and other languages as you can; it never hurts to know other languages and frameworks, and, as a bonus, once you know Python, learning a second or third coding language becomes a whole lot easier, as much of the logic and structures are the same across languages; it is mostly just a matter of learning new syntax and programming styles (e.g., not every language uses indentation).

Video Game Programmer

While this occupation technically falls under the same path as software developer, I thought I would give it special mention. As an avid fan of video games – that is, after all, what got me into programming in the first place – I would be remiss if I did not count this as its own separate career option.

Video game development has really blossomed over the past decade. In fact, when I was in college, there were only a handful of colleges – mostly specialty – that offered courses, much less degrees, in game development. In fact, my college only offered one such course – and just one time a year!

Of course, we used to all chisel our code on giant stones and wore bones in our noses at the time, but still....

If you want to develop for the major consoles, you will need to know more than Python and pygame. In fact, while Python will certainly help you understand some of the logic required, you will really need to branch out into C++ and stick your foot in some C and JAVA as well.

If you opt to go the route of non-console gaming, or PC gaming, you may have more options, but really, C++ is the way to go, at the time of this writing.

Mobile Development

While Python is not the first language you might think of for mobile development, you can, indeed, use the language to create apps and/or tie-in to other languages that are, arguably, better at mobile app development.

Mobile apps consist of any app that you use on your phone or tablet. This can be games, messenger apps, news reader applications, banking software, and even mobile versions of websites – the list goes on and on.

If you choose this important and huge market, you would be well-served to learn the true powerhouse languages for mobile development: C# or Objective-C, C++, JAVA, Swift, or even HTML5. For simplicity's sake, you might want to begin with HTML5, as it may have an easier learning curve than the others on that list. You can also use HTML5 for web development, so it is a pretty handy tool to have in your arsenal if you find mobile app development just isn't for you.

Of course, C++, C, and JAVA will also open other doors for you as well, but they are a little more complicated to learn, so it all depends on your time frame and needs.

Either way, just know that you can use Python for mobile development even if it isn't widely known for that use.

Web Development and Web Applications

If you want to create web-based applications, Python can certainly help in that endeavor. In fact, one of the really strong points of Python is its array of powerful web frameworks, such as Django and Flask. These frameworks act as a sort of blueprint or skeleton that let you rapidly deploy the "bones" of your applications, saving you a ton of time in setup and coding. Basically, they create the basics that you find in web applications for you, so that you don't have to go re-inventing the wheel.

Combine Python and web frameworks with HTML5, and a little JavaScript, and you will be a force to be reckoned with in the world of the Internet. For example, Google, YouTube, and Yahoo all rely on Python for their platforms. If that doesn't tell you how good Python is, I don't know what will!

System Administration

While sysadmins (or system administrators if you dare!) are an interesting lot, they are also a very necessary part of any organization. And Python, as you probably have guessed by now, is exceptionally good at helping sysadmins get the job done.

Systems administrators use Python to create tools and utilities that help them, well, administrate computer systems, control operating systems, and work on networking tasks.

It also allows you to create your own servers and clients, messaging systems, and more. Python is by far the best friend of a sysadmin.

That, and cats, for some reason....

Research, Teaching, and More

Python is also a great tool for research, as the data scientist section touched upon. It features so many libraries and tools for complex equations and handling data sets that it is no wonder NASA relies so heavily upon the language.

What's more, teaching Python in a school or university setting is always a great way to make a living and pass on knowledge to future generations at the same time. It is so easy to learn and, as a by-product, easy to teach, that it is a pretty common first stepping stone in computer science course requirements.

And who knows... if you teach it enough, maybe one day you could write your own book about it.

You know what... scratch that. Leave the book writing to me; I have dogs to feed!

Common Python Interview Questions

For some of you reading this book, you won't have to worry about what sort of questions you might be asked in an interview; for others, this will be a very real concern, sooner rather than later. Either way, whether you are ready to enter the workforce or are still a bit too young to consider such a thing, we suggest you take the time to study and ponder the list of common Python interview questions in this section.

While a good many of these topics were covered in this book, many more were not; remember, this is a beginner's book, designed to teach you what you need to get started programming in Python. It is not meant to send you out into the workforce, fully armed.

If there are any terms or ideas that do not make sense, we urge you to Google them, look them up in other books, and learn as much as you can. These questions and answers are not simply here to help you cheat your way into a job because you are good at memorization; indeed, these questions are common interview questions because the concepts they allude to are important programming principles.

Therefore, knowing the answers to these questions – and further, truly understanding them through study and practice – not only will help you land a job when you are ready, but will help you keep, and even thrive, at that job!

Can You Tell Me Some of the Key Features of Python?

This is a deceptively simple question. The interviewer is going to be looking to see how well you know Python, how interested you really are in the language, and how well you know its common features. While there are quite a few you could point out, the most common are

- Python is an interpreted language, meaning that it does not need to be compiled prior to being run like certain other languages.

- Python is a multi-purpose language, capable of being used in a wide array of fields, including data science, ethical hacking, system administration, web development, mobile app development, video game programming, scientific modeling, and much more.

- Python is highly readable, easy-to-learn, yet powerful. It is an object-oriented language that is dynamically typed (this means there is no need to define the data types of variables that you declare; Python can detect, for the most part, the data type you intend).

What Is the Difference Between a Tuple and a List

We covered this question in an earlier chapter and the answer is pretty simple: tuples are immutable, meaning that their values cannot be changed. Lists, meanwhile, are mutable, which means you can change their values. Another difference is that tuples require round braces ( ), while lists use square brackets []. Finally, while it may not be noticeable to a human, lists are, technically, slower than a tuple.

What Is Inheritance?

We covered the concept of inheritance in our chapter that dealt with objects and classes. As you may recall, classes follow a hierarchical structure, akin to a parent-child relationship. When we have a parent – or superclass – the child class of that parent inherits the attributes and methods of the parent.

Remember: classes and objects – a key feature of object-oriented programming (OOP) – are all about code reusability. A child class can inherit from one parent class or multiple parent classes, allowing for great flexibility and great coding efficiency.

How Do You Generate Random Values in Python?

An important module we used quite a lot in this book was random. It was pivotal to creating the randomized values of our hero stats in our superhero generator program and also used to randomize the selection of superhero names, as well as, powers.

To use it, we first have to import it:

```
import random
```

And then apply it to our code. For instance, we could write:

```
import random
a = random.randint(1, 10)
print(a)
```

This would store a random value between 1 and 10 in the variable a, then print it out.

How Do You Create a List, Tuple, and Dictionary in Python?

This may seem like a simple question, but it can stump a programmer if they have to do it on the spot, so practice creating each of these and know when to use them so that it becomes second nature to you.

The answers are:

```
myList = ['James', 'Mike', 'Spinach Man', 'Mister Kung Food']
myTuple = ('James', 'Mike', 'Spinach Man', 'Mister Kung Food')
myDict = {'Writer' : 'James Payne', 'Student' : 'YourName'}
```

What Is the Difference Between a Local Variable and a Global Variable?

Local variables are meant to be used within a function; that is, we create the variable inside of our function. If a variable is defined outside of a function, it is considered global.

What Are the Different Data Types Python Offers?

There are, in total, five basic data types in Python: numbers, strings, lists, tuples, and dictionaries.

What Is a GUI? What Python Library Is Best for GUI Development?

This two-part question has a simple answer. First, GUI stands for graphical user interface and allows you to incorporate things such as buttons, labels, text boxes, check boxes, radio buttons, and so forth in your programs.

Python's default library for GUI development is known as Tkinter and is arguably the best for those just starting out.

How Do You Open a File in Python?

This is another topic we covered in this book. As you may recall, we use the open( ) function to open a file. We first specify the name and location of the file (if the file is located outside of the root that is), then which mode we are opening the file in. For example:

```
myFile = open("test.py', 'w')
```

opens the file test.py, located in the root directory, in write mode.

How Would You List the Functions of a Module?

Another common interview question you might be asked is how you would view a list of the functions in a given module. For that, we use the dir() method:

```
import random
print dir(random)
```

Using help() is also helpful to view documentation within a module.

Other Python Interview Questions

You never really know what type of Python-specific questions you will be asked in an interview, so be sure you study up well in advance of your interviews. The ones included here are pretty common, but there are plenty more you may be asked.

In addition, you may well be asked to answer some code-specific questions or asked to write code to perform some specific function in the spur of the moment. Be prepared to write the basics and know the most common built-ins and functions.

One great way to prepare for a job interview is to study the company and the types of programming you will be doing there. For instance, if the company develops web applications, you know in advance that you will be asked about web frameworks.

Finally, always be prepared to answer questions not related to Python or programming – those will be asked as well. Career goals, past experience, personality questions, and general manner/attitude will all be considered during the interview process, so be sure you do not ignore basic interview preparation.

And clean behind your ears...your future boss just may inspect behind them!

Best Programming Practices

While much of coding is personal preferences, when you get into the workforce, there are always standards that you must follow. We discussed the importance of good and proper documentation; this section is about the best programming practices to follow.

The tips in this section will help make you a better programmer, make you more efficient, avoid common pitfalls, and reduce your coding errors. This is not a complete list, by far, but it should put you on the path to coding like a superhero!

Follow Style Guides

In his infinite wisdom, the inventor of Python created what is known as a style guide. Just like Python itself, this style guide, known as the PEP – or Python Enhancement Proposals – is a list of suggestions for a wide range of topics in Python. It covers everything from deprecated (removed) modules to style guides, to guidelines on language evolution.

There are a number of PEPs – literally. For example, the style guide is PEP 8 and was originally created by our great leader, Guido Van Rossum, Barry Warsaw, and Nick Coghlan back in 2001.

It covers how to lay out your code, whether or not to use tabs or spaces for indentation, the maximum line length for your code, working with string quotes, and much, much more.

Most jobs that hire you will expect you to be familiar with this particular PEP, particularly the sections covering indentation and naming conventions. Not only will this help your co-workers who have to review and work with your code, but the PEP style guide will also help you code better, more efficient and error-proof code.

You can find PEP 8 at the Python.org website: `www.python.org/dev/peps/pep-0008/`.

You can find a list of all PEPs at:

`www.python.org/dev/peps/`.

As an example, here is what PEP 8 has to say with regard to naming conventions:

Classes: Use capital letters for the first and second word (and any further words) in the name. For example: `VillainType` or `MutateClass`.

Variables, functions, methods, modules, and packages: Use lowercase words separated by underscores. For example: my_hero_name or my_villain_name.

If It's Broken, Fix It (Now, Not Later)

Often, when we are making great headway on a program, we want to keep pushing forward. This is especially true in an office environment, when deadline pressures are looming and you start to feel a time crunch and even get harassed to finish your portion of code and move on to the next part.

This mentality can become a big issue, however. While we may be tempted to ignore minor errors in our code with the thought that we can circle around to fix them later, the truth is, this thought process is more often a trap than it is a help.

An error here or there is expected, but, like an avalanche on a snowy mountain, they can quickly begin to pile up and destroy everything in their path. Errors often lead to other errors, creating a domino effect. If a portion of code doesn't work right or gives you errors, it can make other sections perform oddly. What's worse, those sections that are affected may not even give warnings or errors – causing even bigger problems down the line.

The lesson here is simple: test your code often. If you find a bug, fix it immediately, and do not move ahead in your work unless that problem is solved. You'll thank me later, trust me!

Documentation Is Everything

We touched on this thought many times in the book, but it bears repeating here: always, always, document your code. Clear documentation is key to a successful program – this includes its initial version, as well as any version that follows.

As you know, Python programs can consist of thousands of lines of code. Millions even. Have you ever read another person's letters or e-mails? Under the best of circumstances, people are not always clear, even though they speak the same language as you. Python is no different; while every code (should, at any rate) tries to stick to conventional naming conventions and code structure, the truth is, a lot of coders are self-taught.

We also get lazy over time and assumptive; we assume that anyone looking at our code will understand what we intended to do. Worse, we assume that we will remember what we were trying to do several years in the past.

While documenting your code may take a little more time, in the long run it will save you oodles of time. Whether it does so because it reduces time you spend tracking down bugs and code errors or because you can quickly reuse portions of code, documentation is probably the most important – in my book (and this is my book after all) best practices that you can follow.

And when we say documentation, that includes not just # comments or "" multi-line comments; it includes proper docstring usage as well.

There are tools out there for you to use as well, as you develop into a professional coder, such as Sphinx and reStructuredText. But for now, start off with the basics and practice documenting each section of code you write.

Use Code Repositories and Packages

One of the biggest selling points for using Python is that you get access to a huge library of Python packages, created and tested by the Python community of developers. These pieces of code and functions can save you a lot of time, errors, and grief when you are working on your own projects. As the saying goes, why re-invent the wheel?

You can find packages for use at The Python Package Index (PyPi) repository, located at `https://pypi.org`. There are currently 477,000 projects listed with nearly 736,000 users.

You can search projects, browse them, or see a list of trending projects if you are unsure what you are looking for or are looking for inspiration.

In addition to finding packages to help your programs, you can also learn how to package – and host – your own packages for others to test and use at the PyPi website.

I highly encourage you to visit this site frequently and review what others in the Python community are up to.

You may remember us using pip to install a few packages in this book; this is the repository those packages came from.

Test Often

Just because it needs to be reiterated, I am going to take a whole other paragraph or two to say it: test your code. Test it often.

Anytime you make a new major change or add another section, test the preceding code. Even if it is something as simple as an if block or a small loop. If you have a portion of code that relies on decision-making or a conditional statement, make sure you test each possible answer.

For example, if you have an if block then says "if yes, then X, if no, then Y, else z," make sure you perform each of those conditions. Be thorough in your tests and, as stated above, fix if you find warnings or errors.

Then, once you fix it, test again.

Choose a Side: Indentation or Spaces

This harkens back to our conversation on style guides and PEP recommendations; when writing code, always choose whether you are going to use spaces for indentations or tabs.

Then stick with that decision.

There are arguments – I've witnessed them in person – about which to use, and at the end of the day, I am going to anger half the Python users out there by saying this: it doesn't matter, so long as you use your option consistently.

In addition to personal preference and PEP guidelines, keep in mind that any organization you work for will have their own style guidelines, and those will override anything else – personal preference and otherwise.

But again, when coding, always use the same spacing/tab conventions.

Classes Are Great, But Not Everything Needs to Be One

Anytime you program any structure or *thing* in Python – or any language for that matter – always consider whether or not it is best served as what you are making it as. For example, classes are great for reusability, but so are functions. The same goes for modules.

At the end of the day, your real job is to make everything as simple as it can be. If you do that, then you will achieve the goals we spoke so much about through this book: reusable code, reducing errors, efficient code.

Another benefit of keeping things simple is that it makes everything more readable, and the importance of that can't be overstated. The easier something is to read, the easier you and co-workers will be able to track down issues or append code sections.

That is part of the negative of using too many classes and modules; while they are great in many ways, they tend to break the readability of Pythonic code.

Use them, by all means; just make sure they are necessary and the simplest way to do whatever you are trying to achieve.

The Future of Python

As it stands, Python is, arguably, the most-used programming language on the planet. That trend, which has been trending for quite some time, does not seem to be slowing down. The language is so simple to learn, powerful, and flexible, that the odds of it falling out of favor anytime in the foreseeable future are pretty slim.

There are a few areas that are anticipated to grow pretty rapidly with Python. In part, this is due to the rising popularity of these specific niches or industries. For others, it is due to the fact that Python excels in that general arena.

One example of this is data science, research, and scientific programming applications. Already a powerhouse in this arena, the language will only continue to grow with regard to use as a data science go-to.

Another factor driving the growth of Python is that there are a bunch of corporations that built applications based off of Python 2. With the stability of Python 3, those companies are beginning to update and port their code over to Python 3, which is a much simpler process than, say, switching to a completely new set of code.

Python is not invulnerable, of course. There are some areas where Python definitely needs to grow. One of those is mobile development. Rather than shy away from this realm, however, you can certainly expect the Python community and the Python creators to step up to the plate and ensure that Python is not left in the dust when it comes to mobile app development and tools to help you tackle this field.

Looming on the horizon – or knocking at your door right now depending on where you are at in your programming studies and views of technology – are high-tech fields such as artificial intelligence (AI) (think about the explosion of ChatGPT), virtual reality (VR), augmented reality (AR), and the ever-growing field of IoT (Internet of Things). Smart homes and connected devices are a rapidly growing market, and you can be sure that Python will be a part of this mix.

At the end of the day, Python's learning curve and ease of use make it a language that will be widely used for decades to come. Why? Simple: if you own a business, you can hire someone that can get up to speed coding Python very quickly. Combine that with its flexibility, the vast array of Python packages developed by the community, and all of the other great things we have discussed to death throughout this book and my money is solidly on Python remaining a powerhouse for coders.

And yours should be too.

Python Terms

There are a great many terms discussed in Python. This book, as comprehensive as it may be, does not cover them all. To help sum up the data in this book, and teach you a few new terms, we are including this section to help define some of the more common Python terms you may encounter as you continue to develop as a programmer.

Argument: A value you assign to a function. Also known as a parameter.

Assign: Giving a variable, list, dictionary, tuple, or other object a value.

Boolean: A value equaling either `True` or `False`.

Class: You can think of a `class` as a blueprint for an `object`. There are superclasses – or parent classes – and child classes. A child class can inherit the traits – methods and attributes – of a parent class. Using these blueprints, you can then rapidly create objects based upon one – or more – class.

Comment: A `comment` is used to help document – or explain – what a section or piece of code is being used for. You can comment using a # followed by a whitespace and then text for a `single-line` `comment`, like so:

```
# This is a comment.
```

When Python sees the # symbol, it ignores everything on that line following the whitespace, allowing you to leave notes to yourself or other programmers. If you need more space, you can keep using # for each following line of comments or you can use `'''` or `"""` for a multi-line comment. Here is an example of a multi-line comment:

```
'''
Here is a comment.
Here is another.
Here is more!
'''
```

Conditional statement: A statement that will – or won't – execute depending upon whether or not a certain condition is met.

def: def is used to define – or create – a function. See the term function for more.

Dictionary: A dictionary is a data type that consists of one or more key-value pairs. In this instance, each key corresponds to a value. The key portion of the dictionary is immutable, meaning it cannot be changed. Values in dictionaries can be of any type – number, string, or otherwise and *can* be changed. We define a dictionary like this:

```
example_dict{'Name' : 'Paul', 'Age': '22'}
```

This assigns two items to the dictionary. The first key-value is Name : Paul, where Name is the key and Paul is the value. The second key is Age, which has the value of 22.

Docstring: A documentation string; a piece of documentation that gets embedded in a Python program, module, or function.

Floating-point: A decimal number, such 2.5 or 102.19.

Function: A function is a code that you can call within your program. We usually use functions to save pieces of code we intend to use more than once.

Here is how we define a function:

```
def name_of_function(parameters):
    # Here is where your code would go. For example:
    print("Look, I'm a function!")
```

To call the function, we could type

```
name_of_function()
```

Immutable: If something is immutable, it means that you cannot change its value.

Import: Loading a library into your program.

Integer: A whole number, such as 1, 400, 20,000, or even -50,000.

Iterable: An object that can be iterated (or looped) over.

Len: The len() function is used to count the length of an object, such as a variable containing a string, items in a list, and so forth. If used in a list, it would count the number of items or elements. If used on a string, it would count the characters in the string. Here are some examples:

```
a  = "This is my variable"
some_list = [1,2,3,4,5]
len(a)
len(some_list)
```

This would result in:

```
19
5
```

Note   len() counts whitespaces too.

List: Lists are a Python data type that stores an ordered group of values of any type. Unlike tuples, lists are mutable, meaning that the value they hold can change.

To create a list, you could type this:

```
my_list = [0,1,2,3,4,5]
my_other_list = ['James', 'Super Taco', 'Not So Super Taco', 'Regular Taco Man']
```

Loop: A loop is used to iterate – or repeat – a given piece of code a number of times depending upon a set of criteria. There is a for loop, which iterates however many times you tell it to, and a while loop, which repeats so long as a condition is TRUE.

An example of a for loop:

```
for i in range(0, 5):
    print(i + 1)
```

This would result in

```
1
2
3
4
5
```

Example of a while loop:

```
while a == 4:
    print(" a equals 4! Yay!")
```

Method: A function that belongs to an object.

Mutable: Something that is `mutable` can have its value changed.

Object: What you create using the blueprint of a class.

Parameter: Another name for an argument (though some would argue with that comparison).

print(): The `print()` function lets us display or output something to the user's screen:

```
print("Hello Universe!")
```

would result in:

```
Hello Universe!
```

String: A `string` is a data type that consists of any letter, number, whitespace, or special character.

Syntax error: An error you encounter when you have entered text wrong, spelled a portion of code wrong, or made a mistake in your syntax.

Traceback: A sequential list of calls to a function(s) that caused an error.

Tuple: A `tuple` is a data type that stores ordered collections of values of any type. Unlike lists, they are immutable and their values cannot be changed.

You can create a tuple by using code similar to:

```
my_tuple = ('El Taco Diablo', 'Tiny Monster', 'Guy Focal')
my_other_tuple = ('0', '1', '2', '3', '4')
```

Variable: A `variable` is a data type that stores a single value. That value can be a number, a character, a sentence, and so forth. They can also contain lists, dictionaries, and even functions.

To create a variable, you use the assignment operator:

```
a = 12
b = "Snap, The Cereal Killer!"
```

Index

A

B

C

© James R. Payne 2024
J. R. Payne, *Python for Teenagers*, https://doi.org/10.1007/978-1-4842-9988-3

Printed in the United States
by Baker & Taylor Publisher Services